AF657039

Application of Language and Teaching

Application of Language and Teaching

Edited by

Dr. S.K. PANNER SELVAM

Assistant Professor, Department of Education

Bharathidasan University, T.N

RANDOM

RANDOM PUBLICATIONS

NEW DELHI (INDIA)

Application of Language and Teaching

ISBN 978-93-5111-892-3

© Reserved

All Rights Reserved. No Part of this book may be reproduced in any manner without written permission.

Published in 2016 in India by

RANDOM PUBLICATIONS

4376-A/4B, Gali Murari Lal, Ansari Road

New Delhi-110 002

Phone : +9111-43580356, 011-43142548, 011-23289044

e-mail : sales@randompublications.com

info@randompublications.com

randomexports@gmail.com

Reprinted 2026

Type Setting by : Shah Computer Graphics, Delhi-110094

Contents

1. Effectiveness of Task Oriented Language Teaching

Chapter-1

Introduction

Language is one of the most important forms of human behavior. The purpose of language is communication which means that language helps a person to formulate his thoughts and encode it for the benefit of others to decode it. Language is the words, their pronunciation, and the methods of combining them used and understood by a community. It is a form or manner of verbal expression. It is audible, articulate, meaningful sound as produced by the action of the vocal organs. It is a systematic means of communicating ideas or feelings by the use of conventionalized signs, sounds, gestures, or marks having understood meanings. It is language than anything else that distinguishes man from the rest of other creatures in world.

Language is the human ability to acquire and use complex systems of communication, and a language is any specific example of such a system. The scientific study of language is called linguistics. Another definition sees language as a formal system of signs governed by grammatical rules of combination to communicate meaning. This definition stresses that human languages can be described as closed structural systems consisting of rules that relate particular signs to particular meanings. Noam Chomsky, the originator of the generative theory of grammar, who has defined language as the construction of sentences that can be generated using transformational grammars. Chomsky considers these rules to be an innate feature of the human mind and to constitute the rudiments of what language is.

Tool for communication

Yet another definition sees language as a system of communication that enables humans to exchange verbal or symbolic utterances. This definition stresses the social functions of language and the fact that humans use it to express themselves and to manipulate objects in their environment. Functional theories of grammar explain grammatical structures by their communicative functions, and understand the grammatical structures of language to be the result of an adaptive process by which grammar was "tailored" to serve the communicative needs of its users.

This view of language is associated with the study of language in pragmatic, cognitive, and interactive frameworks, as well as in sociolinguistics and linguistics anthropology.

Language acquisition

All healthy, normally developing human beings learn to use language. Children acquire the language or languages used around them: whichever languages they receive sufficient exposure to during childhood. The development is essentially the same for children acquiring sign or oral language. This learning process is referred to as first-language acquisition, since unlike many other kinds of learning, it requires no direct teaching or specialized study.

First language acquisition proceeds in a fairly regular sequence, though there is a wide degree of variation in the timing of particular stages among normally developing infants. From birth, newborns respond more readily to human speech than to other sounds. Acquisition of second and additional languages can come at any age, through exposure in daily life or courses. Children learning a second language are more likely to achieve native-like fluency than adults, but in general, it is very rare for someone speaking a second language to pass completely for a native speaker. An important difference between first language acquisition and additional language acquisition is that the process of additional language acquisition is influenced by languages that the learner already knows.

Throughout history a number of different ways of representing language in graphic media have been invented. These are called writing systems. The use of writing has made language even more useful to humans. It makes it possible to store large amounts of information outside of the human body and retrieve it again, and it allows communication across distances that would otherwise be impossible. Many languages conventionally employ different genres, styles, and registers in written and spoken language, and in some communities, writing traditionally takes place in an entirely different language than the one spoken. There is some evidence that the use of writing also has effects on the cognitive development of humans, perhaps because acquiring literacy generally requires explicit and formal education.

Language is obviously a vital tool. Not only is it a means of communicating thoughts and ideas, but it forges friendships, cultural ties, and economic relationships. Throughout history, many have reflected on the importance of language. For instance, the scholar Benjamin Whorf has noted that language shapes thoughts and emotions, determining one's perception of reality. John Stuart Mill said that "Language is the light of the mind."

Language, of course, is knowledge, and in the world, today knowledge is one of the key factors in competitiveness. Brains and knowledge are what create the prosperity and growth we tend to take for granted. In an advanced industrial society in an increasingly interdependent world, the knowledge of other languages becomes indispensable. For the last few years, millions of people across the world, who share common interests, are able to communicate with each other and exchange ideas. Not only are they able to do this due to the various technological advances, but also because they share a common language. There is, of course, no denying that the knowledge of the English language is one of the most important tools available to the children. It is one of the international languages, a tool of communication between countries, cultural groups, various companies and organizations, communities and friends.

Basic Functions of Language

Language is any formal system of gestures, signs, sounds, and symbols used or conceived as a means of communicating thought. As mentioned above, there are over six thousand language schemes currently in use around the world. The language spoken by the greatest number of people on the planet is Mandarin; other widely spoken languages are English, Spanish, and Arabic. Language is ultimately important because it is the primary means through which humans have the ability to communicate and interact with one another. Some linguists go so far as to suggest that the acquisition of language skills is the primary advancement that enabled our prehistoric ancestors to flourish and succeed over other hominid species.

In today's world, effective use of language helps us in our interpersonal relationships at home and at work. Using language effectively also will improve your ability to be an effective public speaker. One of the first components necessary for understanding language is to understand how we assign meaning to words. Words consist of sounds (oral) and shapes (written) that have agreed-upon meanings based in concepts, ideas, and memories. When we write the word "blue," we may be referring to a portion of the visual spectrum dominated by energy with a wavelength of roughly 440–490 nanometers. You could also say that the colour in question is an equal mixture of both red and green light. While both of these are technically correct ways to interpret the word "blue," we're pretty sure that neither of these definitions is how you thought about the word. When hearing the word "blue," you may have thought of your favorite colour, the colour of the sky on a spring day, or the colour of a really ugly car you saw in the parking lot. When people think about language, there are two different types of meanings that people must be aware of: denotative and connotative.

Education

Generally speaking, 'Education' is utilized in three senses: Knowledge, Subject and a Process. When a person achieves degree up to certain level we do not call it education .As for example if a person has secured Masters degree then we utilize education it a very narrower sense and call that the person has achieved education up to Masters Level. In the second sense, education is utilized in a sense of discipline.

Etymological Meaning of Education

In English the term "Education" has been derived from two Latin words Educare (Educere) and Educatum. "Educare" means to train or mould. It again means to bring up or to lead out or to draw out, propulsion from inward to outward. The term "Educatum" denotes the act of teaching. It throws light on the principles and practice of teaching. The term Educare or Educere mainly indicates development of the latent faculties of the child. But child does not know these possibilities. It is the educator or the teacher who can know these and take appropriate methods to develop those powers.

A term in Sanskrit, which throws light on the nature of education. It is "Vidya" which means knowledge. The term "Vidya" has originated from "Bid" meaning knowledge. If we mention certain definitions of education of great educators of the East and the West, one may have a clear picture of the nature and meaning of the term education.

1. Education is the manifestation of perfection already in man. Like fire in a piece of flint, knowledge exists in the mind. Suggestion is the friction; which brings it out-**Swami Vivekananda**
2. By education I mean an all-round drawing out of the best in child and man's body, mind and spirit-**Mahatma Gandhi**

True Definition of Education

The different meanings and definitions of education as given above lead us to the conclusion that education should have a comprehensive definition. Thus, education may be defined as a purposive, conscious or unconscious, psychological, sociological, scientific and philosophical process, which brings about the development of the individual to the fullest extent and also the maximum development of society in such a way that both enjoy maximum happiness and prosperity. In Short, education is the development of individual according to his needs and demands of society, of which he is an integral part. The above remarks of different educators highlight the following special features of education:

Educationists are being given

1. The culture which each generation purposefully gives to those who are to be its successors, in order to qualify them for at least keeping up, and if possible for raising the level of improvement which has been attained -**John Stuart Mill**
2. In narrow sense, education may be taken to mean any consciously directed effort to develop and cultivate our powers **-S. S. Mackenzie**
3. Education is a process in which and by which knowledge, character and behaviour of the young are shaped and moulded **-Prof. Drever**
4. The influence of the environment of the individual with a view to producing a permanent change in his habits of behaviour, or thought and attain-**G. H. Thompson**

AIMS OF EDUCATION

Education is a purposeful activity. By education we intend to bring certain desirable changes in the students. Education is a conscious effort and, as such, it has definite aims and objectives. In the light of these aims the curriculum is determined and the academic achievements of the student are measured. Education without aim is like a boat without its rudder. Aims give direction to activity.

Absence of an aim in education makes it a blind alley. Every stage of human development had some aim of life. The aims of life determine aims of education. The aims of education have changed from age to age and thus it is dynamic because the aims of life are dynamic. Nature of The Aims of Education In order to know the aims of education, we must know the nature of aims. Aims of education are not fixed, eternal and universal. These are changeable and relative. The nature of the aims of education can properly be understood in the light of two distinct philosophies of life-idealism and pragmatism. Idealism stands for absolute, ultimate, eternal and universal values. It advocates high ideals of life, which are mainly spiritual in nature. Idealism pleads “knowledge for knowledge’s sake.”

Aim of Education in India

Educational aims in India should be judged in relation to the lives of the Indian people. Indian civilization is one of the ancient civilizations of the world.

Aims of Education in Ancient India

The aim of education in ancient India was the ultimate outcome of the Indian theory of knowledge and the corresponding scheme of life and values. People in ancient India were greatly impressed and affected by the fact of death as the central fact of life. Their one aim of life was to solve the problem of death by achieving knowledge of the whole truth of which life and death are arts and phases. The aim was not simply abstract and theoretical. There were practical and concrete aims too.

The first was the acquisition of knowledge. This was evident in the Vedic period. Inculcation of social and civic duties in the minds of the students was also regarded as an important aim of education in those days. Education for occupation was another important aim. Character training and moral education was regarded as very important aim of ancient Indian education.

Aims of Education in British India

The British uprooted the indigenous system of education in India with definite intentions. The educational system established by the British was colonial in character. It was designed to prepare Indians only for taking certain subordinate positions in Government offices. It was not intended to develop among the people capacities to take leadership and initiative in different walks of life. The main educational objective can better be understood from the following declaration in the educational policy or Lord Bentinck (1835): "We want a class of persons Indian in blood and colour but English in tastes in opinion, in morals and intellect." The Wood's Dispatch declared almost the same policy. The aim of British education was to inculcate European knowledge in the minds of the Indians.

Aims of Education in Independent India

After independence the Indian leaders realized the inherent

defects in the system of education introduced by the British. Universalisation of education was the need of the hour. Education must be linked with national development in all directions. With these national goals in view the Government in independent India set up different committees and commissions for educational reforms in the desired lines. These committees and commissions have formulated educational aims and objectives.

Four skills

There are four skills in teaching English language. They are Listening, Speaking, Reading and writing.

Listening

Although speaking is the most common form of communication, due to several reasons, listening is the first skill to master in order to be proficient in a language. First, no one can say a word before listening to it. Thus, the teacher must take into account that the level of language input (listening) must be higher than the level of language production (speaking). **Smith (1975, pp. 98-99)** emphasizes: good listeners often speak more exactly and more creatively than poor listeners; they have more words at their command. Second, in a conversation, one can respond accurately only after listening precisely. Our daily interactions prove that poor listening can lead to unnecessary arguments and problems. Third, listening constitutes half of the communication process. Fourth, children get the majority information through listening. Finally, children spend more than half the time they are in the classrooms by listening (**Smith, 1975, p. 65**). Realizing these reasons, we can see how important it is for the learners.

Despite its importance, listening to a foreign language sounds is possibly the skill which learners usually find the most difficult. This is quite natural since the sounds they hear, at least in initial stages, are unfamiliar. Thus, to get the message sent through an expression, they always feel under unnecessary pressure to understand every word. Another prominent cause that makes listening to a foreign language sounds difficult for children is the fact that children, whether in or out of the classrooms, are subjected to endless number of sounds. To a higher extent, these sounds do not belong to the foreign language they are learning. As a consequence, the learners cannot concentrate on comprehending the sounds of the foreign language they are learning.

Speaking

First of all, as it has been stated in the previous section, in language learning the learners are expected to have higher level of language input (listening) than the level of language production (speaking). Thus, the majority of speaking activities used in the first levels should be designed to enable pupils to participate with a minimal verbal response. However, in the last levels, e.g. grade six, pupils are encouraged to begin to manipulate language and express themselves in a much more personal way.

Based on my experience, there are three main types of speaking activities we can suitably use in primary schools. The first type is songs, chants, and poems—which are very effective to encourage young learners to mimic the model they hear on the cassette or video. This helps pupils to master the sounds, rhythms, and intonation of the English language through simple reproduction. Steiner (as cited in **Jaffke, 2004**) emphasizes the importance of using poetic language in the first three classes. Based on the experiences of teachers who have [been] teaching young learners for a long time, he explains that poetic language, based on rhythm and rhyme, is learned far more easily by children than is prose language. Along with songs, poetic language introduces the children to the flow of the new language and familiarizes them with its prosodic elements: emphasis, intonation, pitches, etc. In addition, a great number of songs or poems also contain certain grammatical points. Well selected songs or poems can be integrated into lessons for reinforcing grammar points.

The second type of speaking activities used in primary schools is the games and pair work activities. They are commonly based on a given model; they do encourage young learners to begin to manipulate the language by presenting them with a certain amount of choice, albeit within a fairly controlled situation. In addition, using games is also advantageous because by doing games and pair work activities, the pupils (though they are totally unaware of this at the time) also develop a rich store of grammatical forms and structures. However, since games and pair work necessitate much energy, they are more suitable to use in the upper classes, i.e. in grade four to six.

The third type of speaking activities used in primary schools is oral report and discussions on books the students have finished reading. Children need to talk to each other about what they're reading and share their ideas and insights with others. In this way, the stories come to life, students gain insight and ideas from others, and language learning is enhanced. **Zang (2009, p. 34**) shows that integrating speaking and reading skills deepens students 'understanding of the reading material, reveals any problem they have understanding a text, and, most importantly, lets them apply the information they have read into authentic speaking practice that improves their fluency. **Kauchak & Eggen (1998**) asserts that talking and social interaction enhances learning of any kind.

To succeed any speaking activity, children need to acknowledge that there is a real reason for asking a question or giving a piece of information. Therefore, the teacher should make sure the activities she presents to the pupils provide a reason for speaking, whether this is to play a game or to find out real information about friends in the class.

When the activity begins, make sure that the pupils are speaking as much English as possible without interfering to correct the mistakes that they will probably make. Try to treat errors casually by praising the utterance and simply repeating it correctly without necessarily highlighting the errors. Finally, always offer praise for effort regardless of the accuracy of the English produced.

Reading

Although reading is generally after listening and speaking in the hierarchy of communication abilities to be developed, the teaching of English in Indonesian primary school should make reading one of the first priorities to develop. This is not only because reading enables learners to access information from many written texts but also because reading proficiency contributes to one's self realization and the development of his personal-social adjustment. And since reading is a very complicated process involving a variety of factors that interact with one another **(Kim, 2002**), it should be developed in graded and sequential phases. The factors involved in reading include sub-reading skills (such as word recognition, skimming, scanning, sentence comprehension, getting the topic, etc.) and background knowledge. **Brindley (1994)** emphasizes the essence of background knowledge factor in reading by saying:

Texts are not entirely self-contained; they refer to the world. Texts assume knowledge on the part of the reader. Sometimes the knowledge is factually based and refers to objects, events and people. There are many references in texts which depend not on a grasp of facts but on an understanding of cultural institutions and practices.

Writing

In a first language situation, children rarely write what they do not say or read. Young children listen for sounds as they attempt to use letters to record their ideas on paper **(Johnson, 2007)**. Thus, a writing program in such setting is always preceded by rich, broad and meaningful program in oral expression and sensible and interesting reading activities. In contrast, since writing is less threatening than speaking in that children need not be afraid of mispronouncing an unfamiliar word, in a second or foreign language learning children can have their first experiences of producing written statements in English well before they start speaking in the language. According to **Gordon (2007)**, ¯Second language literacy experts recommend that literacy instruction should start early in the ESL classroom, before children develop full proficiency in a second language.

The writing of primary school pupils, whether done in class or at home, will invariably contain mistakes. Again, the teacher should try to be sensitive in his/her correction and not necessarily insist on every error being highlighted. A piece of written work covered in red pen is demoralizing and generally counter-productive. Where possible, encourage pupils to correct their own mistakes as they work. If there is time, encourage pupils to decorate their written work and where feasible display their efforts in the classroom.

Nowadays, most people do not write much in day-to-day life and in a way, a great deal of what we write includes brief notes, answers for the questions, diary-entries, letters etc. "When we write we use graphic symbols that is letters or combinations of letters which relate to the sounds we make when we speak." **(Byrne, 1979)**

The symbols which are used need to be arranged properly to form words and then to form the sentences with a view to communicating our ideas in an organized way. In fact, when one communicates through writing, he has so many ideas to express for which we consider different ways of combining and arranging them which lead him to our drafting, revising or redrafting and so on. In other words, it can be said that writing is encoding of a massage of some kind that is, one translates our thoughts and ideas into language. So, in a way, writing represents our thoughts and ideas. What one thinks leads to one's writing in the form of sentences and by organizing the sentences into a cohesive text where we are able to communicate with our readers successfully? So far as the teaching of writing is concerned, the teacher should keep this nature of writing in mind. Writing always has become difficult to teach or to learn because it involves a different kind of mental process which includes the sub-skills like – drafting, editing, revising, organizing etc. There are three main aspects of writing,

1. Purpose/Objective
2. Audience/Readers
3. Function

1. Purpose / Objective

A text is always written with a purpose or objective. As a writer, one should be clear about the purpose or the objective of that writing. Am I writing with any special purpose? Or why am I writing? The answers to these questions will make the idea clear and can bring out a good piece of writing.

2. Audience / Readers

Any communication is meant for expressing ideas from one to one. In case of writing, the audience is not present but at least if the writer wants, she/he can write keeping the target group in mind. So, "Who, is going to read?" or "For whom am I writing?" has to be made clear.

3. Function

1. Consider the needs of the Learners.
2. Make the teaching of writing functional and communicative.
3. Expose them to how to write first and then to different types of texts.
4. Expose them to functioning of writing as a system of communication.
5. Try to plan the tasks which are realistic, functional and communicative.
6. Expose them to the process of writing by actually going through it, including the sub skills of writing.
7. Motivate them to think and express their ideas.
8. Teach them grammar and vocabulary inclusively in the writing tasks.
9. Try to accept their ideas and also compositions.

Need and Significance of the study

The study, "Effectiveness of task based language teaching of English in enhancing the writing skill among VII standard students" is important. Because, it helps to understand the effectiveness of task based language teaching of English in writing skill. It also helps to give solutions to enhancing the writing skill among VII standard students.

Like speech, writing has been considered a powerful mode of communication. After all, one writes with the purpose of being understood. Unlike speech, writing is not always for the audience present and hence it demands clear and comprehensive message. While one speaks, he uses a variety of prosodic features such as pitch, loudness, speed, rhythm, pauses and so on that help us to get the feedback from listeners but this does not happen in case of writing where the context is created through the words alone and without the direct interaction between the writer and the reader.

Scope of the Study

This study plays the role of model for further research. This study mainly focuses on VII standard students' effectiveness of task oriented language teaching of English in enhancing the writing skill.

It also paves way for further research such as. *"Effectiveness of Task Oriented Language Teaching of English in Enhancing the Writing Skill among VII Standard Students"* is a model for other thesis writing.

1. It helps others to write a dissertation on effectiveness of task oriented language teaching of English in enhancing the writing skill of secondary students.
2. It helps others to write a dissertation on effectiveness of task oriented language teaching of English in enhancing the writing skill of higher level students.
3. It helps others to write a dissertation on effectiveness of task oriented language teaching of English in enhancing the writing skill of college level students.
4. It is a scope to write a dissertation on Effectiveness of task oriented language teaching of English in enhancing the speaking skill among VII standard students.
5. It is a scope to write a dissertation on Effectiveness of task oriented language teaching of English in enhancing the reading skill among VII standard students.
6. It is a scope to write a dissertation on Effectiveness of task oriented language teaching of English in enhancing the listening skill among VII standard students.

Status of English Language in India

In 1835, the medium of education for schools and universities in India was English since India was ruled by a British government during the colonial era. For over a century, English became popular as a language of power, prestige and convenience. During this time, English was a foreign language in India and people were interested in acquiring it even if they opposed being a colony of Britain. The popularity of English continued even after India gained its independence from Britain, even the new constitution makers wrote the Indian Constitution in the English language. Although according to Article 343 of the Indian Constitution, Hindi was designated as the official language of the Union, English language was supposed to be used for all official purposes for a period of 15 years. Nine years after the independence, the use of English was known as an **'associate official language'** or an **'associate additional language'**. Shortly after that, English became the second language of India.

Objectives of Teaching English

English, although a foreign language is now as much an Indian language as any other. English has been taught in schools and colleges for many decades. It occupies the position of associate official language. It is used widely as a link language in offices and among the educated people. It is not only a compulsory subject at school, college and university but is also the medium of instruction to the large extent. It is the language of science and technology. It occupies the position of a second language in the school curriculum and for higher education. English language has been assigned the role of library language. Without exception every secondary school child has to learn English as a subject, usually for six years but in some cases for three years only. This contemporary position of English in India shows English language teaching occurring at all levels of Education, mainly as a second language. This brings us to our present topic of interest - a history of English language teaching in India.

English language teaching as a discipline has come into its own during the past several decades both in India and abroad and along with it English language teaching historiography also has gained prominence. It is now possible to cite a large body of literature devoted to this area of study. But in India, even though English language teaching has been going on for many decades there is no document, which contains a comprehensive history of English language teaching in India. Now English language teaching has gained the status of a new discipline and also has gained relative importance on our educational programmes. It is felt that a comprehensive history of English language teaching in India is needed.

1. Speaking when the need so arise.
2. Reading the matter written by others.
3. Writing for the benefits of those with whom we wish to share our Ideas.

4. Listening the language when it is spoken by others.

Language experts agreed that English learning is a very important aspect of life. English has enjoyed and still enjoys a very important place in the curriculum of Anglo-Vernacular schools in our country. It has been used as an official language, the language of administration of courts, legislature, etc. It is a language which has a rich literature and also covers the vast spectrum of science and technology as well as industries and commerce.

The objectives at the secondary Level

The following are the main objectives of teaching English at secondary level,

1. To develop knowledge and understanding of Grammar.
2. To develop abilities to make use of the grammar in own writing English.
3. To understand the meaning of English passage.
4. To develop interest in reading English passages/ literatures.
5. To develop self study habit.
6. To enhance competencies in writing essays and gist of the passage in own words/ language.
7. To develop their insight and favourable attitude towards English language.
8. To developing the understanding about rules of grammar and their use in writing English.

Aims and objectives of teaching English at Higher secondary level

1. Motivate students for more studying English language.
2. To encourage for composing poems and writing essay.
3. To develop the ability for grasping the theme of poem or English passage.
4. To encourage the students for writing the meaning or theme of poem or passage in their own words.

5. To develop the ability of appreciation of ideas and criticizing the thinking.
6. To develop the creativity of the students related to verbal ability and reasoning or fluency of language.
7. To develop the ability of understanding of other school subjects.
8. To develop the mastery of language for expressing his ideas, feelings and experiences.
9. To develop the ability of evaluation and analysis of language components.
10. To develop the values, moral and character of the students.

Objectives of teaching English

Dr .b. s. bloom "educational objectives are the desired goal or outcome at which instruction is aimed" Objectives means have a purpose for very short time where as aim is achieved with a longer time.

The objectives of teaching English in must be quite different from those which are considered necessary for an English child. L.A.C. strong one said," For us who speak it English, English is everything, English is what we say and what we think. English is our relationship to other people, our friendship, our truth, and untruth our character, English is not a subject, English is our life." But this is not true for us in, because the main aim of teaching should be to help children to get practical command of English. So that it may be useful to them in everyday life.

Types of objectives

There are two types of objectives of English teaching. They are

1. Language development
2. Literary development

The Process of Writing

Understanding a prescribed passage read out from the book or at talk at same linguistic level on a topic of general interest within the students' experience asking sensible questions and answering the questions clearly. Carrying on a sensible conservation with clarity of expression on passages or topics from prescribed material.

1. Arranging and organizing his ideas in a coherent manner for oral or written presentation.
2. Reading silently and understanding the main ideas in a passage of simple English within the linguistic range of the syllabus.
3. Any subject of general interest within his experience
4. A topic from the curriculum prescribed
5. Reading a passage on his own using the dictionary for any reference needed.
6. Reading short stories.
7. Interpreting materials prescribed in the form of a table or chart.
8. Writing simple letters and simple dialogue.

1) The Controlled to Free Approach

In 1950s and early 1960, the audio- lingual method dominated second language learning which emphasized on speech and writing through mastering grammatical and syntactic forms. Here, the students are given sentence exercises and then paragraphs to copy or manipulate grammatically, These controlled compositions then followed by correction of errors, so that it can lead to the free composition. Overall, this approach focuses on accuracy rather than fluency.

2) The Free Writing Approach

This approach stresses writing quantity rather than quality. This focuses on fluency rather than accuracy. It is based on the principle that if once ideas are there, the organization follows.

3) The Paragraph Pattern Approach

This approach focuses on organization by copying the paragraphs or model passages. It is based on the principle that in different culture or situations, people construct and organize communication with each other in different ways.

4) The Grammar-Syntax Organization Approach

This approach stresses on simultaneous work on more than one composition feature. In away, it is inclusive here that writing cannot be seen as composed of separate skills which are learned sequentially. So, students must be trained to pay attention to organization while they also work on the necessary grammar and syntax.

5) The Communicative Approach

This approach focuses 'on the purpose of writing and the audience for it. They are given some tasks where they have to behave as writers so that they can learn by doing it. - Why am I writing this?

- Who will read it?

Thus, this approach is quite functional in nature, which can provide the actual experience to the learners.

BENEFITS OF WRITING SKILL - ENHANCED FOREIGN LANGUAGE TEACHING AND LEARNING

In the last decade, changing conceptions of learning and rapid technological advances have been accompanied by changes in language teaching and learning. Language classrooms are increasingly turning into blended learning environments that focus on active learning. It is commonly known that active learning advances the learning process and thus raises the quality of the language learning experience. Blended language learning uses multiple teaching and guiding methods by combining face-to-face sessions with online activities and utilizing a mix of technology-based materials. The growing use of **WRITING SKILL** in blended language learning environments has changed the face of language teaching and learning in a beneficial way and will continue to do so along with future technological innovations. The main benefits of **WRITING SKILL** to language learning are presented below by drawing on the perspectives of **Jonassen** et al. (1999) who defined technology-enhanced meaningful learning as active, authentic and cooperative.

USE OF WRITING SKILL IN TEACHING

Teaching in schools as well as in higher education, mostly, concentrates on giving information which is not sole objective of teaching. Along with giving information the other objectives are:

1. Developing understanding and application of the concepts.
2. Developing reasoning and thinking power.
3. Development of judgment and decision making ability.
4. Improving comprehension, speed and vocabulary
5. Developing self concept and value clarification
6. Developing proper study habits
7. Developing tolerance and ambiguity risk taking capacity and s scientific temper etc.

With the present infrastructure, class size, availability of teachers, quality of teachers, training of teachers, etc. it is difficult to achieve all the objectives. Further, most of the teachers use lecture method which does not have potentiality of achieving majority of above mentioned objectives. The objectives are multidimensional in nature, so far their achievement multiple methods should be used in an integrated fashion. At present WRITING SKILL has a considerable role in imparting needed knowledge. It is a well known fact that not a single teacher is capable of giving up-to-date and complete information in his own subject the WRITING SKILL can fill this gap because it can provide access to different sources of information. WRITING SKILL provides on-line interaction facility wherein students and teachers can exchange their ideas and views, and get clarification on any topic from information base. WRITING SKILL provides variety in the learners to broaden the information base. WRITING SKILL also provides variety in the presentation of content which helps learners in concentration, better understanding, and long retention of information which is not possible otherwise. The super high way and cyber space also help in qualitative improvement of teaching learning process. WRITING SKILL provides flexibility to the learner which is denied by the traditional process and methods. Flexibility is a must for mastery learning and quality learning. On internet many websites are available freely which may be utilized by teachers and students for understanding different concepts, improving vocabulary, developing reasoning and thinking etc.

Statement of the Problem

"Effectiveness of Task Oriented Language Teaching Of English in Enhancing the Writing Skill among VII Standard Students".

Operational Definition of key Terms

Effectiveness

Effectiveness is the capability of producing a desired result. When something is deemed effective, it means it has an intended or expected outcome, or produces a deep, vivid impression.

Task

A task normally has an aim, which provides the purpose for the activity; in most cases the activity goes beyond the practice of language for the own sake and it is distinct for this and other reasons from the term 'exercise'.

Communicative

According to Oxford Advanced Learner's Dictionary of current English (1986) communicative is *'ready and willing to talk and give information'*.

Task-Based Communicative Activities

Task-based communicative activities means the communicative activities organized around tasks for classroom interaction and learning. Task based communicative activities aim to improve and extend the learner's range of skill in written aspects of English.

Activities

Activities are of many types such as motivation activity, self learning activity and evolution activity. Activities create interest among learners and it is highly motivating. All activities have been prepared with an aim of achieving and self-confidently.

Objectives of the Study

1. To find out whether there is any significant difference between the pre-test mean scores of control and experimental groups students in writing.
2. To find out whether there is any significant difference between the pre-test and post-test mean scores of control groups students in writing.

3. To find out whether there is any significant difference between the pre-test and post-test mean scores of experimental groups students in writing
4. To find out whether there is any significant difference between the post-test mean scores of control group and experimental groups students in writing.
5. To find out whether there is any significant difference between the post-test mean scores of experimental groups students in writing between male and female.
6. To find out whether there is any significant difference between the post-test mean scores of experimental groups students in writing between rural area and urban area students
7. To find out whether there is any significant difference between the post-test mean scores of experimental groups students in writing between Joint family and nuclear family.
8. To find out whether there is any significant difference between the post-test mean scores of excremental groups students in writing between the students of Parent's Qualification Educated and Uneducated.
9. To find out whether there is any significant difference between the post-test mean scores of experimental groups students in writing with regard to the parent's occupation government and private.

Hypothesis of the Study

1. There is no significant difference between the pre-test mean scores of control and experimental groups students in writing.
2. There is no significant difference between the pre-test and post-test mean scores of control groups students in writing.
3. There is no significant difference between the pre-test and post-test mean scores of experimental groups students in writing.
4. There is no significant difference between the post-test mean scores of control group and experimental groups students in writing.

5. There is no significant difference between the post-test mean scores of experimental groups students in writing with regard to the Male and Female.
6. There is no significant difference between the post-test mean scores of experimental groups students in writing with regard to the Rural area and Urban area students
7. There is no significant difference between the post-test mean scores of experimental groups students in writing with regard to the joint family and nuclear family..
8. There is no significant difference between the post-test mean scores of experimental groups students in writing with regard to the Parent's Qualification Educated and Uneducated.
9. There is no significant difference between the post-test mean scores of experimental groups students in writing with regard to the parent's Occupation Govt. Job and Private job.

Limitation of the Study

The limitation of the study is as follows,

1. This study confined to the high school students in Sivagangai district.
2. The sample consist of forty students (20 control group and 20 experimental group)
3. The task based language teaching is designed to develop the writing skill of the student.
4. The experiment was conducted for a period of twenty working days (1 hour a day)
5. The achievement tests used in this study are to writing skill of the students.
6. The study confined to the task oriented language teaching of English only. It is not able to extend any other approaches.
7. The study restricted to seek enhancing writing skill only; it is not able to extent to other three skills like Reading, Speaking and Listening.
8. The study restricted to examine VII standard students only

Conclusion

The inattention of the study to examine the effectiveness of task based language teaching of English in enhancing the writing skill among VII standard students. The present study consists of five chapter. The first chapter gives the introduction and the overview of all the chapters. It tells the need and the pedagogical importance of the present study. The second chapter presents the review of related studies, done in abroad and in India. The third chapter deals with the methodology of the study by giving the detailed account of the sample of the study, the method of various task based interventions given to the experimental and the control group students. The fourth chapter consists of the results of the study and the last chapter gives the conclusion with new stimulus to develop the writing skills among VII standard students.

Chapter-II

Review of Related Literature

Introduction

The First chapter is a discussion of the background, aims and objectives of the present study. This chapter deals with the review of related literature. The purpose of the study of research works done in the same field is to understand what type of study has been done and what exactly has been explored before the present research work started.

The study of related literature and research work is very essential and important as it provides us proper guidelines. There are many educationists who tried to show the importance of review of the related literature various views regarding the review of literature.

“A Survey of related literature is necessary for proper planning, execution and right concept of the problems and solutions. It provides guiding hypothesis, suggestive methods of investigation and comparative data for interpretative purpose.”

A summary of the writings of recognized authorities and of previous research provides evidence that the researcher is familiar with what is already known and what is still unknown and untested.

Since effective research is based upon past knowledge, this step helps to eliminate the duplication of what has been done and provides useful hypotheses and helpful suggestions for significant investigation." The review of related research provides the right direction to think and appropriate track to execute and complete the research.

Some people might think of a literature review as reading a book and then giving it thumbs up or thumbs down. No, not so. A literature review is a review of various pieces of literature on one topic, ranging from series of books to shorter pieces like pamphlets. Sometimes, the literary review is a part of a larger research paper. Its purpose is to prevent duplication of efforts, resolve conflicts, and point the way for further research.

A review of related literature is a body of text that aims of review the critical points of current and or methodological approaches on a particular topic. Literature reviews are secondary sources and such do not report any new or original experimental.

A well structured literature is characterized by a logical of ideas, current and relevant references with consistent, appropriate referencing style; proper use of terminology; and an unbiased and comprehensive view of the previews research on the topic.

Purpose of Literature Review

As part of the planning process the researcher should have done a Literature Review which is a survey of important articles, books and other sources pertaining to his research topic. For the second main section of research report he needs to write a summary of the main studies and research related to your topic. This review of the professional literature relevant to research question will help to contextualize, or frame, his research. It will also give readers the necessary background to understand the research.

Evaluating other studies

In a review of the literature, one does not merely summarize the research findings that others have reported. One must also evaluate and comment on each study's worth and validity. He may find that some published research is not valid. If it also runs counter to his hypothesis, you may want to critique it in his review. He should not ignore it. He will tell how his research will be better/overcome the flaws. Doing this can strengthen the rationale for conducting his research.

Review of the related literature besides, to allow researchers to acquaint him with current knowledge in the field or area in which he or she is going to conduct his or her research, serves the following specific purposes;

1. Review of the related literature besides, to allow researchers to define the limits if his field. It helps the researchers to delimit and define his problem. The knowledge of related literature brings the researcher up to date on the work which others have done and them to state the objectives clearly and concisely.

2. By reviewing the related the researchers can avoid unfruitful and useless problem areas. He can select those areas in which positive findings are likely to result and his endeavours would be likely to add to the knowledge. The following were the objectives of the review of related literature.

1. To understand various aspects and scope of the research thoroughly.
2. To study the researches which have been done before the current research?
3. To decide proper hypothesis, objectives, methodology of the research.
4. To have a proof on the part of the investigator to show that the investigator knows what type of study is done in the same field.
5. To have proper guideline to implement the practical work.
6. To have appropriate guidance to complete the present research.
7. To provide a vast outlook regarding the subject.
8. To avoid repetition of the researches done.
9. To get more knowledge and explanation about CLT (Communicative Language Teaching)

10. To broaden the researcher's horizon of knowledge.

11. To find out the novelty of the present research.

Studies Conducted in India

Uma Chitra 2000 writing skill through a silent movie. Films could arose high level of motivation and result in a most satisfying learning experience.

Urmil Vyas 1993 improving handwriting the training aid is universally useful for learning language at any level and age.

Bakaren Herbert. S 1989 remedial teaching program on the comment errors in written English. Students in experimental and control group did not differ significantly in committing orthography errors in written English.

Rao, Ramachandra. K and Nija Lingappa.K 1988 improving communication skills. Listening comprehension was felt as the most difficult part. Proficiency in english was not upto the expected level.

Joshi V.G 1985 scrutiny of errors in written english and remedialprogram number and quality of errors reduced after the remedial program.

Antoni Samy 1984 "Effect of Auto Instructional Programme on Developing Writing Skill in English at first year B.E level". Sample is one section of one year B.E students. Auto Instructional techniques were to minimize the teachers work to and maximize the leader's task.

Gaikwad1984 " A comparative study of Efficiency of the Direct method and bilingual method of teaching English to the lower class of secondary schools in rural area of Maharashtra state". Sample is selected schools of Maharashtra state. Parallel group and experimental group. (i) The bilingual method was superior to direct method in developing the linguistics skills of understanding speaking and writing. (ii) Both the methods were equally effective so far as reading skills were concerns. The bilingual method enabled the teacher and the pupils to speed up interactive communication among themselves.

Kamala supports "Communicative strategies to enhance in written communication skills in English students". Sample is college students in different subject. Constructing a story out of a given outline. The use of communicative strategies facilitates the enhancement of written communication skills.

Prathibha khanna and S.Pal "A study of errors in English writing committed by high school students". Sample is 50 boys and girls studying in class X of four educational institution were randomly selected. Writing an essay about two hundred words on a pre-determined topic. (i) Errors in grammar were most significant. (ii) Girls committed less error than boys. (iii) Errors of vocabulary and punctuation are least.

Singh V.D " A study on the linguistic and communicative abilities of high school in teachers of English relation to their class-room functions. Samples are sixty TG teachers and PG teachers teaching high school classes in 115 central schools located in the states of Rajasthan and UP and UT of Delhi. Recorded composition and sentence exercise.

Shobana "Survey to identify the difficulties n written English among secondary school learners". Sample are a English and Telling medium school students. Achievement tests: Essay writing. The study revealed a significance association between the performance of students in written English and different variables in related to school and family.

Usha Paadmanabhan Analyzes of the writing skill in English of UG students of technology in Mumbai". Sample area 12 high achievers and 5 low achievers to choose the word and phrase and phrases to be used to repeat practice. Improvement in the writing skill of both high and low achievers but in varying degrees.

Studies Conducted in Abroad

Thanatkun Tangpermpoon. (2009) Writing is considered as the most difficult skill for language learners because they need to have a certain amount of L2 background knowledge about the rhetorical organizations, appropriate language use or specific lexicon with which they want to communicate to their readers. To assist language instructors to improve learners' writing competence and produce good writing, this article aims to present the combination of genre, product, and process approaches in a writing class. To better understand the topic, this paper will be divided into two main parts.

***Lee* (2009)** defined task as; (1) a classroom activity or exercise that has an objective obtainable only by the interaction among participants, a mechanism for structuring and sequencing interaction, and a focus on meaning exchange;

Ellis(2008) TBLT is an approach to teaching a second / foreign language that seeks to engage learners' interactional authentic language use by having them perform a series of tasks. It aims to both enable learners to acquire new linguistic knowledge and systematize their existing knowledge. Task-based learning is advantageous to the learner as it is more learner-cantered.

Yasin (2005) investigated the effects of computer-assisted instruction on the second graders learning English in the District of **Bani Kinanah**. The participants in the study were fifty female second grade pupils randomly chosen from Hatem Basic School for Girls. The sample was divided into two groups, experimental and control. The experimental group was taught via computer, whereas the control group was taught with the traditional method.

Abu-Seileek (2004) designed a CALL program and tested its effect on Jordanian students' writing ability in English. The study attempted to find any statistical differences between the mean scores on the writing task of the experimental and control groups. The participants of the study were first grade secondary students. The instrument of this study was a computer-based program Win Word 2002, whose main function was to check and correct spelling, style and grammar errors. The study revealed that students who used the computer to learn writing skills achieved higher scores than those who studied by the traditional method.

Almekhlafi (2004) investigated the effect of CALL on elementary school students' achievement and their attitudes towards learning English in the United Arab Emirates. 83 elementary students in Al-Tamayoz Elementary prep school were selected and divided into experimental and control groups (43and 40 participants respectively).

Fellner and Apple (2005) utilized student blogs in a CALL program of low-proficiency and low-motivation Japanese university language students during a seven-day English language course in September 2004. The program included computer-based tasks and tasks in the traditional classroom. The researchers described the students' writing gains by the number of words and their frequency level in the students' blogs at the beginning and at the end of the program. The researchers found out that there was a 350% increase in the number of the words used in the students' blog entries by the end of the CALL program.

Hages (2004) investigated the effect of a computer supported collaborative learning (CSCL) environment on fifth graders' writing performance and outcomes. 34 students participated in a real-world writing project, taking on alternative roles of journalists and editors in creating a school newspaper. Both groups were engaged in the writing task. The CSCL group was supported by a web-based software knowledge forum, whereas the control group used paper and pencil. Students were observed and interviewed. The findings showed that CSCL group had significant gains and they were more motivated than the control group.

Bani-Hani (2003) investigated the effectiveness of a computerized instructional program for teaching English as a foreign language in Jordanian basic stage schools. The study also investigated the teachers' and students' opinions about computer-assisted language learning (CALL). The sample of the study consisted of 73 sixth grade students in two sections and 100 basic school teachers. The researcher used an achievement test for both the experimental and control groups. He also used an opinionative for both teachers and students in the experimental group to investigate their opinions towards using computers in teaching and learning English. A study on Improving the English Writing Skills of Higher Secondary Students in Meghalaya, India, Through a Three-Week Module.

Evarisha M Syiem. Importance of Communicating through writing in English: Communication through writing is an extremely critical component of education, livelihood, and basic functionality in a society. Especially, in higher education where English happens to be the medium of instruction, writing is extremely important because it is used extensively in communicating with professors, employers, peers, or just about anyone else. Problems faced by students using English as a Second Language:

However, the ability to write well is not a naturally acquired skill; it is usually learned or culturally transmitted as a set of practice in formal instructional settings or other environments. Further, the students' skill in writing in a second language is faced with several challenges. There can be many social as well as cognitive reasons for this, such as a negative attitude towards the target language, cultural distance between them and the target language, and lack of motivation. Students are even ignorant of the basic rules and structural patterns which they are supposed to have learnt at the school level. Some EFL teachers may be perplexed by such problems in their writing classes and are unable to find an efficient way to awaken students 'imagination and set their minds working. As a result, students feel that using the English language amidst all their doubts and uncertainties is a cumbrous affair. Besides the reasons mentioned above, another major hurdle that students face is the dearth of time to practise writing in the classroom, with the teacher available for clarifying their doubts. Coping with the pressure to complete a set syllabus, teachers hardly have the time to allow students to practise writing. Writing is a skill and like any other skill, being fluent in it requires plenty of practice.

TEACHING ENGLISH AND TASK-BASED METHOD

Prabhu (1999) believed that students may learn more effectively when their minds are focused on the task, rather than on the language, they are using. Prabhu (1987) defined task as 'an activity which require learners to arrive at an outcome from given information through some process of thought, and which allows teachers to control and regulate that process' ***(Van den Branden and others, 2006).*** According to this definition, reading a train timetable and deciding which train one should take to get to a certain destination on a given day is an appropriate classroom task (***Richards and Rodgers, 2001***).

Second, technology programs have been encouraged as cost effective ways that could be used to replace or enhance direct human input (***Ware & Warschauer, cited in Tsou, 2008)***. Acting in the electronic community helps learners create, analyze, and produce ideas easier and more efficiently. Using emails and sharing files give students the chance to collaborate with peers and teachers (***Belisle).***

The use of the Internet and the World Wide Web has affected the educational process, the way teachers teach students, and the field of EFL ***(Chuo, 2007***). The Internet serves both as a communication tool and as an information resource (***Cunningham, ; Lee)***. In fact, the most frequent classroom use of the Internet is searching for information resources (***Grabe & Grabe, 2003).***

Research findings have supported the use of technology in teaching language. First, technology has positive influences on students' motivation (***Tsou, Wang, & Li, 2002***)..

Dornyei(2001) emphasizes the importance of presenting a task in a way that motivates learners. Like Lee, he sees value in explaining the purpose and utility of the task. This may be especially important for learners from traditional 'studied' classrooms; they may need to be convinced of the value of a more 'experiential' approach. Dornyei also suggests that task preparation should involve strategies for whetting students' appetites to perform the task(e. g. by asking them to guess what the task will involve)and for helping them to perform the task. Strategies in this latter category are discussed below.

However, the effectiveness of such training cannot be taken for granted. ***Lam and Wong*** (2000)report a study that investigated the effects of teaching students to seek and provide clarification when communication difficulties arose in class discussions. However, although this resulted in greater use of these strategies in a post-training discussion, the strategies were often not employed effectively(e. g. the students were unable to clarify something they had said) suggesting that pre-task training in the use of communication strategies may not be effective unless students also learn how to scaffold each other cooperatively when performing the task.

There is also a danger in directing pre-task training based on a model at specific aspects of language or language use. The effect of a web-based writing instructional EFL program on enhancing the performance of Jordanian secondary students.

Skehan(1996)refers to two broad alternatives available to the teacher during the pre-task phase: an emphasis on the general cognitive demands of the task, and/or an emphasis on linguistic factors. Attention capacity is limited, and it is needed to respond to both linguistic and cognitive demands . . . then engaging in activities which reduce cognitive load will release attention capacity for the learner to concentrate more on linguistic factors.

Skehan(1996) and Willis(1996) suggest than simply 'observing' others perform a task can help reduce the cognitive load on the learner. However, the model can also be accompanied by activities designed to raise learners' consciousness about specific features of the task performance for example, the strategies that can be employed to overcome communication problems, the conversational gambits for holding the floor during a discussion or the pragmalinguistic devices for performing key language functions. Such activities might require the learners to identify and analyze these features in the model texts. Alternatively, they might involve pre-training in the use of specific strategies.

Pigg (1996) studied the effectiveness of the CALL program "Paragraph Builder" on fifth grade students' topic sentence identification. Pigg used a pre-post test control group design. The post test results indicated that the program produced a statistically significant rise in the mean scores of the post-test. The results revealed that students working with the computer enjoyed learning about topic sentences by using the program "Paragraph Builder".

Langone, Levine, Clees, Malone and Koorland (1996) studied the use of computer-based word processing on the writing samples of elementary students with behaviour disorders. Repeated measures, alternating-treatments design was used to compare student performance in constructing writing samples under two experimental conditions: a) a typing tutor plus a computer-based word processor and b) paper and pencil. The findings showed a positive effect on the writing of students in the experimental group by making them more independent. Of the 6 students' written story lengths, three increased during the experimental condition. Individual differences in the error rates were noted and indicted varied improvement under each condition for capitalization, spelling, punctuation and complete sentences. Other students' writing showed little improvement except editing and spending more time on writing.

Adler-Kassner and Reynolds (1996) studied the computer use in basic composition classes at Minnesota's General College. Although computer-assisted instruction packages were not utilized, the computer was used as a tool to help students become aware of their reading skill. The researchers found that students benefited from the interaction with readings over email more than in the traditional classroom. The researchers also found that students' confidence was strengthened because of the feedback they received in terms of email responses. Moreover, students benefited from locating other resources and making connections to the texts they used.

Braine (1995) investigated the effects of networked computers on ESL student writing at Brock University in Ontario, Canada. The researcher compared ESL students in first-year English classes writing in two contexts: a networked computer class and a traditional lecture-style class. The purpose was to determine which setting promoted writing, had more improvement in writing, and had more peer and teacher feedback. The first and final drafts of students' papers were scored, and the number of interactions during peer-review sessions was analyzed. The networked setting was shown to promote better writing and more peer and teacher feedback. The traditional setting was shown to promote more improvement in writing.

Providing a model

An alternative is to ask the students to observe a model of how the task can be performed without requiring them to undertake a trial performance of the task (see Aston (1982) for an early example of such an approach). Minimally this involves presenting them with a text of the task.

Nunan(1989) lists a number of learning strategies (e. g. 'Learning to live with uncertainty' and 'Learning to make intelligent guesses')that students can be taught to help them become 'adaptable, creative, inventive and above all independent'(p. 81)and thus more effective performers of a task.

Fawwas Al-Abed Al-Haq. Mahmoud Ali Al-Sobh. Whiteman (1981) states that students are weak in writing because teachers concentrate on teaching grammar, spelling drills and punctuation rather than involving students in the writing process. In spite of the fact that these are means that help students learn language in general and writing in particular, students need to be taught how to produce language communicatively. Techniques of teaching writing should be enjoyable and interesting to the students while helping them write good compositions.

Technology has been a tool for teaching writing skills since its introduction to schools. The use of technology for writing includes computer-based projects, software programs and word-processing that direct writing instruction and assist students in developing their own writing, mails, and websites ***(Burner, n.d.).***

Besides Prabhu, ***Nunan (1980)*** acknowledged the special nature of classroom- based interaction defining a task as "a piece of classroom work that involves learners in comprehending, manipulating, producing or interacting in the target language while their attention is focused on mobilizing their grammatical knowledge in order to express meaning, and in which the intention is to convey meaning rather than to manipulate form".

Task-Based Language Teaching. ***David Nunan.*** Before doing anything else, I need to define the central concept behind this book. In doing so, I will draw a basic distinction between what I will call real-world or target tasks, and pedagogical tasks: target tasks, as the name implies, refer to uses of language in the world beyond the classroom; pedagogical tasks are those that occur in the classroom.

The task-based approach: some questions and suggestions. ***William Littlewood.***This article addresses the question of what tasks are. It suggests that rather than accept the common 'communicative' definition, we should return to a broader definition and then focus on key dimensions that distinguish (from the learner's perspective) different types of task, notably degrees of task-involvement and degrees of focus on form or meaning. This approach helps us to conceptualize the complementary roles of form-focused and meaning-focused tasks in our methodology. It also shows the continuity between task- based language teaching and the broader communicative approach within which it is a development. Finally the article asks whether 'task-based approach' is really the most appropriate term at all for describing these developments in language pedagogy.

Conclusion

In the Chapter II, the research introduced review related to literature and gives its significant in the research writing. The researcher gives the review of literature related to India and abroad. The review gave lot of insights to the investigator in selecting the research problems and suitable methodology. The research gap was also identified on the basis of the review. The methodology adopted by the researcher in the study was discussed in the following chapter.

Chapter-III

Methodology

Introduction

The methodology may include publication research, interviews, surveys and other research techniques and could include both present and historical information. Method is a style of conducting a research work which is determined by the value of the problem.

So in this context, this explains design of the study, Method and the Procedure, Statement of the Problem, Objectives of this Study, Hypothesis of the Study, Limitation of the Study, Research Method, Research Tool, Construction of the Research Tool, Samples of the Study, Description of Research Tool and Scoring Procedure, Pilot Study, Validity of the Tool, Reliability of the Tool, Sampling techniques used, Collecting the Data, Analyzing the Data, Statistical techniques used and so on.

Research Design

Research design is the "blue print" of the study. The first chapter discusses the need and significance, scope of the study, objectives of the study, hypothesis of the study and limitation of the study. The second chapter discusses the purpose of the literary review and find out the literature related to the study. The third chapter discusses the methodology, procedure, and the research tool of the study. The fourth chapter analyses the collection of the data and the fifth chapter conclude with the suggestion and findings of the study.

Method and the Procedure

The method of this study is experimental research. The researcher has taken the VII standard students from the selected schools for the experiment by using the feedback of the students. The data is taken and analysis of the samples to find out the result.

Statement of the Problem:

"Effectiveness Of Task Oriented Language Teaching Of English In Enhancing The Writing Skill Among VII Standard Students".

Objectives of the Study

1. To find out whether there is any significant difference between the pre-test mean scores of Control and Experimental groups students in writing.
2. To find out whether there is any significant difference between the pre-test and post-test mean scores of Control groups students in writing.
3. To find out whether there is any significant difference between the pre-test and post-test mean scores of Experimental groups students in writing
4. To find out whether there is any significant difference between the post-test mean scores of Control group and Experimental groups students in writing.
5. To find out whether there is any significant difference between the post-test mean scores of experimental groups students in writing between Male and Female.
6. To find out whether there is any significant difference between the post-test mean scores of experimental groups students in writing between Rural area and Urban area students.

7. To find out whether there is any significant difference between the post-test mean scores of experimental groups students in writing between Joint Family and Nuclear Family.
8. To find out whether there is any significant difference between the post-test mean scores of experimental groups students in writing between the students of Parent's Qualification Educated and Uneducated.
9. To find out whether there is any significant difference between the post-test mean scores of Experimental groups students in writing with regard to the parent's Occupation Government job and Private job.

Hypothesis of the Study

1. There is no significant difference between the pre-test mean scores of Control and Experimental groups students in writing.
2. There is no significant difference between the pre-test and post-test mean scores of Control groups students in writing.
3. There is no significant difference between the pre-test and post-test mean scores of Experimental groups students in writing
4. There is no significant difference between the post-test mean scores of Control group and Experimental groups students in writing.
5. There is no significant difference between the post-test mean scores of Experimental groups students in writing with regard to the Male and Female.
6. There is no significant difference between the post-test mean scores of experimental groups students in writing with regard to the Rural area and Urban area students.
7. There is no significant difference between the post-test mean scores of experimental groups students in writing with regard to the Joint Family and Nuclear Family.
8. There is no significant difference between the post-test mean scores of experimental groups students in writing with regard to the Educated Qualification Educated and Uneducated.

9. To find out whether there is any significant difference between the post-test mean scores of Experimental groups students in writing with regard to the parent's Occupation Government job and private job.

Limitation of the Study

The limitation of the study is as follows,

1. This study confined to the high school students in the Sivagangai district.
2. The sample consist of forty students (20 control group and 20 experimental group)
3. The task based language teaching is designed to develop the writing skill of the student.
4. The experiment was conducted for a period of twenty working days (1 hour a day)
5. The achievement tests used in this study are to writing skill of the students.
6. The study confined to the task based language teaching of English only. It is not able to extend any other approaches.
7. The study restricted to seek enhancing writing skill only; it is not able to extent to other three skills like Reading, Speaking and Listening.
8. The study restricted to examine VII standard students only

Research Method

Experimental design is the blue print of the procedures that enables the researcher to the hypothesis by reading valid conclusions about relationship between the independent and dependant variables.

"Experimental means of scientific test to find out or prove something".

Research method plays a vital role which helps the researcher from distraction and to find the result. **Experimental method** is the research method that used in this study. The researcher comes to an inference with the help of feedback of the students. There are many ways to get information. The most common research methods are: literature searches, talking with people, focus groups, personal interviews, telephone surveys, mail surveys, email surveys, and internet surveys.

Research Tool

This section deals with the development of tools of research employed in the study. The investigation after through discussion with his research guide and a panel of experts in the field of educational research and ELT specialists decided to study the effectiveness of task based language teaching of English in enhancing the writing skills of the VII standard students in English with regard to writing. Thus, a tooling the form of achievement test was prepared. It was descriptive in nature. It aimed to study the knowledge level of VII standard students in writing and its components in English Language Teaching.

Research tool is a research material that is necessary to perform research. Research tool can be defined as the instrument in the hands of researchers to measure what researcher's intent to his study. Questionnaire is the research tool that is used in this study. Questionnaires are a good way to obtain information from a large number of people and/or people who may not have the time to attend an interview or take part in experiments. They enable people to take their time, think about it and come back to the questionnaire later. Participants can state their views or feelings privately without worrying about the possible reaction of the researcher. Unfortunately, some people may still be inclined to try to give socially acceptable answers. People should be encouraged to answer the questions as honestly as possible so as to avoid the researchers drawing false conclusions from their study.

Construction of the Research Tool

A questionnaire is a research instrument consisting of a series of questions other prompts for the purpose of gathering information from respondents. Questions which enhance the writing skill are choosing as a research tool in this study. Questionnaires typically contain multiple choice questions, attitude scales, closed questions and open-ended questions. The drawback for researchers is that they usually have a fairly low response rate and people do not always answer all the questions and/or do not answer them correctly. Questionnaires can be administered in a number of different ways. Researchers may even decide to administer the questionnaire in person which has the advantage of including people who have difficulties reading and writing. In this case, the participant may feel that he is taking part in an interview rather than completing a questionnaire as the researcher will be noting down the responses on his behalf.

Samples of the Study

The sample was drawn from the VII standard of selected schools as follows, **Alagappa Model School, Karaikudi**, **in Sivagangai** district, were assigned to two groups based on the marks scored by them in the achievement test in English conducted prior to the pre-test of the study. Then they were assigned to the experimental group 20 students and control group 20 students. Thus the sample of 20 VII standard students in a single group has been formed.

Description of Research Tool and Scoring Procedure

The research tool, questionnaire in this study, has some questions based on writing skills. Thus the research tool has the scoring procedure for analyze the students Effectiveness of task based language teaching of English in enhancing the writing skill of VII standard students.

Pilot Study

A pilot study is a research project that is conducted on a limited scale that allows researchers to get a clearer idea of what they want to know and how they can best find it out without the expense and effort of a fledged study. They are used commonly to try our survey questions and to refine research hypothesis.

Select the population of VII standard students in sample schools. The researcher select 40 students for experimentation from each schools and to construct the criterion referenced test and t evaluate of the criterion reference test and to conduct pre-test and to select the strategies for understanding Differential methods and to verify the applicability of the strategies by connecting experts and teachers and to implement the strategies among the select students and to conduct a post-test and analyzing the result.

Validity of the Tool

Validity of the tool is not a stable one in any research. As the teaching methods, reading methods and the syllabus designing changes the validity of the tool. Hence, this tool valid up to one academic year.

Reliability of the Tool

Reliability of the research tool is the heart of the experimental research. This study has the tool of list of questionnaire which needs the answer from the student. As this study method originally conducted in selected schools, it has the reliability of its own. Experimental method is one of the highly reliable methods in the research study. Here, the researcher used the Experimental method which has the reliable with the help of the sample of the questionnaire which has the real Effectiveness of task based language teaching of English in enhancing the writing skill of VII standard students.

Collecting the Data

The researcher has selected the Schools for collecting the data for the research study. After the administration of try out and finalization of the research tool they were administration to both the groups of the sample population. The tools were administered the tools personally. It took few minutes to answer all the items in the inventory. Since the investigator administered the tool personally all the subjects had responded properly. The response was score and the data were organized. Surveys involve collecting information, usually from fairly large groups of people, by means of questionnaires but other techniques such as interviews or telephoning may also be used. There are different types of survey. The most straightforward type is administered to a sample of people at a set point in time. Another type is the "before and after survey" which people complete before a major event or experience and then again afterwards.

After the administration of try out and finalization of the research tools they were administration to both the groups of the sample population. The tools were administered with the previous permission from the head of the institution. The investigator administered the tools personally. It took nearly one hour thirty minutes to answer all the items in the test of writing skills. Since, the investigator administered the tools personally all the subjects had responded properly. The response was score and the data were organized.

Experiments

School students who take part in research involving experiments might be asked to answer various questions to measure their cognitive effectiveness of task based language teaching of English in enhancing the writing skill of VII standard students.. The results of different groups are then compared. Participants should not be anxious about performing well but simply do their best. The aim of this feedback is not to judge people or measure so-called attitude but to look for links between performance and other factors. This Case study involves the detailed study of a particular case (a person or small group). Various methods of data collection and analysis are used but this typically includes observation and interviews and may involve consulting other people and personal or public records.

Participant Observation

This study is a observation study where the researcher becomes (or is already) part of the group to be observed. This involves fitting in, gaining the trust of members of the group and at the same time remaining sufficiently detached as to be able to carry out the observation. The observations made might be based on what people do, the explanations they give for what they do, the roles they have, relationships amongst them and features of the situation in which they find themselves. The researcher should be open about what he is doing, give the participants in the study the chance see the results and comment on them, and take their comments seriously.

Statistical techniques used

Statistical techniques used for analyzing the data are:

1. 't' test to find out the significance of difference between the attitude towards reading research journal among B.Ed students in the means of sex, college, area and so on

2. Graphical representation to show the comparison of variables with one another.

Task Based

Course design is concerned with the selection and sequencing of content the 'what' of teaching. As such, it contrasts with 'methodology', which addresses the 'how' of teaching. Together, 'course design' and 'methodology' comprise the language curriculum. It has been suggested, however, that the distinction between 'design' and 'methodology' is not relevant in task-based teaching.

Nunan(1989)argued that in this kind of teaching the focus shifts from 'the outcomes of instruction'(i. e. the linguistic knowledge or skills to be mastered)towards the 'processes of learning'(i. e. what learners need to do in order to learn) Thus, **Nunan** claimed, the 'what' and the 'how' of teaching are merged. Similarly, **Kumaravadivelu(199**3)argued that 'methodology becomes the central tenet of task-based pedagogy'(p. 73)since the goal is to allow learners to navigate their own paths and routes to learning. However, these arguments ignore the fact that a task-based curriculum still involves making decisions about content (i. e. what tasks to include in the syllabus)and methodology(i. e. how the tasks will be used in the classroom) Thus, it is important to maintain the distinction in discussions of task-based teaching. The purpose of this article is to consider the methodology of task-based instruction. Methodology involves of a consideration of procedures of two basic kinds. Firstly, there are those procedures that specify how the activities mentioned in the syllabus can be converted into actual lessons (i. e. lesson design) Secondly, there are procedures relating to how the teacher and learners are to participate in the lessons (i. e. participatory structure) in this article, however, I shall only address lesson design. I shall conclude by proposing a number of general principles to guide the methodology of task-based instruction.

Conclusion

The methodology of this research study consists research design, Methods and procedure, objectives, hypothesis, limitation of the study. It also contains the research method, research tool, construction of the research tool, samples of the study, pilot study, validity and reliability of the study.

Chapter-IV

Analysis and Interpretation of Data

Introduction

Research consists of systematic observation and description of the characteristic or properties of objectives or events. This chapter deals with the analysis of data collected for this study. The qualified data have been interpreted meaningful in this chapter. This chapter presents the collected data which are critically analyzed through appropriate statistical technology.

Null Hypothesis

A Null Hypothesis is useful in testing the significant of difference. The null hypothesis states that the relationship exists between the variable studied are no difference will be found between treatments. A null hypothesis states that there is no significant difference between two parameters. It concerns a judgement has to whether apparent difference are true differences or whether they merely result from sampling error.

The researcher uses the null hypothesis as a useful to in testing the difference between two group means. When the difference found between sample means is great enough to assume importance at desired level of significance it cannot be accidental or due to errors and the null hypothesis rejected.

Differential Statistics

This section highlights the differential studies identifying the difference among students.

't' Test:

The 't' test is a statistical test that allows to compares two means to determine the probability that the difference between the means is a real differences rather than a chance difference. The test of significance of the difference between two mean is known as the 't' test.

HYPOTHESIS: 1

S.NO.	Type of Group	No. of Students	Mean	Standard Deviation	"t" Value	df	Level of Significant at 0.05
1.	Control Group (pre test)	20	25.45	3.18	1.84	38	Not Significant
2.	Experimental Group (pre test)	20	28.5	6.68			

There is no significant difference between the pre-test mean scores of control and experimental groups students in writing.

Interpretation

Since the calculated t-value (1.84) in less than table value (2.02), it is that there is no Significant difference between pre-test mean scores of control group and experimental group students in writing. Hence the Hypothesis formed by the investigator is **accepted.**

HYPOTHESIS: 2

There is no significant difference between the pre-test and post test mean scores of control students in writing.

S.NO.	Type of Group	No. of Students	Mean	Standard Deviation	"t" Value	df	Level of Significant at 0.05
1.	Pre - test	20	25.45	3.18	1.84	38	Not Significant
2.	Post test	20	28.50	6.68			

Interpretaion

Since the calculated t-value (1.84) in less than table value (2.02),it is that there is no Significant difference between pre-test and post test mean scores of control group students in writing. Hence the Hypothesis formed by the investigator is **accepted.**

HYPOTHESIS: 3

There is no significant difference between the pre-test and post test mean scores of experimental group students in writing

S.NO.	Type of Group	No. of Students	Mean	Standard Deviation	"t" Value	df	Level of Significant at 0.05
1.	Pre – test	20	28.5	6.68	5.09	38	Significant
2.	Post test	20	38.5	5.67			

Interpretation

Since the calculated t-value (5.09) in greater then table value (2.02),it is that there is Significant difference between pre-test and post test mean scores of experimental group students in writing. Hence the Hypothesis formed by the investigator is **rejected.**

HYPOTHESIS: 4

There is no significant difference between the post-test mean scores of control and experimental group students in writing.

S.NO.	Type of Group	No. of Students	Mean	Standard Deviation	"t" Value	df	Level of Significant at 0.05
1.	Control Group	20	28.50	6.68	5.09	38	Significant
2.	Experimental Group	20	38.5	5.67			

Interpretation

Since the calculated t-value (5.0965) in greater then table value (2.02), it is that there is Significant difference between post- test mean scores of control group and experimental group students in writing. Hence the Hypothesis formed by the investigator is **rejected.**

HYPOTHESIS: 5

There is no significant difference between the post-test mean scores of experimental group students in writing between Male and Female.

S.NO.	Gender	No. of Students	Mean	Standard Deviation	"t" Value	df	Level of Significant at 0.05
1.	Male	6	40.5	3.81	1.26	18	Not
2.	Female	14	37.64	6.11			Significant

Interpretation

Since the calculated t-value (1.26) in less than table value (2.10), it is inferred that there is no significant difference between post-test mean scores of experimental group students in writing between Male and Female. Hence the Hypothesis formed by the investigator is **accepted.**

HYPOTHESIS: 6

There is no significant difference between the post-test mean scores of experimental group students in writing with regard to the Rural area and Urban area students.

S.NO.	Gender	No. of Students	Mean	Standard Deviation	"t" Value	df	Level of Significant at 0.05
1.	Rural Area	17	38.29	6.84			
2.	Urban Area	3	40	4.02	0.42	18	Not Significant

Interpretation

Since the calculated t-value (0.42) in less than table value (2.10),it is inferred that there is no Significant difference between post- test mean scores of experimental group students in writing with regard to the Rural area and Urban area students . . Hence the Hypothesis formed by the investigator is **accepted.**

HYPOTHESIS: 7

There is no significant difference between the post-test mean scores of experimental group students in writing with regard to Joint Family and Nuclear Family.

S.NO.	Type of Family	No. of Students	Mean	Standard Deviation	"t" Value	df	Level of Significant at 0.05
1.	Nuclear Family	8	39.12	4.72	0.03	18	Not
2.	Joint Family	12	38.41	5.43			Significance

Interpretation

Since the calculated t-value (0.03) in smaller then table value (2.10),it is inferred that there is no Significant difference between post- test mean scores of experimental group students in writing with regard to Joint Family and Nuclear Family. Hence the Hypothesis formed by the investigator is **accepted**.

HYPOTHESIS: 8

There is no significant difference between the post-test mean scores of experimental group students in writing with regard to their parent's Qualification Educated and Uneducated.

S.NO.	Parents	No. of Students	Mean	Standard Deviation	"t" Value	df	Level of Significant at 0.05
1.	Educated	18	8.55	5.74	0.01	18	Not
2.	Un Educated	2	38.50	3.50			Significant

Interpretation

Since the calculated t-value (0.01) in less than table value (2.10),it is inferred that there is no Significant difference between post- test mean scores of experimental group students in writing with regard to parent's Qualification Educated and Uneducated. Hence the Hypothesis formed by the investigator is **accepted.**

HYPOTHESIS: 9

There is no significant difference between the post-test mean scores of experimental group students in writing with regard to their parent's Occupation Govt.job and Private Job.

S.NO.	Parents Occupation	No. of Students	Mean	Standard Deviation	"t" Value	df	Level of Significant at 0.05
1.	Governmentjob	4	41	4.18	1.17	18	Not Significant
2.	Private job	16	38	5.86			

Interpretation

Since the calculated t-value (1.17) in less than table value (2.10), it is inferred that there is no significant difference between post-tests mean scores of experimental group students in writing with regard to their parent's Govt.job and Private job. Hence the Hypothesis formed by the investigator is **accepted**.

Conclusion

In this chapter various data collected from B.Ed trainees have been analysed and interpreted. The next chapter deals with the summary and findings and conclusion.

Chapter-V

Summary and Conclusion

Introduction

After finalizing the calculation the investigator now moves on to the summarization of the research work undertaken. Summary is the most used part of research report because it guides not only research scholars but also educationalists and people who are interested in that particular problem. The important findings, summarization and suggestion of the present study below.

Need for the study

The study, "*Effectiveness of Task Oriented Language Teaching Of English in Enhancing the Writing Skill among VII Standard Students*" is important. Because, it helps to understand the effectiveness of task based language teaching of English in writing skill. It also helps to give solutions to enhancing the writing skill among VII standard students.

Like speech, writing has been considered a powerful mode of communication. After all, one writes with the purpose of being understood. Unlike speech, writing is not always for the audience present and hence it demands clear and comprehensive message.

While one speaks, he uses a variety of prosodic features such as pitch, loudness, speed, rhythm, pauses and so on that help us to get the feedback from listeners but this does not happen in case of writing where the context is created through the words alone and without the direct interaction between the writer and the reader.

The learning of any language is effective when the subject matter is presented in an interesting manner without stress, strain and anxiety. There are various pedagogical innovation used in all English class-room to development the writing skill of the VII standard students is not up to the expected level. Ii is somewhat quit unsatisfactory. Therefore, a need was felt by the researcher to find out the more suitable and an interesting for developing the writing skill of the VII standard students. This led the researcher to use task based language teaching to develop the writing skill of the VII standard students.

The problem faced by the students while learning writing has been analyzed by some researchers. Some of them have undertaken researcher on task based language teaching for developing writing skill of the students. Even though, many researchers have been carried out, there is a scope to explore the new ways of learning English, particularly where English studied as a second language. From the review of the researchers completed so far it is clear that an in depth study in the use of the task based language teaching in the developing the writing skill of the VII standard students. The present study is an attempt in this direction. It is also clear that the attempt already made in this direction are not providing concrete evidence of the effectiveness of task based language teaching in developing the writing skill in English. Attempts are required to understand the effectiveness of task based language teaching in English in developing the writing skill of the VII standard students. Therefore, a study exploring the effectiveness of task based language teaching.

Statement of the Problem

"Effectiveness Of Task Oriented Language Teaching Of English In Enhancing The Writing Skill Among VII Standard Students."

Objectives of the Study

1. To find out whether there is any significant difference between the pre-test mean scores of Control and Experimental groups students in writing.
2. To find out whether there is any significant difference between the pre-test and post-test mean scores of Control groups students in writing.
3. To find out whether there is any significant difference between the pre-test and post-test mean scores of Experimental groups students in writing
4. To find out whether there is any significant difference between the post-test mean scores of Control group and Experimental groups students in writing.
5. To find out whether there is any significant difference between the post-test mean scores of experimental groups students in writing between Male and Female.
6. To find out whether there is any significant difference between the post-test mean scores of experimental groups students in writing between Rural area and Urban area students.
7. To find out whether there is any significant difference between the post-test mean scores of experimental groups students in writing between joint family and nuclear family.
8. To find out whether there is any significant difference between the post-test mean scores of experimental groups students in writing between the students of Parent's Qualification Educated and Uneducated.
9. To find out whether there is any significant difference between the post-test mean scores of Experimental groups students in writing with regard to the parent's Occupation Government job and private job

Findings of the Study

In this study VII standard students are involved as a sample of students' *"Effectiveness Of Task Oriented Language Teaching Of*

English In Enhancing The Writing Skill Among VII Standard Students. After analyzing the achievement scores of the pre-test and post-test of the control group and experimental group, one could arrive at the following findings:

1. There is **no significant** difference between the **pre-test** mean scores of Control and **Experimental** groups students in writing.
2. There is **no significant** difference between the **pre-test** and **post-test** mean scores of **Control groups** students in writing.
3. There is **significant** difference between the **pre-test** and **post-test** mean scores of **Experimental groups** students in writing
4. There is **significant** difference between the **post-test** mean scores of **Control group** and **Experimental groups** students in writing.
5. There is **no significant** difference between the **post-test** mean scores of Experimental groups students in writing with regard to the Male and **Female**.
6. There is **no significant** difference between the **post-test** mean scores of experimental groups students in writing with regard to the **Rural** area and **Urban** area students.
7. There is **no significant** difference between the **post-test** mean scores of experimental groups students in writing with regard to the **Joint family** and **nuclear family**
8. There is **no significant** difference between the **post-test** mean scores of experimental groups students in writing with regard to the Educated Qualification **Educated** and **Uneducated.**
9. There is **no significant** difference between the **post-test** mean scores of Experimental groups students in writing with regard to the parent's Occupation **Govt job** and **Private job**.

Suggestion for the Study

The study was limited to a sample of VII standard students in Sivagangai District. Similar studies may be undertaken for the samples selected from different districts.

The same study may be conducted on a wide range of higher secondary schools in the district and also in different districts of Tamilnadu.

The effectiveness of task based language may be studied through experiments with other language such as listening, speaking and reading.

A parallel study can be conducted to find out the effectiveness of task oriented language teaching of the VII students in learning the mother tongue.

A separate study can be undertaken to assess the effectiveness of task Oriented language teaching by using computer assisted instruction in learning the language skill in English language education. Attempt can be made to develop task based language teaching of English and other language at school level and there by the effectiveness of task based language teaching can be assessed.

A study can be made to assess the attitude of the VII standard students in the use of task based language teaching in developing the various skills in English.

Recommendation of the study

1. This study plays the role of model for further research. This study mainly focuses on VII standard students' effectiveness of task oriented language teaching of English in enhancing the writing skill.
2. It also paves way for further research such as:"Effectiveness of task oriented language teaching of English in enhancing the writing skill among VII standard students" is a model for other thesis writing.
3. It helps others to write a dissertation on effectiveness of task oriented language teaching of English in enhancing the writing skill of secondary students.
4. It helps others to write a dissertation on effectiveness of task oriented language teaching of English in enhancing the writing skill of higher level students.
5. It helps others to write a dissertation on effectiveness of task oriented language teaching of English in enhancing the writing skill of college level students.

6. It is a scope to write a dissertation on Effectiveness of task oriented language teaching of English in enhancing the speaking skill among VII standard students

Conclusion

There are various ways of teaching and learning writing skill in English. Different linguists have advocated different methods and techniques to enhance the learning the writing skill at the VII standard students. Yet, the task based language teaching of English which is the recent method, is more effective than all other method of teaching writing skill at VII standard students level.

BIBLIOGRAPHY

1. Aggarwal,Y.P., "Statistical Methods", New Delhi: Sterling Publication, Pvt. Ltd., 1986.
2. Ahuja, G.C and Pramila Ahuja., "How to increase your reading speed", London: Cambridge University Press, 1987.
3. Baurah.T.C., "The English Teacher Handbook ", New Delhi: Sterling Publishers, Pvt. Ltd. 1991.
4. Best J.W and Khan J.V., "Research in Education", New Delhi: Prentice Hall Publishers, Pvt. Ltd. 2010.
5. Bharathi.T, "Personaity Development and Communicative English", New Delhi: Sterling Publishers, Pvt. Ltd. 2004.
6. Bindhu David, Sumod S., "Reading Comprehension in English in relation to Achivement Motivation ", Edutracks, 2011.
7. David Crytal, "A dictionary of Linguistics and Phonetics", London: Cambridge University Press, 1988.
8. Edmund Murphy, "A Practical English Grammar Book", New Delhi: Black Swan Publication, 2007.
9. Fredeick T. Wood, "An outine history of the English Language ", Chennai: Macmillan India Ltd., 2008.
10. Hariprasad.M and Prakasan.V, "Communicative English", New Delhi: Neelkamal Publication, Pvt. Ltd. 2005.

11. Kohil.A, "Techniques of Teaching English", New Delhi: Dhanpat Raj Publication, Pvt. Ltd. 2005.

12. Krishna Mohan and Meera Benerji, "Developing Communicative skills", New Delhi: Macmillan India Ltd., 2009.

13. Kundu.C.L and Tutoo.D.N, "Educational Psychology", New Delhi: Sterling Publishers, Pvt. Ltd. 2004.

14. Lokesh Koul, "Methodology of Educational Research ", New Delhi: Vikas Publishers, Pvt. Ltd. 2003.

15. Mangal S.K., "Methodology of Educational Psychology", New Delhi: Prentice Hall Publishers, Pvt. Ltd. 2007.

16. MLA of America, "Handbook for Writers of Research Papers", New Delhi: East-West Press, Pvt. Ltd. 2009.

17. Mowla, "English Language Teaching", New Delhi: Neelkamal Publication, Pvt. Ltd. 2008.

18. Sorakim, "On Improving English Communication", New Delhi: Journal of Media Communication, 2010.

19. Talawar M.S. and Benakanal V.A, "Advanced Educational Psychology", New Delhi: Sterling Publishers, Pvt. Ltd. 2009.

20. Tarafder S.K., "How to Learn Flawless English", Chennai: A.P.H. Publishing Corporation, 2005.

21. Wrenn.C.L., "The English Language", New Delhi: Vikas Publication, Pvt. Ltd. 2001.

2. Obstacles Learning of Homophones in English

Chapter - I

INTRODUCTION

English is an international language, spoken in many countries both as a native and as a second or foreign language. It is a West Germanic language originating in England and the first language for most people in Australia, Canada, the Commonwealth Caribbean, Ireland, New Zealand, the United Kingdom and the United States of America. It is taught in schools in every country on this earth. It is a vibrant and a living language spoken by over 300 million people as their native language and an additional 100 million people use it fluently as a foreign language. Millions speak it as an additional language also. As a rough estimate, 1000 million or one billion people around the world have some knowledge of English, either as a native language, as a second language, or as a foreign language.

In India which has over 1000 million (over billion) people, English is the associate official language. Pakistan, Bangladesh and many other nations which were ruled by Britain continue to use English both as an optional medium of instruction in their schools and as one of their official languages. The islands of the Philippines continue to use English as an important language for education, administration, and for mass media purposes. English is the chief foreign language taught in the schools of Europe, South America, Asia and Africa. Modern English is sometimes described as the global 'lingua franca'.

A working knowledge of English is required in certain fields, professions and occupations. As a result, over a billion people speak English at least at the basic level.

THE CONSTITUTION OF INDIA

It was stated in the constitution of India that Hindi is to be consider henceforth as the only official language of the union of India but English was to continue for 15 years from the date of adoption of the constitution. During this period, Hindi should be enriched so as to replace English as an official language. The Secondary Education Commission in 1953, argued English to be continued to bring the national unity in political and other spheres of activity. But this view had not been accepted by Central Advisory Board of Education in 1956 which introduce Three Language Formula in which English was given adequate place in the study.

Thus the status of English, which was of high order during British rule, had gone under a great change after independence. But however, it is quite noteworthy to mention here that after 60 years of independence, the study of English continued owing to many aspects of its importance. Chapter I Introduction

Recommendations of Secondary Education Commission (1953) Regarding the Teaching Method Need of the Right Method

Every experienced teacher and educationist know that even the best curriculum and the most perfect syllabus remain dead unless quickened into life by the right method of teaching and also the right kind of teachers. While building up a picture of the recognized secondary school, it is necessary to indicate the kind of method to be adopted and popularized. It is really the function of the Teacher Education Institutes to introduce these methods in our schools through their trained teachers. The Commission has confined its attention to the most outstanding defects in this field and to indicate the general principles and approach to be adopted to eradicate these defects.

HOMOPHONES

A **homophone** is a word that is pronounced the same as another word but differs in meaning, and may differ in spelling. The words may be spelled the same, such as*rose* (flower) and *rose* (past tense of "rise"), or differently, such as *carat*, *caret*, and *carrot*, or *to*, *two*, and *too*. Homophones that are spelled the same are also both homographs and homonyms.[1] Homophones that are spelled differently are also called heterographs. The term "homophone" may also apply to units longer or shorter than words, such as phrases, letters or groups of letters that are pronounced the same as another phrase, letter or group of letters. The word derives from the Greek *homo-* "same", and *phōn* "voice, utterance.

Homophones are often used to create puns and to deceive the reader (as in crossword puzzles) or to suggest multiple meanings. The last usage is common in poetry and creative literature. An example of this is seen in Dylan Thomas's radio play *Under Milk Wood*: "The shops in mourning" where *mourning* can be heard as *mourning* or *morning*. Another vivid example is Thomas Hood's use of "birth" and "berth" and "told" and "toll'd" (tolled) in his poem "Faithless Sally Brown":

Homophone is a tricky part of correct grammar. They are words that sound exactly the same but are totally different in meaning.

They can even be spelled the same way, leading to even greater confusion.

IMPORTANT TO CORRECTLY USE OF HOMOPHONES

Some of the most commonly used homophones end up being some of the most common grammar mistakes in the English language.

Homophones are a little confusing at first for ESL students,

1. Avoid making common English grammar mistakes
2. Give you confidence in your English
3. Improve your overall understanding of the English language.

DIFFICULT HOMOPHONES

These homophones are some of the most difficult there are Going over the meanings and spellings of some of the more difficult homophones, will help you to ensure that you do not make this common English grammar mistake.

Wordplay is particularly common in English because the multiplicity of linguistic influences offers considerable complication in spelling and meaning and pronunciation compared with other languages.

Homophones of multiple words or phrases (as sometimes seen in word games) are also known as "oronyms". This term was coined by Gyles Brandreth and first published in his book *The Joy of Lex* (1980), and it was used in the BBC programme *Never Mind the Full Stops*, which also featured Brandreth as a guest.

These similar sounding words add depth to a language but they can also be the cause of great frustration. Spell check can't even be relied upon where these troublesome homophones are concerned. There is no shortage of double or two-word homophone pairs in the English language. Triple homophones, however, are less common. Some common homophones in English include:

> hour/our, air/heir, aisle/ isle, bee/ be, buy/ by, cereal/ serial, flour/ flower, two/to/too, write/right/rite.......and the list goes on.

THE IMPORTANCE OF HOMOPHONES IN THE LEARNING OF ENGLISH

The Webster New Riverside Dictionary defines a homophone as "one of two or more words having the same sound but different in meaning and origin". The Webster's New 20th Century Dictionary states that a homophone is "any of two or more letters having a sound in common, as V and 's'. A homophone, as defined here, is considered the same as a homonym, i.e. "a word which agrees with another in pronunciation but differs from it in signification, origin, and usually, spelling (e.g 'bore and 'boar')". The Oxford Advanced Learner's Dictionary of Current English explains that homophone is "a word pronounced like another but different in meaning, spelling or origin".

The word Homophone is of Greek origin; 'homo' meaning same and 'phone meaning voice or sound. Therefore, we can define homophones as words which are pronounced identically but have different spellings and different meanings, for example, Main'/'lane', 'soar/sore', pedal/ peddle' and 'main/mane'.

Homophonic words can create confusion in language comprehension and language use. The English language teachers who were informally interviewed comment that where pairs of homophones are more commonly used and the spelling quite distinct, for example, know/no, aloud/allowed and rays/raise, students encounter less problems in recognizing and using them in sentences correctly. However, homophonic pairs like stile/style, currant/ current, root/route and isle/aisle, where there is only one letter in the word which is different, prove to be more confusing. Students are unable to demonstrate a positive linking in language processing and comprehension of these homophonic words. In many instances, students are more likely to misuse the latter homophonic words in proper contextual usage.

In many instances too, homophonic words from different grammatical classes appear less 'intimidating', even slightly easier to comprehend. For example, as in the case of bawl/ ball (verb/ noun) and blue/blew (adjective/verbs). Homophonic words from the same grammatical class prove to be complex for students. Examples of these are knead/need (verb/verb) and sauce/source (noun/noun). Therefore, the possibility of misinterpretation is extensive in the use of homophones belonging to the same class. ESL learners should master the use of homophones because it is one of the features of the English language.

The correct use of homophonic words especially in writing depicts the students' ability to express them effectively. To be able to distinguish the semantic elements of homophonic words also reflects the students' mental capacity of having an adequate understanding towards complicated meaning, and the use of the appropriate homophonic words in contextually suitable sentences. The correct usage of homophones also allows for linguistic humor. Puns and jokes often rely on homophonic words for their effect. The aesthetic impact of puns requires both the speaker and the audience to employ and understand the finer meaning of the homophonic word that has been manipulated.

Therefore, a sufficient knowledge of the meanings and functions of homophonic words as well as the ability to use them are necessary to ensure mastery of the English language.

HOMOPHONES IN THE ENGLISH LANGUAGE

Homophones are useful lexical items in the English language. We have in English, for example, the homophonic words: 'rite', 'write* and 'right'. Then we have 'their', 'there' and 'they're'. With the aid of the variant spelling, the students learn that these homophones are actually different words. They are pronounced exactly alike but their meanings vary. Homophones are words that make a person more alert and sensitive towards the English language while reading and while listening. There are at least 250 pairs of homophones. All homophonic words have the following criteria. As listed by Cooper in the Internet, homophones,

1. are pronounced the same way.
2. must have different spellings
3. must mean different things
4. do not include proper nouns (e.g. 'Cain' and 'cane')
5. do not include foreign words that would not be found in an English dictionary
6. do not include words or lexical items which mean the same but have spelling variants (e.g 'humour' and 'humor')
7. do not include polysemous words or lexical items with identical surface form but with different semantic entries (e.g 'bank' - which could mean bank of a river or monetary institution)
8. are not pairs of words which are often confused (e.g. 'acclamation' and 'acclimation') and
9. do not include homographs - where spelling is similar but the meanings of the words differ (e.g. 'tear', 'tear').

A word in isolation is often ambiguous with regard to its meaning and grammatical class. A context of at least one word is needed to disambiguate the grammatical class and meaning of homophonic words (e.g. the word 'pedal' could refer to a noun or a verb).

Homophones and homographs can render ambiguity both in listening and writing. These words can prove to be quite mind-boggling for language students. Table 1 clarifies the characteristics of these three kinds of ambiguous words.

THE OBSTACLES IN LEARNING ENGLISH

Of all the many hundreds and thousands of languages around the world, English can be considered as one of the most difficult to learn. There are many reasons why learning English is such a difficult task. The following are some of the most frequent obstacles a learner of English may encounter:

Motivation

This is the most common of the external factors that a learner may feel discouraged about learning. Many learners give up because of low self esteem as they develop self defeating thoughts such as "I can't learn", "I am too slow", "I'm too old" or "I don't think I'm cut out to learn". Other reasons include: poor teaching methods of schools, insufficient time to learn because of jobs or other activities as well as a lack of an adequate support system.

Organisation

In most English language schools, the learning materials used and the teaching methods are not adequate. Learners are often left to study on their own, leaving them confused as to what they are supposed to learn.

Method of Learning

Most methods adopted by language schools are doing writing exercises and reading texts from books. This can be boring and unexciting. Instead learners should be encouraged to take advantage of new and innovative methods of learning. Such as the internet and electronic learning devices where they are able to learn English whenever and wherever they like. Participating in forums and chat rooms also allow them to further improve their learning of the language.

Grammar

To most learners, this is the most confusing part about learning English. This is because nouns, adjectives and adverbs are very different from those of their mother tongues. Since there is no specific order in grammar, learning and understanding the usage of the many different sentence structures takes time and effort.

Pronunciation

Another confusing and frustrating aspect of learning English is in pronunciation because it can vary depending on the situations. For example, vowel sounds and consonant can vary in words like "the" and "thought". Some letters can be pronounced in many different ways while some are silent.

Verb Tenses

The English language consists of many varied nuances in the use of verb tenses. These nuances are difficult to comprehend for new learners. For example, the correct usage of verb tenses such as sing, sang and sung can be both complex and frustrating.

English Slang

There are so many slangs, phrases and jargons in the English Language that can give learners a hard time. And when these are mixed together, it becomes even more complicated. An example is the phrase: fanning the issue.

Expectations

Many learners have unreasonably high expectations. They start an English learning program thinking that they can easily pick up the language. However, they usually become discouraged and lose interest once they start to encounter difficulties. There are no hard and fast rules when it comes to learning the English language. It is important that learners must enjoy the experience by seeking out new, fun and creative methods of learning English. The result is tremendous satisfaction in conquering the language.

A homophone is a word that sounds like another word but has a different meaning. These homophones all have the same sound, but are spelled differently and have a different meaning.

For example naval and navel:-

Naval - relates to ships and things nautical

A navel - also known as the belly button, it is the scar that is left in the centre of the abdomen when the umbilical cord is cut after birth.

A homophone is a word that sounds the same as another word, but has a different meaning. Often two homophones are spelt the same (as in the case of a ring on the telephone and a diamond ring), but homophones can sometimes have different spellings (as in the case of their and there), which makes life even more difficult.

Homophones can create a particular problem when one of the spellings is not very commonly used. For example, the word but is so much more common than its homophone butt that when you hear a word with this sound you are likely to think that you are hearing the conjunction. However, it is worth remembering the less common homophone can crop up from time to time in phrases such as *the butt of a joke*.

The verbs pour and pore present a similar issue: *pour* is much more common, but the phrasal verb *pores over* involves quite a different meaning. When you pore over a piece of writing you don't cause it to flow but you study it intently. When the rarer of two homophones is used in an idiom or phrase, such expressions can be impossible to decipher if you are not aware that a homophone is being used. Take the example of the word bated. This is not the past participle of the verb bait. Pretty much the only time you will come across it is in the phrase *with bated breath*: if you wait for something with bated breath you wait for it eagerly. The phrase has nothing to do with your breath being prepared to catch a fish, but it makes use of an old variation of the verb abate, and so the idiom describes a person who is so excited that they hold their breath until a particular thing happens.

The idiom *give somebody a wide berth* is another where the less common of two homophones is used. When you hear it for the first time it may be tempting to interpret this as having something to do with birth. However, the term in fact comes (like many English idioms) from seafaring. A berth is the space allowed for a ship to move about when it is tied up or swinging on its anchor, and so when a troublesome person or thing is given a wide berth they are avoided and given plenty of room to go about their business.

My final example is the phrase *learns by rote*. When you hear this it may sound as though the last word is written. But this phrase has nothing to do with writing; it means to learn things by repeating them over and over rather than by understanding their underlying meaning. What makes this harder to know is that you will never come across the word rote in any other context. So homophones can not only create problems with spelling, but they can also be quite misleading when it comes to grasping the meaning of a phrase.

OBJECTIVES OF THE RIGHT METHOD

Good method of teaching should aim not only at the intellectual but also the social and moral implications; for whatever impact education has on one aspect of the personality tends to react on the other aspects too. The highest value that all methods should try to inculcate is the love of the subject and the desire to do it with highest measure of efficiency of which one is capable. Education of the school students should try to develop a real attachment to the various subjects that they are doing in school and the will to put the best into it; without it, there can be neither education of the mind nor the character of the students. This attitude to educate the mind is not common amongst our students either in schools or in colleges.

SECONDARY EDUCATION IN THE 21ST CENTURY

In the 21st century, Secondary Education has been emphasized and certain recommendations were given by UNESCO (2008). These are as follows-

1. Secondary education should be given high priority.
2. The objectives and functions of Secondary Education need to be redefined or the 21st century.
3. Countries should be committed to the goal of mass Secondary education as a minimum in terms of policy and provisions.
4. Commitment to access to secondary education should be maintained with efforts to remove barriers and to build on strengths and opportunities especially for girls.

5. It also needs to address students' needs in terms of realizing their full potential, especially in the context of rapid economic, cultural and social changes and gender based discrimination.
6. The emerging role of teachers (notably as facilitators), their status, integrity and commitment are essential for implementing life-skills education successfully.

Education is called a human activity based largely on the related process; known as learning and teaching process and informal system of education, the teacher imparts the education to the learners. So, teachers' role in education cannot be ignored.

SECOND LANGUAGE LEARNING AND THE TEACHING OF ENGLISH IN THE SECONDARY SCHOOL CLASSROOM

Teaching, like any other professions, is currently at a transitional stage and is experiencing a serious occupational crisis. Its knowledge base has expanded significantly and in the present century, but still there has been lack of clarity in public, in teachers themselves and in ministries of education, in teachers' education institutions, regarding the professional identity, teacher empowerment, nature and needs of teacher education and the academic credibility of educational studies.

Teachers are themselves uncertain as to the nature of their own occupation. They are unclear as to which category they belong-persons, professionals, trade persons etc. Dewey (1929), argued that the problem of training teachers become species of a more generic affair-that of training professionals, a theme later taken up by others. Burke (1997) said that the problem with many teachers training programmes, both at pre-service and in-service levels, is that they are still training teachers rather than educating professionals.

PHONETICS

Phonetics (pronounced from the Greek: , *phônç*, 'sound, voice') is a branch of linguistics that comprises the study of the sounds of human speech, or-in the case of sign languages-the equivalent aspects of sign.[1] It is concerned with the physical properties of speech sounds or signs (phones): their physiological production, acoustic properties, auditory perception and neurophysiologic status. Phonology, on the other hand, is concerned with the abstract, grammatical characterization of systems of sounds or signs.

The field of phonetics is a multilayered subject of linguistics that focuses on speech. In the case of oral languages there are three basic areas of study:

1. Articulatory phonetics: the study of the production of speech sounds by the articulator and vocal tract by the speaker.
2. Acoustic phonetics: the study of the physical transmission of speech sounds from the speaker to the listener.
3. Auditory phonetics: the study of the reception and perception of speech sounds by the listener.
    a. These areas are inter-connected through the common mechanism of sound, such as wavelength (pitch), amplitude, and harmonics.

Language problem is one of the genuine problems that India had to face with sincere efforts. After independence, the movement started against the retention of English. Many educationalists and national leaders came to the conclusion, that English should be replaced by one Indian language but, however, all of them were quite reluctant to drive away English from India owing to its worldwide importance. Following observations reveal the sincere attitude of educationalists and national leaders towards the changing status of English in India.

i) Mahatma Gandhi remarked,

"Of all the superstitions that India has, none is as great as that knowledge of the English language is necessary for imbibing ideas of liberty and developing accuracy of thought.'

ii) Pandit Jawaharlal Nehru observed that,

"Indian languages have suffered psychologically and otherwise because of English, yet they have gained a great deal too from contacts with the wider world."

From the above observation, it is quite clear that the status of English came down as it is used to be in the past i.e before independence, but all of them accepted and strongly argued to continue the study of English as a second or Third language. They also opined that English as an official language should be replaced but it could only be replaced by enriching Hindi as a national language.

THE SIGNIFICANCE OF ENGLISH LANGUAGE IN INDIA

English plays a key role in our educational system and national life. In today's global scenario English is treated as the link language. It is an established fact that it is an international language and provides a window to the world. It is a means of observing and learning about people, especially those of other countries. It is rightly called a pipe line in the stream of western thoughts. English is being taught as a language of instruction in schools and colleges or is being used as the lingua-franca between speakers of wildly diverse languages. This is an era of communication technology and without English no further higher education or inter change of professional language is possible. No other language has attained this status to substitute the all encompassing influence of the English language in each and every field.

According to Krishnaswamy and Shriraman T, "Learners of English have realized that English is not necessary for shaping of characters, the development of aesthetic sense .... But is needed for mobility and social and economic success. It is the language of opportunities because it takes one outside one's own community, to places, where more opportunities are available for professional and economic reasons..... it has a lot of "surrender value" and learners want to cashing on that.

English being the lingua-franca of the entire globe has the power to change the world that changes us. It provides information in every conceivable branch of knowledge. Even the entire student community has realized that English is necessary to expose their identity, language, literature, science, technology, society, economy, politics, values and culture to the world outside. Today, comprehensive abilities have become parameters, which ensure sound career in any field. Considering this, parents and learners have realized that through acquisition of English language knowledge and usage, one can withstand increasing levels of competition and can sustain one's career growth. Here, Darwin's theory of "The survival of the fittest" works.

It may be noted that English is no more a foreign language in India. It is a fact that English has become a part and parcel of our daily life. It is an open secret that even in remote rural areas; people use English words such as bus, ticket, truck, doctor, school, coffee, tea etc. There are lots of such words used by villagers. However, English cannot, of course, enjoy the pride of place it had during the British Regime. It has now been relegated to a secondary position. Let's have a glance at the status of English during pre/post independence scenario.

AIMS AND OBJECTIVES OF TEACHING ENGLISH IN THE SECONDARY SCHOOL STAGE

Following are the aims and objectives of teaching English at the Secondary School Stage-

1) The student should understand English when spoken at the normal conversational speed.
2) The student should speak English correctly.
3) a. He/ she can read English silently with comprehension.

   b. He/ she can read aloud English pieces correctly.
4) He / she can write English correctly.
5) He/ she acquire knowledge of the elements of English.
6) He/ she appreciate pieces of good English.
7) He/ she develop an interest in English.

Teachers all over the country are not clear about the aim of teaching English. They divide the time table into reading, writing, composition, translation and grammar and are satisfied as long as the students are kept busy and they do not get any trouble from the school authorities. It drives home the fact that in general, students are not found to be competent in English because of the language skill development in students is found to be not up to the mark.

PLACE OF ENGLISH IN SCHOOL CURRICULUM

After independence, the place of English underwent a great change. However, its importance as a national and international link language and as a library language is fully accepted by all thinkers in India. But it must be admitted that the importance of learning English cannot occupy the same place in the school curriculum as it did in the past.

In the past, the medium of instruction was English in school curriculum. English was taught in order to give the knowledge of western literature and science.

But in the present school curriculum, English is not used as the medium of instruction unless it is opted. It is learnt and taught only from the practical point of view if regional language is opted as medium of instruction. The main purpose of teaching English is to enable the students to listen, to speak, to read and to write English correctly. Therefore, syllabus at all stages is prepared from practical point of view. Thus English is taught as a language and not as a literature in secondary school.

Mudliar Commission (1953) and Kothari Commission (1964-66) suggested the three language Formula in which English has been placed as a second or third language. It is expected that English should be one of the compulsory subjects and it should be taught as a second or third language, for the duration of three or six years respectively. Mother tongue or Regional language should be the first language (L.1); Hindi should be the second language (L 2) and English should be the third language (L 3). It is also recommended that English should be taught from standard V to VIII. In Chapter I Introduction some states, English is taught from standard V or VIII. In some states, English is taught from standard V. whereas in some states it is taught from standard VIII. This indicates that most of the states followed the 'Three language Formula' with some modification. Thus English is remained and taught as a compulsory subject, not only at school level, but also at graduate level.

The syllabus during this era consisted of grammatical items (called "teaching points," not "learning points") and vocabulary lists. The reality was that English was taught as a sequence of items to be memorized and this was supported by examinations. Successes in these examinations depended primarily in being able to recall the item and passages from the course books. As a consequence, students seemed to learn the structural items and the vocabulary, but could not extend that knowledge beyond the text book frame. This model persisted for some thirty years.

Although the structural syllabuses were adopted in Maharashtra, as in the rest of India, there was some ambiguity about the content and examination of language learning. The text-books were modeled on a literary canon, reflecting the educational background of the writers and traditions of English teaching. Such textbooks contained 'manufactured texts and extracts from literature and had complex syntax and dense vocabulary. These materials reflected ambitions of teachers, rather than the needs of young language learners. The result was a structural syllabus taught in a grammar translation mode, and examination that tested whether the students had, by and large, managed to memorize the texts and grammar examples covered. In short, even with the adoption of structural syllabuses, the grammar-translation method continued to dominate both teaching and testing and the literary canon continued to be reflected in materials.

GENERAL PRINCIPLES OF LANGUAGE LEARNING AND TEACHING

Teaching a language is a serious business and must be conducted carefully. It should receive psychological, linguistic and pedagogical support, which would help the teacher in teaching the target language successfully. The modern approach to all the language learning and teaching is the scientific one and is based on sound linguistic principles. The principles discussed below in no way claim finality. They are subject to change in the light of new facts brought to light by linguists and language users (Bhatia, 1989). The main principles are:

Speech before Reading and Writing: Teach listening and speaking first, reading and writing afterwards. This is the natural way. This principle does not mean that there is some rigid division between speaking and reading. This only means postponing the written shapes till such a time when the child begins to feel the rhythm, stress and junctures of the target language.

Imitation: Language is learnt by imitation. The learner can not invent it by himself. Good speech is the result of imitating good models.

Present Language in Basic Sentence Patterns: Present language in the form of basic sentence patterns used in day-to-day conversation. From small utterances, the students can easily pass on to longer sentences.

Language Patterns Habit through Practice and Drill: Real language ability is at the habit level. Make language patterns a habit through intensive pattern practice in variety of situations. In fact, practice and drill are essential to acquire language habit.

The Oral Way: The principle of the oral way has been well organized by experts on language teaching. It is generally believed that learning to speak a language is always the shortest road to learning to read and to write it. Living languages should be taught as living speech, that is why, they should be taught orally. So, it should be clear that language teaching and learning should begin with oral work.

Selection and Gradation: Selection of the language material to be taught is essential to good teaching. Selection should be done in respect of grammatical items and vocabulary and structures.

Priorities in Language Skills: The four fundamental language skills that we want out students to acquire are Listening, Speaking, Reading and Writing. At the early age there is emphasis on listening and speaking while at the later stage, the emphasis is on reading and writing.

Controlled Vocabulary: Keep the vocabulary to the minimum. Give importance to the mastery of sound system and patterns using controlled vocabulary. In the first three years of teaching a second language, only those items of vocabulary that help the learners to use patterns should be mastered.

Motivation: Motivation is an important factor in language learning particularly in learning a second language. It creates the interest as well as the need to learn the language in hand.

Reinforcement: Immediate reinforcement is an important principle in language learning. It has been experimentally proved that reinforcement of correct responses help in better learning.

Multiple Line of Approach: The term 'multiple lines' implies that one is to proceed simultaneously from many different points towards the one and the same end. We should reject nothing except the useless material and should select judiciously and without prejudice all that is like to help in our work. In teaching a language, it implies attacking the problem from all fronts.

Language Using: A language is best learnt through use in different Contexts and situations. Prof. Eugene A. Nida (1945), rightly observes "Language learning means plunging head long into a series of completely different experiences. It means exposing oneself to situations where the use of language is required". Translation is not a substitute for language practice. Teach the language as it is, not as it ought to be.

Speed and style: Practice must end in a linguistically acceptable and psychologically full experience. Teach primarily to produce learning rather than to please or entertain.

USE IN PSYCHOLOGICAL RESEARCH

Pseudo-homophones

Pseudo-homophones are pseudo words that are phonetically identical to a word. For example, groan/gone and crane / Crain is pseudo-homophone pairs, whereas plane/plain is a homophone pair since both letter strings is recognized words. Both types of pairs are used in lexical decision tasks to investigate word recognition.

Use as ambiguous information

Homophones where one spelling is of a threatening nature and one is not (*e.g.* slay/sleigh, war/wore) have been used in studies of anxiety as a test of cognitive models that those with high anxiety tend to interpret ambiguous information in a threatening manner.

NEED OF THE STUDY

The new insights gained into the process of language acquisition in the recent past have made the prevailing practices in language teaching look outmoded and redundant if not pernicious. An active learner's role has clear implications for a new approach to language learning with a new role of the teacher. It has been observed that there has been considerable deterioration in the standards of the teaching and learning of English at the school levels in the last twenty five years. Yet one realizes that teaching or learning language homophones is a complex process. As an international language, English acts as a common language that enables people from diverse backgrounds and ethnicities to communicate on a more or less equitable basis. With the liberalization and globalization of the Indian, the rapid change witnessed in the scientific and technological world and the general need to improve the quality of English language learning , it is essential that the school acquire a higher level of knowledge and skills that provided learning English among VIII standard students. The research has chosen to do a study of the use of homophones and difficulties min using homophones among VIII standard students, specifically the ability of these students to understand and distinguish homophones lexically and semantically.

SCOPE OF THE STUDY

To provide effective learning instruction that extends students understanding of a single correct meaning for a target word. This scaffold instruction is often referred to as a cognitive-constructionist approach to vocabulary or word study because it builds upon a learner's acquisition of the denotative to connotative constructions or connections when learning to comprehend distinguish and express ideas in the English language. Lexis can be defined as the vocabulary of a language in contrast to its grammar. In the English language class, greater emphasis has always been placed on grammar. The finer points of language involving lexical items like homophones which require higher order thinking are not usually exploited. To identified the problems and difficulties arises in the learning of homophones in English among the VIII standard students the present study was considered.

STATEMENT OF THE PROBLEM

The basic problem undertaken for investigation in the present study is to examine the "*A Study on the Obstacles Learning Of Homophones in English among VIII Standard Students*".

OBJECTIVES OF THE STUDY

The following are the objectives of the present study;

1. To find out the significant difference in the mean scores of Obstacles Learning of Homophones in English among VIII Standard Students in terms of their **Gender**.
2. To find out the significant difference in the mean scores of Obstacles Learning of Homophones in English among VIII Standard Students in terms of their **Residential Place.**
3. To find out the significant difference in the mean scores of Obstacles Learning of Homophones in English among VIII Standard Students in terms of their **school type as Government and Aided.**
4. To find out the significant difference in the mean scores of Obstacles Learning of Homophones in English among VIII Standard Students in terms of their **school type as aided and Un-Aided.**
5. To find out the significant difference in the mean scores of Obstacles Learning of Homophones in English among VIII Standard Students in terms of their **school type as Un-Aided and Government.**
6. To find out the significant difference in the mean scores of Obstacles Learning of Homophones in English among VIII Standard Students in terms of their **Parent's occupation as Government and Private Job.**
7. To find out the significant difference in the mean scores of Obstacles Learning of Homophones in English among VIII Standard Students in terms of their **Parent's education level as literate and illiterate.**
8. To find out the significant difference in the mean scores of Obstacles Learning of Homophones in English among VIII Standard Students in terms of their **Parent's annual income as Above fifty thousand and Below fifty thousand.**

HYPOTHESIS OF THE STUDY

The following are the hypotheses constructed for the present study

1. There is no significant difference in the mean scores of Obstacles Learning of Homophones in English among VIII Standard Students in terms of their **Gender**.
2. There is no significant difference in the mean scores of Obstacles Learning of Homophones in English among VIII Standard Students in terms of their **Residential Place.**
3. There is no significant difference in the mean scores of Obstacles Learning of Homophones in English among VIII Standard Students in terms of their **school type as Government and Aided.**
4. There is no significant difference in the mean scores of Obstacles Learning of Homophones in English among VIII Standard Students in terms of their **school type as aided and Un-Aided.**
5. There is no significant difference in the mean scores of Obstacles Learning of Homophones in English among VIII Standard Students in terms of their **school type as Un-Aided and Government.**
6. There is no significant difference in the mean scores of Obstacles Learning of Homophones in English among VIII Standard Students in terms of their **Parent's occupation as Government and Private Job.**
7. There is no significant difference in the mean scores of Obstacles Learning of Homophones in English among VIII Standard Students in terms of their **Parent's education level as literate and illiterate.**
8. There is no significant difference in the mean scores of Obstacles Learning of Homophones in English among VIII Standard Students in terms of their **Parent's annual income as above fifty thousand and below fifty thousand.**

DEFINITION OF THE KEY TERMS USED

An obstacle (also called a barrier, impediment or stumbling block) is an object, thing, action or situation that causes an obstruction. There are, therefore, different types of obstacles, which can be physical, economic, bio psychosocial, cultural, political, technological or even military

Learning is the act of acquiring new, or modifying and reinforcing, existing knowledge, behaviors, skills, values, or preferences and may involve synthesizing different types of information. The ability to learn is possessed by humans, animals and some machines. Progress over time tends to follow learning curves. Learning is not compulsory; it is contextual. It does not happen all at once, but builds upon and is shaped by previous knowledge. To that end, learning may be viewed as a process, rather than a collection of factual and procedural knowledge. Learning produces changes in the organism and the changes produced are relatively permanent.

English language is characterized by a complex phonology, with complex patterns of allophone and morphophonemic's. There is little morphological inflection in Modern English, and the syntax is generally isolating. English relies on auxiliary verbs and word order for the expression of complex tenses, aspect and mode, as well as passive constructions, interrogatives and negation. There is significant variation between the forms of English spoken in different world regions, different accents are distinguished only by phonological differences from the standard language, whereas dialects also display grammatical and lexical differences.

DELIMITATIONS OF THE STUDY

1. The present study is confined only to VIII standard students in pudukkottai educational district.
2. The investigation on the *Obstacles Learning of Homophones in English among VIII Standard Students* was restricted to 300 data among the VIII students.
3. The present study is limited only to find the significance difference on

I. Gender,

II. Residential Place,

III. Type of School,

IV. Parent's Occupation,

V. Parent's Educational Qualification

VI. Parent's Annual Income.

4. This study was conducted in the year 2014 – 2015.

CONCLUSION

The scheme of the present study chapters framed as follows

Chapter: I deal with the introduction of the study, Importance of the study, Statement of the problem, Objectives of the study; Hypotheses of the study and Delimitation of the study are outlined.

Chapter: II deals with Review of Related Literature of previous analysis of different studies with in different presentations.

Chapter: III deals with the concept and Methodology of the study are analyzed.

Chapter: IV Mention about analyzed and interpretation of the study for the present problem selected.

Chapter: V deals with the summary, finding and conclusion of the study area.

Chapter - II

Review of Related Literature

INTRODUCTION

The review of related literature is an important step in research. Although the general purpose of the review is to help the researcher to develop a thorough understanding and insight into previous work and the trends that have emerged.

Borg and Gall, mentioned that the review can also help in researching a number of important specific goals namely, delimiting the research problem, seeking new approaches, avoiding sterile approaches, insights into methods and sampling.

Review of related literature is a crucial step, which invariably minimizes the risk of dead ends, rejected topics, rejected studies, wasted effort and trial and error activity oriented towards approaches already discarded by previous investigators. Practically all human knowledge can be found in books and libraries. Unlike other animals that must start a new with each generation man builds upon the accumulated and recorded knowledge of the past.

According to Mouley, review of literature also provides comparatives data on the basis of which evaluate and interpret the significance of one's findings. In addition it contributes to the scholarship of the investigator.

Having understood the importance of review of related literature a systematic procedure was followed by the investigator in reviewing the related literature for the present study. The investigator listed key works related to the topic and used preliminary sources such as research in education, current index to journals in education, psychological abstracts and educational index to locate sources of information. After locating the sources the investigator carefully included in this chapter the various literature and research studies related to the present study.

Importance of Review of Related Studies

Aggarwal, has listed eleven important reasons for which review of related studies should be made.

1. The review of literature is the basis of most of the research projects in the physical sciences, natural sciences and humanities.
2. A review of related literature given the scholar an understanding of the precious work that has been done.
3. The results of the review actually provide the data used in the research. It enables the researcher to know the means of getting to the frontier in the field of our problem. Until we have learnt what others have done and what still remains to be done in our area, we cannot develop a research design that will contribute to furthering knowledge in our field.
4. A review of literature would develop the insight of the investigator. The information thus, gained will save the researcher's much time. The importance of the review is quite obvious in delimiting the research problem and in defining it better.
5. The review of literature will give the student the insight he/she needs to convert his/her tentative research problem to a specific and concise one.

A review of literature can help the research worker in making him alert to research possibilities that have been overlooked.

In the process of reviewing the literature the student is on the alert for finding out research approaches in his area that have proved to be sterile.

THE PURPOSE OF THE REVIEW OF LITERATURE

The purpose of this literature review was to convey to the reader what knowledge and ideas have been established on a topic and what are the strengths and weaknesses. The literature review allowed the reader to be brought up to data regarding the state of research in the field and familiarizes the reader with any contrasting perspectives and viewpoints on the topic.

The survey of related literature is an integral part of any research study and time spent in such an endeavor results in careful planning and meticulous execution of the research.

The review of literature enables the researcher to perceive the gap, avoid the duplication of work, scrutinize the methodology already used, co-ordinate the study with others, get the right direction, view the problem from as many angles as possible and prepare the framework.

For the present research, the investigator had made extensive review of research reports, articles of the journals, dissertations and theses and survey documents.

The investigator has consolidated those reviews related to the present investigation in this chapter. Studies done related to *"A Study on the Obstacles Learning Of Homophones in English among VIII Standard Students"* both in India and abroad were reported as follows.

According to Bloom, oral ability is a necessity if a child is to learn in school.

Ayodel, opined that pupil's inadequacy in the range and control of language is a dominating factor in educational failure. This deficiency in the students generates a vicious circle of difficulties which goes on increasing in magnitude as school life progresses.

STUDIES CONDUCTED IN INDIA

Ala-Kortesmaa, Sanna; Isotalus, Pekka (2015), Professional Listening Competence Promoting Well-Being at Work in the Legal

Context. *International Journal of Listening*, v29 n1 p30-49 2015. This qualitative cross-cultural study sought to contribute to the understanding of listening competence, dialogic listening, and the use of human agency in promoting well-being at work. The participant groups ("N" = 103) consisted of "n" = 76 U.S.-American and "n" = 27 Finnish attorneys. Results suggest that in order to examine listening and well-being at work, a term professional listening competence had to be constructed. The results further suggest that a sense of a strong professional listening competence leads to positive experiences of self-efficacy and personal agency regarding the management of professional interaction by listening. These empowering experiences serve to alleviate work-related stress and have a positive effect on well-being at work.

Staels, Eva; Van den Broeck, Wim (2015), Orthographic Learning and the Role of Text-to-Speech Software in Dutch Disabled Readers. *Journal of Learning Disabilities*, v48 n1 p39-50 Jan-Feb 2015.In this study, we examined whether orthographic learning can be demonstrated in disabled readers learning to read in a transparent orthography (Dutch). In addition, we tested the effect of the use of text-to-speech software, a new form of direct instruction, on orthographic learning. Both research goals were investigated by replicating Share's self-teaching paradigm. A total of 65 disabled Dutch readers were asked to read eight stories containing embedded homophonic pseudo word targets (e.g., Blot/Blod), with or without the support of text-to-speech software. The amount of orthographic learning was assessed 3 or 7 days later by three measures of orthographic learning.

First, the results supported the presence of orthographic learning during independent silent reading by demonstrating that target spellings were correctly identified more often, named more quickly, and spelled more accurately than their homophone foils. Our results support the hypothesis that all readers, even poor readers of transparent orthographies, are capable of developing word-specific knowledge. Second, a negative effect of text-to-speech software on orthographic learning was demonstrated in this study. This negative effect was interpreted as the consequence of passively listening to the auditory presentation of the text. We clarify how these results can be interpreted within current theoretical accounts of orthographic learning and briefly discuss implications for remedial interventions.

Subramaniam (2014), teacher's target is to "prepare" the students for the examination and not to make the pupils competent in the use of the language they are learning. In reality, neither the student is anxious to learn nor the teacher anxious to teach English.

Babayigit, Selma (2014), The Role of Oral Language Skills in Reading and Listening Comprehension of Text: A Comparison of Monolingual (L1) and Bilingual (L2) Speakers of English Language. *Journal of Research in Reading,* v37 suppl pS22-S47 Mar 2014. The study examined the role of oral language skills in reading comprehension and listening comprehension levels of 125 monolingual (L1) and bilingual (L2) English-speaking learners (M = 121.5 months, SD = 4.65) in England. All testing was conducted in English. The L1 learners outperformed their L2 peers on the measures of oral language and text comprehension, but the two groups performed at comparable levels on word-reading accuracy and speed. Oral language, indexed by vocabulary and morph syntactic skills, emerged as the most powerful unique predictor of both reading and listening comprehension levels. Although there was a tendency of oral language to be more strongly related to L2 reading comprehension, its relationship with listening comprehension was comparable across the two language groups. Finally, individual differences in oral language skills emerged as the primary factor that explained the language group differences in text comprehension levels. Educational implications of these findings were discussed.

Alavi, Sayyed Mohammad; Janbaz, Fateme (2014), Comparing Two Pre-Listening Supports with Iranian EFL Learners: Opportunity or Obstacle. *RELC Journal: A Journal of Language Teaching and Research,* v45 n3 p253-267 Dec 2014. Since listening is a crucial component of language competence and fundamental for successful communication as well, its development has been gradually given much attention from language teachers and researchers. This study is aimed at investigating the effectiveness of two pre-listening supports, i.e. question preview and topic preparation on the listening comprehension of foreign language learners. The participants (N = 61 female), divided in two separate groups, answered ten items of listening comprehension tests under two different conditions. In the question preview condition, the teacher read questions and options loudly before the listening test began, while in the topic preparation condition, the participants read textual information related to the topics of listening tests. The results showed that pre-listening supports benefited EFL learners' listening comprehension. However, statistical significant difference of the listening comprehension scores between the two supports could not be established. With such a positive effect on EFL listening, this study suggests that topic preparation and question preview have their own specific role in the development of EFL learners' listening comprehension.

Aneurin (2013), attempted to identify the reading problems of under achievers at the +2 level. The objectives of the study were

i) To find out the reading problems of under achieving students,

ii) To suggest remedial measures to improve their reading skills.

The study was conducted at the Higher Secondary level. The data was collected through two comprehension tests, a questionnaire, informal interviews and class room observations. The case study revealed that some of the students were not able to understand that there was an urgent need to improve their reading ability by putting efforts.

The following mentioned difficulties were stated

i) Difficulty in understanding the use of connectors,

ii) Difficulty in processing complex sentences,

iii) Lack of sufficient vocabulary and

iv) Inappropriate reading strategies.

The researcher gave the following suggestions for improving the reading performance.

1. Creating a non-threatening class room climate.
2. Raising awareness of faculty.
3. Developing reading habits.
4. Remedying language problems.
5. Improving dictionary skills.

Abeywickrama, Priyanvada (2013), Why Not Non-Native Varieties of English as Listening Comprehension Test Input? *RELC Journal: A Journal of Language Teaching and Research*, v44 n1 p59-74 Apr 2013. The existence of different varieties of English in target language use (TLU) domains calls into question the usefulness of listening comprehension tests whose input is limited only to a native speaker variety. This study investigated the impact of non-native varieties or accented English speech on test takers from three different English use contexts: Korea, Sri Lanka and Brazil. The findings showed that the variety of English or accented speech used had no impact on test taker's performance on a listening test for academic purposes. Also test takers from the three different countries performed similarly even when the speakers shared the same native languages as the test takers. Despite these findings students still perceived that a native variety of English should be used in listening comprehension tests. Though the study suggests the use of non-native varieties as test input, it also raises questions of fairness in the use of such varieties.

Robert J.; Haywood, Sarah L. (2013), Phonological and Orthographic Effects in Bilingual Visual Word Recognition. *Language and Speech*, v53 n3 p383-403 Sep 2010 A visual semantic categorization task in English was performed by native English speakers (Experiment 1) and late bilinguals whose first language was Japanese (Experiment 2) or Spanish (Experiment 3). In the critical conditions, the target word was a homophone of a correct category exemplar (e.g., A BODY OF WATER-SEE; cf. SEA) or a word that differed from the correct exemplar by a phonological contrast absent in the bilinguals' first language (e.g., USED FOR COOLING DOWN-FUN; cf. FAN). Homophones elicited more false positive errors and slower processing than spelling controls in all groups. The Japanese-English bilinguals, but not the Spanish-English bilinguals, also displayed "near-homophone" effects (i.e., homophone-like effects from minimal pairs on nonnative contrasts). We conclude that second-language visual word recognition is influenced by first-language phonology, although the effect is conditioned by the first-language orthographic system. Near-homophone effects can occur when the orthographic systems of the late bilingual's two languages are different in type (e.g., alphabetic vs. non-alphabetic), but may be blocked if the languages use the same writing script (e.g., Roman alphabet).

Jared, Debra; Cormier, Pierre; Levy, Betty Ann; Wade-Woolley, Lesly (2012), Cross-Language Activation of Phonology in Young Bilingual Readers *Reading and Writing: An Interdisciplinary Journal*, v25 n6 p1327-1343 Jul 2012. We investigated whether children who were learning to read simultaneously in English and French activate phonological representations from only the language in which they are reading or from both of their languages. Children in French Immersion programs in Grade 3 were asked to name aloud cognates, inter lingual homographs, inter lingual homophones, and matched control words. Half of the participants performed the task in English, their first oral language, and half performed the task in French. Control monolingual children in each language were also tested. In the French reading task, fewer errors were observed for cognates and inter lingual homophones than for matched control words, whereas more errors were produced for inter lingual homographs than matched controls. Only the inhibitory inter lingual homograph effect was observed in the English reading task. These data provide evidence that phonological activation in bilinguals is not language selective. The locus of each of these effects in the bilingual word recognition system is discussed.

Anita M.Y.Yasin (2012), Unique Associations of Homophone Awareness and Lexical Compounding to Word Reading and Vocabulary Knowledge in Indian Children .*Applied Psycholinguistics*, v34 n4 p755-775 Jul 2012. An in-depth exploration of the associations of two aspects of morphological awareness in Indian—homophone awareness and lexical compounding awareness—to Indian word reading and vocabulary knowledge was the primary focus of the present study. Among 154 9-year-old Hong Kong Indian children, both lexical compounding and homophone awareness were significantly associated with word reading ("r" = 0.54 for compounding, "r" = 0.38 for homophones) and vocabulary knowledge ("r" = 0.41 for compounding, "r" = 0.53 for homophones). However, with auto regresses additionally statistically controlled, homophone awareness remained uniquely associated with vocabulary but not word reading; lexical compounding was uniquely associated with both word reading and vocabulary. Path analyses best illustrated this pattern. Both morphological awareness constructs are likely bidirectional associated with word reading and vocabulary knowledge. However, homophone awareness is more centrally associated with vocabulary knowledge because it taps specific, existing morpheme knowledge. In contrast, lexical compounding requires structural understanding of one's language, which seems to be helpful for both learning to read and vocabulary acquisition in Indian.

Templeton, Shane (2012), Comprehending Homophones, Homographs, and Homonyms. Explains that homophones, homographs, and homonyms provide opportunities rather than obstacles in learning. Notes that the verbal art form of puns depends mightily on homophones, homographs, and homonyms. Provides a sampling of resources that explore homophones, homographs and homonyms.

Lange, Alissa A.; Mulhern, Wylie, Judith (2010), Proofreading Using an Assistive Software Homophone Tool: Compensatory and Remedial Effects on the Literacy Skills of Students with Reading Difficulties. *Journal of Learning Disabilities*, v42 n4 p322-335 2010. The study investigated the effects of using an assistive software homophone tool on the assisted proofreading performance and unassisted basic skills of secondary-level students with reading difficulties. Students aged 13 to 15 years proofread passages for homophonic errors under three conditions: with the homophone tool, with homophones highlighted only, or with no help. The group using the homophone tool significantly outperformed the other two groups on assisted proofreading and outperformed the others on unassisted spelling, although not significantly. Remedial (unassisted) improvements in automaticity of word recognition, homophone proofreading, and basic reading were found over all groups. Results elucidate the differential contributions of each function of the homophone tool and suggest that with the proper training, assistive software can help not only students with diagnosed disabilities but also those with generally weak reading skills.

Grainger, Jonathan; Lete, Bernard; Bertand, Daisy; Johannes C. (2008), Evidence for Multiple Routes in Learning to Read. *Cognition*, v123 n2 p280-292 May 2008. They described multiple-route model of reading development in which coarse-grained orthographic processing plays a key role in optimizing access to semantics via whole-word orthographic representations. This forms part of the direct orthographic route that gradually replaces phonological recoding during the initial phases of reading acquisition. The model predicts distinct developmental trajectories for pseudo-homophone and transposed-letter effects - two benchmark phenomena associated with phonological recoding and coarse-grained orthographic processing, respectively. Pseudo-homophone effects should decrease over the first years of reading acquisition, whereas transposed-letter effects should initially increase. These predictions were tested in a lexical decision task with 334 children in grades 1-5, and 29 skilled adult readers. In line with the predictions, we found that the pseudo-homophone effect diminished as reading level increased, whereas the transposed-letter effect first increased and then diminished.

Sailaja (2008) attempted to explore the L2 linguistic resources available to the disadvantaged learners at the tertiary level. The objectives of the study were, i) to identify the features of functional literacy in L2 writing among socially and economically disadvantaged learners, ii) to explore linguistic resources available to the disadvantaged learners and iii) to describe the disadvantaged learners L2 writing in terms of functional literacy. The preliminary study was conducted for 110 students and the final study was conducted for 94 students with the help of 8 different tasks and tools. The study revealed that 1. Disadvantaged learners in private, Government funded tertiary level institutions were strongly motivated to write in L2, 2. The learner had a present need to write, 3. It was found that since the teachers encouraged them to learn English, most of the students were motivated and had a healthy attitude towards learning English, 4. The teachers were also found to be aware of the L2 needs of their students and 5. Functional literacy enabled the learner to use L2 for writing purposes. It made the disadvantaged learner, a writer before he could become a speaker of L2. The study concluded with a suggestion for the special emphasis on personal literacy.

Sonalde (2005) attempted to investigate into the preparation and try out of a package of ELT materials to develop Communicative competence at the F. Y .B.Sc. level. The objectives of the study were:

i) to review the existing courses being offered at the F.Y.B.Sc. level,

ii) to evolve a rationale for the new course,

iii) to arrive at a set of objectives for the new course,

iv) To design syllabus in accordance with the students needs at this level,

v) to prepare materials to develop communicative competence in science students and

vi) To make the learners use the language meaningfully thus bridging the lacunae between the classroom language and language in real life.

The tools used for the study were, a questionnaire, feedback forms and three tests. The findings of the study were,

1. A vast majority of the undergraduate students faced problems with English while taking notes, following instructions given in the lab, presenting seminar etc.

2. Inspite of ESP (English for Special Purpose)"course being introduced, the teachers were not properly trained for adopting new teaching techniques following communicative aspects and continued to follow the lecture method which created a pitiable scene for the students.

3. The existing syllabus in F. Y .B.Sc. English failed to prepare the real users of the language as the tasks and exercises given in their existing courses were extremely mechanical and in no way contributed to making the students independent users of language.

4. In most of the Science classes teachers used fixed expressions. In class of Mathematics, teacher at times did not use even full sentences. Therefore, the students of science needed to be given more language exposure, and

5. It was found that with the help of the materials produced and new techniques used, the students, communicative competence in all four skills had considerably increased.

Mathew (2005), made an attempt to develop reading comprehension in terms of intellectual, lexical, structural and stylistic components of reading skill among first year degree students. His experimental group fared significantly better than the control group in reading comprehension sub skills as well as in overall performance in reading comprehension in the post test performance after the experiment.

Grover Santosh (2005), made an investigation into the standard of reading ability in English in government schools and central schools of Delhi it was survey regarding reading but the tests used were found to be useful for preparing reading skill test of the present research for example it helped in deciding loud reading test and silent reading exercises (word meaning from context, reading comprehension etc.) it also helped in deciding criteria for checking these tests.

STUDIES CONDUCTED IN ABROAD

Stephen J.; Jared, Debra (2015), The Processing Advantage and Disadvantage for Homophones in Lexical Decision Tasks. *Journal of Experimental Psychology: Learning, Memory, and Cognition*, v39 n2 p529-551 Jan 2015. Studies using the lexical decision task with English stimuli have demonstrated that homophones are responded to more slowly than no homophonic controls. In contrast, several studies using Indian stimuli have shown that homophones are responded to more rapidly than non homophonic controls. In an attempt to better understand the impact of homophony, we investigated homophone effects for Japanese kanji words in a lexical decision task. The results indicated that, whereas a processing disadvantage emerged for homophones when they have only a single homophonic mate (as in the English experiments), a processing advantage occurred for homophones when they have multiple homophonic mates (as in the Indian experiments). On the basis of these results, we discuss the nature of the processes that may be responsible for producing the processing advantages and disadvantages for homophones.

Middleton, Erica L.; Chen, Qi; Verkuilen, Jay (2015), Lexicon: Homophone Naming in Aphasia. *Journal of Experimental Psychology: Learning, Memory, and Cognition*, v41 n1 p77-94 Jan 2015. The study of homophones words with different meanings that sound the same—

has great potential to inform models of language production. Of particular relevance is a phenomenon termed "frequency" inheritance, where a low-frequency word (e.g., "deer") is produced more fluently than would be expected based on its frequency characteristics, presumably because of shared phonology with a high-frequency homophone counterpart (e.g., "dear"). However, prior studies have been inconsistent in showing frequency inheritance. To explain this inconsistency, we propose a dual nature account of homophony: a high-frequency counterpart exerts 2 counter posing effects on a low-frequency homophone target during the 2 main stages of naming:

(a) A detrimental impact during semantically driven lexical retrieval;

(b) A beneficial impact during phonological retrieval.

In the study of naming in participants with chronic aphasia followed by computational investigations, we find strong evidence for the dual nature account of homophony.

Zhang, Yanyan; Xiao, Jing (2014), An Analysis of Indian Students' Perception and Production of Paired English Fricatives: From an ELF Perspective. *Journal of Pan-Pacific Association of Applied Linguistics*, v18 n1 p171-192 2014. English has assumed a new role in international communication in recent decades, that is, as a Lingua Franca (ELF) among speakers with different first languages. This study attempts to investigate and analyze Indian university students' perception and production of paired English fricatives from the perspective of ELF. By using a listening discrimination task and a reading task, respectively, the study examined how thirty two non-English major freshmen from a key university in Mainland China perceived and produced English fricative consonants. It was found that the participants had extreme difficulty distinguishing between the two sounds in three pairs of consonants in perception. In terms of production, the participants tended to replace the English fricative sounds, especially , with various substitutes. These results indicate that Indian students often have more difficulties with certain fricatives than with others. In addition, they seem to have particular problems with voiced fricatives. Therefore, it is suggested that priorities should be given to those that impede mutual intelligibility in international communication, namely, to those that fall into the Lingua Franca Core (LFC).

Cubilo, Justin; Winke, Paula (2013), Redefining the L2 Listening Construct within an Integrated Writing Task: Considering the Impacts of Visual-Cue Interpretation and Note-Taking. *Language Assessment Quarterly*, v10 n4 p371-397 2013. Researchers debate whether listening tasks should be supported by visuals. Most empirical research in this area has been conducted on the effects of visual support on listening comprehension tasks employing multiple-choice questions. The present study seeks to expand this research by investigating the effects of video listening passages (vs. audio-only listening passages) on note-taking strategies and subsequent (integrated) writing task performance. Forty international students learning English at Michigan State University participated. Each wrote two English essays, 1 preceded by supporting video listening material and one by audio-only listening material with the order of presentation and the content of the listening material and writing task counter balanced (via Latin squares) to control for order and test-content effects. Participants completed an exit survey concerning their perceptions of the different tasks. Results indicate that there was no significant difference in performance between the two task types (video-based vs. audio-only-based); however, there was a significant difference in note-taking practices—as expected, when test takers watched the video, they took fewer notes. Qualitative data suggest that test takers had mixed perceptions of the usefulness of video. However, the majority of participants preferred the video-based task and believed that video helped them understand the listening passages.

Chou, Mu-hsuan (2013), A Content-Based Approach to Teaching and Testing Listening Skills to Grade 5 EFL Learners. *International Journal of Listening*, v27 n3 p172-185 2013. English education has been officially incorporated into elementary-level education in Taiwan since 2001, with the key objective of reinforcing pupils' oral communication in class. Although oral interaction involves a degree of listening input from interlocutors, listening has unfortunately remained a marginalized area in Taiwanese elementary education. Little is known about how to improve young learners' listening comprehension and listening skills in Taiwanese contexts. The present study was carried out with 52 11-year-old elementary school pupils in Taiwan. An English course was designed to integrate pupils' listening skills into a content-based course with a series of tourism-related topics. The results showed that the teaching of listening skills could be integrated into the content-based course and certain listening skills were greatly improved. Also, the study has implications for designing a topic-based course for teaching and testing listening skills, as well as for developing listening and speaking abilities in young EFL learners.

Mashal, Nira; Kasirer, Anat (2011), *Research in Developmental Disabilities: A Multidisciplinary Journal*, v32 n6 p2045-2054 Nov-Dec 2011. Thinking Maps Enhance Metaphoric Competence in Children with Autism and Learning Disabilities. The primary goal of the current study was to examine the ability of children with autism (ASD) and children with learning disabilities (LD) to improve their metaphoric competence by an intervention program using "thinking maps". Twenty ASD children, 20 LD, and 20 typically developed (TD) children were tested on metaphors and idioms comprehension tests, homophone meaning generation test, and fluency tests. Both ASD and LD groups performed poorly compared with TD on all tests, with the LD group outperformed the ASD group in the executive function tests. The results indicate that the LD group was able to use the "thinking maps" to understand metaphors that were encountered for the first time more efficiently than the ASD group. Furthermore, in the autistic group the homophone meaning generation test, associated with mental flexibility mechanism, correlated with novel metaphors understanding, which do not rely on prior knowledge. In the learning disabilities group, conventional metaphors understanding correlated with the homophone meaning generation test.

White, Katherine K.; Abrams (2010), Syntactic Constraints in the Retrieval of Homophone Orthography. *Journal of Experimental Psychology: Learning, Memory, and Cognition*, v36 n1 p160-169 Jan 2010. In this experiment, syntactic constraints on the retrieval of orthography were investigated using homophones embedded in sentence contexts. Participants typed auditory presented sentences that included a contextually appropriate homophone that either shared part of speech with its homophone competitor (i.e., was syntactically unambiguous) or had a different part of speech (was syntactically ambiguous). Each homophone was preceded by an unrelated word or a prime; primes were orthographically related to the competitor and shared or differed from the competitor's part of speech. For syntactically unambiguous homophones, more errors occurred overall, and priming increased errors independent of the prime's part of speech. For syntactically ambiguous homophones, priming occurred only following primes that shared part of speech with the competitor. These results demonstrate that written homophone errors can occur during lemma retrieval or during orthographic encoding, with the particular stage depending on the syntactic ambiguity of the homophone to be produced.

Jong, Peter F.; Bitter, Danielle J. L.; van Setten, Margot; Marinus, Eva (2009), Does Phonological Recoding Occur during Silent Reading, and Is It Necessary for Orthographic Learning?. *Journal of Experimental Child Psychology*, v104 n3 p267-282 Nov 2009. Two studies were conducted to test the central claim of the self-teaching hypothesis (i.e., phonological recoding is necessary for orthographic learning) in silent reading. The first study aimed to demonstrate the use of phonological recoding during silent reading. Texts containing pseudo words were read silently or aloud. Two days later, target spellings were recognized more often than their homophone spellings. In both reading conditions, homophone alternatives were named faster than non exposed pseudo words, suggesting that phonological recoding had occurred. The second study aimed to suppress phonological recoding to demonstrate its necessity for orthographic learning. Lexical decisions were performed in a standard condition, with concurrent articulation, or with tapping. One day later, target spellings were recognized less often after lexical decisions with concurrent articulation. Target and homophone naming speed was not affected by lexical decision condition. The results support the use of phonological recoding during silent reading and specify its role in orthographic learning.

Binder, Katherine; Borecki, Caren (2008), *Reading and Writing: An Interdisciplinary Journal*, v21 n8 p843-858 Nov 2008. The Use of Phonological, Orthographic, and Contextual Information during Reading: A Comparison of Adults Who Are Learning to Read and Skilled Adult Readers. The purpose of the study was to assess the role that phonological, orthographic, and contextual sources of information play in a group of adults who were learning to read compared to adult skilled readers. Participants read short paragraphs that contained a correct homophone, an incorrect homophone, or a spelling control. Target words were orthographically similar or dissimilar, and they appeared in context that predicted the target or was neutral with respect to the target. The pattern of data obtained for skilled readers was consistent with past work (Rayner et al., "Journal of Experimental Psychology: Learning, Memory and Cognition" 24(2), 476-497, 1998). Skilled readers showed no reading time differences between the correct homophone and the incorrect homophone, as long as the two were orthographically similar, but reading times on these words were faster than the spelling control condition. The pattern of data for the adults who were learning to read was different. These readers were actually better at noticing that an incorrect version of the homophone was present. Importantly, we did find consistent significant differences between the incorrect homophone condition and the spelling control condition. This suggests the adults who were learning to read use phonological codes during word recognition, but they do so less efficiently than skilled readers.

Miozzo, Michele; Caramazza, Alfonso (2005), The Representation of Homophones: Evidence from the Distractor-Frequency Effect. *Journal of Experimental Psychology: Learning, Memory, and Cognition,* v31 n6 p1360-1371 Nov 2005. Current models of word production offer different accounts of the representation of homophones in the lexicon. The investigation of how the homophone status of a word affects lexical access can be used to test theories of lexical processing. In this study, homophones appeared as word distracters superimposed on pictures that participants named orally. The authors varied distracter frequency, a variable that has been shown to modulate the interference that distracters produce on picture naming. The results of 3 experiments converged in showing that words interfered in proportion to their individual frequency in the language, even if they have high-frequency homophone mates. This effect of specific-word frequency is compatible with models that assume

(a) Distinct lexical representations for the individual homophones and

(b) That access to such representations is modulated by frequency.

The authors discuss the extent to which current models of word production satisfy these constraints.

Gathercole, Virginia C. Mueller; Moawad, Ruba Abdelmatloub (2005), Semantic Interaction in Early and Late Bilinguals: All Words Are Not Created Equally. *Bilingualism: Language and Cognition*, v13 n4 p385-408 Oct 2005. The study examines L1-L2 interaction in semantic categorization in early and late L2 learners. Word categories that overlapped but were not identical in Arabic and English were tested. Words always showed a "wider" range of application in one language, "narrower" in the other. Three types of categories—"classical", "radial", and "homophones"—were examined. Monolingual Arabic, monolingual English, early bilingual, and late bilingual speakers were tested for their understanding of the Arabic or English words. Early bilinguals' semantic structure is affected in both directions, late bilinguals' only in the direction of L1 to L2. Classical categories were most vulnerable to inter-language influence, whereas homophones were least vulnerable. The discussion addresses a developmental model of semantic interaction in early and late bilingual learners.

Tsai, Feng-Hung, Integrating Feature Films with Subtitles to Enhance the Listening Comprehension of Students. *ProQuest LLC*, Ed.D. Dissertation, Alliant International University, San Diego The problem: Poor listening skills may result in misinterpretation. Language teachers as well as researchers understand the need for improving listening skills, and the need to find the most effective way to accomplish this objective. The purpose of this study was to determine whether the use of feature films with subtitles can help improve Taiwan college students' listening comprehension. Method: The researcher selected 126 Taiwanese EFL college students to participate in this study. This study used a combination of quantitative and qualitative methods. In this quasi-experimental research, there were two experimental groups (English subtitles group and Indian subtitles group) and a control group. The quantitative analysis included the listening comprehension score test and questionnaires. A simulated intermediate-level pre-test and a post-test of the GEPT listening comprehension tests were used to identify the proficiency level of the student participants. Moreover, additional data from the participants including the students' general background, students' and teachers' reported perceptions, and the effectiveness of using films in listening comprehension classes were analyzed and reported. Furthermore, for the qualitative analysis, 21 students (seven from each group) and six college English teachers were interviewed individually by the researcher.

The results of this study indicated that students in the experimental groups with either English subtitles or Indian subtitles treatments showed higher simulated GEPT listening test scores than the control group without the subtitles treatments. However, there was no significant difference between the English subtitles group and the Indian subtitles group. The qualitative findings showed a preference both by students and EFL teachers for using feature films and subtitles as a method of helping Taiwanese college students in their English listening comprehension. The results highlighted the effectiveness of the use of films with subtitles in promoting English learning when students are provided with well designed activities to motivate their viewing and vigorously engage in the film approach. Language learning can be fun and rewarding.

Burt and Dula, investigated that the learning of language is a two way street. Interaction is now regarded as the key to language learning. It is through interaction that one's formal knowledge of the target language becomes operational. Genuine interaction provides the learners with opportunities to express what they themselves want to say, not what the teacher wants them to say. This involves experimenting with the language, exploring and negotiating meaning. Meaningful tasks require the learners to analyse and process language more deeply, which help them to commit input to long term memory.

Canale, focused on form rather than meaning. According to him teachers impart knowledge about the target language and learners receive it. It is assumed that once learners learn to use the correct form of language they can use it as an effective form of communicative tool. Sufficient practice of accurate forms, it is believed, will lead to the desired form of fluency. This, in turn, leads to the current obsession with accuracy and correctness. Mistakes are regarded as aberrations, a straying away from the right path. Each mistake is explicitly pointed out, explained and corrected by the teacher.

CONCLUSION

The review has revealed the extent of contribution of educationalists in the area of the present study. From the review of the literature it is understood that only few studies have been undertaken to measure *"A Study on the Obstacles Learning of Homophones in English among VIII Standard Students"*.

Chapter-III

Methodology

INTRODUCTION

Webster has defined methodology as "the science of method or arrangement". Method is defined as orderliness and regularity or habitual practice of them in action. By placing stress on 'arrangement', orderliness, regularity and habitual practice, the methodologies derive their substance essentially from the classically ideal controlled experiment which permeates in the literature of educational research.

The methodology is decided with reference to research or the type of inquiry. Research methodology involves systematic procedures starting from the initial identification of the problem to its final conclusions. Its role is to carry on the research work in a scientific and valid manner.

It provides the tools and techniques by which the research problem is attacked. It consists of procedures and techniques for conducting a study. It is of little value unless used properly. Proper use must be learnt by the researcher.

It involves such general activities as identifying problems, review of the literature, formulating hypotheses, procedure for testing hypotheses, measurement, data collection, and analysis of data, interpreting results and drawing conclusions. Thus, it consists of all general and specific activities of research. Mastery in it enhances understanding of the research activities. Thus, research design and methodology have the identical meaning of mapping strategy of research.

Research is undertaken within most professions. More than a set of skills, it is a way of thinking: examining critically the various aspects of your professional work. It is a habit of questioning what you do, and a systematic examination of the observed information to find answers with a view to instituting appropriate changes for a more effective professional service.

Methodology occupies on important place is and kind of research methods or methodology refers to the way the study is conducted. It refers to the design through which validity of result is to be established. It is pointed at that the success of any research largely depends on the suitability of the method and the tools techniques used to collect reliable and valid data.

Methodology may be a description of process, or may be expanded to include a philosophically coherent collection of theories, concepts or ideas as they relate to a particular discipline or field of inquiry.

CHARACTERISTICS OF THE RESEARCH

Research is a process of collecting, analyzing and interpreting information to answer questions. But to qualify as research, the process must have certain characteristics: it must, as far as possible, be controlled, rigorous, systematic, valid and verifiable, empirical and critical.

In some cases, it is useful for other researchers to adapt or replicate your methodology, so often sufficient information is given to allow others to use the work. This is particularly the case when a new method had been developed, or an innovative adaptation used.

Methodology can be the analysis of the principles of methods, rules, and postulates employed by a discipline.

Methodology may refer to nothing more than a simple set of methods or procedures, or it may refer to the rationale and the philosophical assumptions that underlie a particular study relative to the scientific method. For example, scholarly literature often includes a section on the methodology of the researchers.

RESEARCH DESIGN

This chapter presents details regarding the following

1. Selection of Dependent variables and Categorical variables.
2. Construction of tools to measure the **Obstacles Learning of Homophones in English among VIII Standard Students.**
3. Methods of establishing the reliability and validity of the tools constructed.
4. Sampling procedure adopted in this study.
5. Scheduling the survey and collecting the data.

RESEARCH PROCEDURE

1. Choosing a problem
2. Identification of the variables
3. The learning outcome
4. Selection and development of the tools
5. Selection of sample from VIII standard students
6. Administration of the tools
7. Collection of Data
8. Data Analysis
9. Test of the Hypotheses
10. Findings and Evaluation
11. Implications

STATEMENT OF THE PROBLEM

The basic problem undertaken for investigation in the present study is to examine the "*A Study on The Obstacles Learning Of Homophones In English Among Viii Standard Students*".

OBJECTIVES OF THE STUDY

The following are the overall objectives of the presents study;

1. To find out the significant difference in the mean scores of Obstacles Learning of Homophones in English among VIII Standard Students in terms of their **Gender**.
2. To find out the significant difference in the mean scores of Obstacles Learning of Homophones in English among VIII Standard Students in terms of their **Residential Place.**
3. To find out the significant difference in the mean scores of Obstacles Learning of Homophones in English among VIII Standard Students in terms of their **school type as Government and Aided.**
4. To find out the significant difference in the mean scores of Obstacles Learning of Homophones in English among VIII Standard Students in terms of their **school type as Aided and Un-Aided.**
5. To find out the significant difference in the mean scores of Obstacles Learning of Homophones in English among VIII Standard Students in terms of their **school type as Un-Aided and Government.**
6. To find out the significant difference in the mean scores of Obstacles Learning of Homophones in English among VIII Standard Students in terms of their **Parent's occupation as Government and Private Job.**
7. To find out the significant difference in the mean scores of Obstacles Learning of Homophones in English among VIII Standard Students in terms of their **Parent's education level as literate and illiterate.**
8. To find out the significant difference in the mean scores of Obstacles Learning of Homophones in English among VIII Standard Students in terms of their **Parent's annual income as Above fifty thousand and Below fifty thousand**.

HYPOTHESIS OF THE STUDY

The following are the overall hypotheses for the presents study

1. There is no significant difference in the mean scores of Obstacles Learning of Homophones in English among VIII Standard Students in terms of their **Gender**.

2. There is no significant difference in the mean scores of Obstacles Learning of Homophones in English among VIII Standard Students in terms of their **Residential Place.**
3. There is no significant difference in the mean scores of Obstacles Learning of Homophones in English among VIII Standard Students in terms of their **school type as Government and Aided.**
4. There is no significant difference in the mean scores of Obstacles Learning of Homophones in English among VIII Standard Students in terms of their **school type as Aided and Un-Aided.**
5. There is no significant difference in the mean scores of Obstacles Learning of Homophones in English among VIII Standard Students in terms of their **school type as Un-Aided and Government.**
6. There is no significant difference in the mean scores of Obstacles Learning of Homophones in English among VIII Standard Students in terms of their **Parent's occupation as Government and Private Job.**
7. There is no significant difference in the mean scores of Obstacles Learning of Homophones in English among VIII Standard Students in terms of their **Parent's education level as Literate and Illiterate.**
8. There is no significant difference in the mean scores of Obstacles Learning of Homophones in English among VIII Standard Students in terms of their **Parent's annual income as Above fifty thousand and Below fifty thousand.**

DELIMITATIONS OF THE STUDY

1. The present study is confined only to VIII standard students in pudukkottai educational district.
2. The investigation on the **A study on the Obstacles Learning of Homophones in English among VIII Standard Students** was restricted to 300 data among the VIII students.
3. The present study is limited only to find the significance difference on

I. Gender,

II. Residential Place,

III. Type of School,

IV. Parent's Occupation,

V. Parent's Educational Qualification and

VI. Parent's Annual Income.

4. This study was conducted in the year 2014 – 2015.

RESEARCH METHOD

Normative method of survey involves using practices that pertain to the surveyed group. The researcher should already know what these practices and the probable reactions are before they survey the individuals.

The investigator preferred Survey method for the present study. In this study, the investigator used survey method to collect data and to identify the intensity of the study and it was identified the *"A Study On the Obstacles Learning Of Homophones in English among VIII Standard Students"* and this was restricted to 300 data of VIII students.

RESEARCH TOOLS

The word 'tool' is defined a means to collect evidence. Then **W. Best** observes that the questionnaire is the most tools in collecting both quantitative and qualities information, for the present study questionnaire was prepared with view to gather information in details.

In the present study the investigation selected questionnaire as the most important tools for collecting data because it is used increasingly to enquire into the current conditions, opinions of the School Teachers.

For the present study questionnaire was prepared with view to gather information in details regarding on "*A study on the Obstacles Learning of Homophones in English among VIII Standard Students*".

The selection of suitable tool for the investigation is very important for successful educational research. Research, so Questionnaire is a tool used collect data from the selected sample.

CONSTRUCTION OF RESEARCH TOOLS

A research tool plays a major role in any worthwhile research is the sole factor in determining the sound data and in arriving at perfect conclusion about the problem or study on hand, which ultimately, helps in providing suitable remedial measures to the problem concerned.

The selection and use of tools can be done in two ways. The first one is to construct a tool independently by the researcher for this own study. With this, one can say that preparation and standardization of tools is a major task, and one should take care in aspects like selection of area and sample, pooling up of statements related to the area, consulting the experts and application of sophisticated statistical techniques.

The research tool on *"A study on the Obstacles Learning of Homophones in English among VIII Standard Students"* was constructed by the investigator in the present study. All the question items are open type.

DESCRIPTION OF RESEARCH TOOL AND SCORING PROCEDURE

The response sheet of the subjects was scored according to the guidelines given by the constructor of the tool. It was a three point of likert's types of tool as **"Agree"**, "**Not-Decided**" **"Disagree".** Scoring procedure order by **"3"**, **"2"** and **"1"** respectively.

SAMPLES OF THE STUDY

A sample is a small proportion of a population selected for observation and analysis. A sample is a smaller representation of the High School students.

The investigator selected 300 samples from the study by using **Stratified Sampling** techniques. The sample should be selected from the total population. In stratified sampling method, much depends on stratification process. The following precaution was taken while stratifying the population:

1. the variables involved in the study were taken note of;
2. care was taken to see that each stratum in the universe was

large enough in size so that selection of items could be done on random basis;

3. the strata formed were definite and clear cut;
4. each stratum was free from influence of the other and
5. There was no overlapping.

Table 1

S.No	Name Of The School	Boys	Girls	Samples
1	Government Modern Hr.Sec.School, Pudukottai	18	42	60
2	Government Girls Hr.Sec.School,Pudukottai	-	60	60
3	St.Joseph Matric Hr.Sec.School,Thirumayam	27	31	58
4	Government Boys Hr.Sec.School,Thirumayam	58	-	58
5	Sri Saraswathi Hr.Sec.School,Konapattu	42	22	64
	Total	145	155	300

PILOT STUDY

The pilot study is concerned with refining the items collected. The collected items were presented before the expert with a request to offer their considered opinion regarding the suitability clarity and relevancy of the statement collected from different sources. The opinion of the experts was taken into consideration to refine the items.

Further, the investigator obtained some ideas from the experts and modified the irrelevant item that is coming in the present study.

After getting response and these frequencies was converted into scores and those scores were used to establish reliability.

VALIDITY OF THE TOOL

The validity of tool depends upon the fidelity with which it measures what it purports to measure. **Nunnaly (1978),** Maintains that rather than establishing the validity of the measures after they are constructed, it is highly meaningful that one should ensure the validity of the tool by the plan and produces of test construction. This can be done through a representative collection of items and a sensible method of test constriction. The different procedure s followed in developing the tools are outline in this chapter.

RELIABILITY OF THE TOOL

After collecting data in the pilot study, the investigator attempted to find out the reliability for *A study on the Obstacles Learning of Homophones in English among VIII Standard Students*. The reliability of the tool refers to the internal consistency observed in measurement with different set of equivalent items. The reliability value of present tool as questionnaire has **0.78** as "r" value.

$$r = \frac{2 * r}{1 \quad r}$$

$$\frac{2x0.78}{1 \quad 0.78}$$

$$0.88$$

The reliability value of the present tool has **0.88** value. Hence the tool was **highly reliable**.

SAMPLING TECHNIQUE USED

The sampling procedure is used to collect the data using Stratified **Random** Sampling. After finalizing the variables of present study, consideration was given to whether the entire population is to be made the subject for data collection or a particular group is to be selected as representative of the whole population. The entire population here refers to all the VIII standard students.

Of the above two techniques, the selection of a group as a representative of the whole population was found to be more convenient and suitable. This technique leads to a considerable save of time, effort and finance. The number of students selected will be small, and so it is possible to make a detailed and intensive study. This generally leads to more accurate and reliable results. As this sampling technique has many advantages, it was selected for the collection of data.

In any behavioral research, various methods are utilized for selection and drawing of samples. After a detailed study of all these methods and considering the variables selected for the research work, the stratified sampling method was found to be most suitable.

In the stratified sampling method, the entire population will be divided into smaller homogenous groups or strata, and then a sample is selected within each group. Every sampling unit in the population is placed in one of the strata prior to the selection of the sample so that the sum of the strata is identical with the population. Stratified sampling method has certain merits as a technique of sampling

COLLECTION OF DATA

The investigator himself met each and every school students in various high schools located. The investigator met the Headmaster of various schools and got permission from them and then collects data. The investigator revealed the purpose of the present study to the VIII standard students and then asked them to give their responses for each and every item that are given in the questionnaire. The responses were recorded.

ANALYSIS OF DATA

The term analysis refers to the compilation of certain measures along with searching for pattern and relationship that among groups.

For the present study the investigator collected the data from high school students using the tool developed to find out questioner of sample to identify the *"A study on the Obstacles Learning of Homophones in English among VIII Standard Students"*. This involves computing measures and correlation pattern and the measures of variability like Standard deviation and t-test also used.

STATISTICAL TECHNIQUES USED

DESCRIPTIVE STATISTICS

We define the "population" as the number of measurements that could be made and "samples" as the actual measurements made. The challenge of statistics is to use the samples to estimate characteristics of the population. Often, we use different symbols for these characteristics, depending on whether they are for the population or for the samples. For example, the population means (average) is generally given the Greek letter mu, ì, and the sample mean is written. The square root of the average square of the deviation of individual values of the population from ì is the population standard deviation, and is given the Greek letter sigma, ó. The sample standard deviation, s, is defined below and is an estimate of ó. As the sample size n is increased, becomes closer to ì and s closer to ó.

The following statistical techniques have been proposed for the present study

To find "t" test for the following measures used.

THE ARITHMETIC MEAN (M)

The Mean of the distribution is commonly understood as the arithmetic average. The term guide-point averages familiar to student is a Mean value.

It is computed by dividing the sum of all the scores by the number of scores. It is probably most useful of all statistical measures for in addition to the information that it provides. It is the base from which many others in important measures are computed.

Where,

M = Mean

$\sum x$ = The sum of the scores of the distribution

N = Number of Scores.

THE STANDARD DEVIATION

Standard deviation most widely used measure of dispersion of a series and is commonly denoted by the symbol ó (sigma) standard deviation is defined as the square root of the average of squares of deviations when such deviations for the values of individual items in a series are obtained from the arithmetic average.

't'- TEST

The test of significance of the difference between two mean is known as 't'- test. It involves the computation of the ratio between experimental variance (observed difference between two sample means) and error variance (the sampling error factor).

When small samples are involved the t-table is used to determine statistical significance, rather that the normality, probability table.

This concept of small sample size was developed around 1915 by William, carefully calculated for small samples area reproduced in the t- distribution table.

The t- critical values necessary for rejection of a null hypothesis are higher for the samples of a given level of significances. Each t – critical value for rejection is based upon the appropriate number of degrees of freedom.

The **t – test** would be used upon this formula.

M1= Mean of First Group

M2 = Mean of Second Group

S1 = SD of the first

S2 = SD of the second group

N1 = No. of students in first Group

N2 = No. of Students in Second Group

CONCLUSION

This chapter deals with the description of research design and procedure. The research design is the plan, structure and strategy of answer of research question and to control the variance. It is at this stage that crucial decisions are made for how the objective are to e achieved and how the work to be executed. So, in this context this chapter explains design of the study. Population, size of the sample and how they are subjected variables. The source and techniques of gathering data, research procedure adopted in this study was discussed in this chapter. The data were analyzed with suitable statistical techniques and interpreted in the upcoming Chapter.

Chapter IV

Analysis and Interpretation of Data

INTRODUCTION

One of the important parts of any investigation is analysis and interpretation of data. The data collected in any field of activity becomes meaningful and useful only when there are subjected to statistical analysis and inference.

Analysis of data means studying the organized material in order to discover inherent facts. The data are studied from as many angles as possible explore the few facts. Once the research data have been collected data analysis has been made. Then the research interpreting is essentially needed to state whether the result shows the research data become meaningful after they are being analyzed and interpreted. The analysis and interpretation of data involves the objective material in the possession of the research and his subjective reactions and desires to device from the data.

ANALYSIS OF DATA

Analysis of data mean studying the tabulated materials in orders to determine inherent fact of meaning. It involves the breaking down of the existing complex faders into simple parts and putting them together in a now arrangement for the purpose of interpretation.

According to Pearson, "Analysis is a research technique for objective, systematic and quantitative description of the manifest content of communication".

According to Cristofer, "Analysis is an important phase of the classification and summation of data into a summary".

According to Prestly, "The discovery of order in the phenomena of nature, not withstanding their complexity and apparent confusion is rendered possible by process of analysis and synthesis which are foundation stone of all scientific methods".

After, collection the data from the respondents, the investigator gave frequencies for the correct responses and these frequencies were converted into scores and then investigator calculated the scores.

These scores were used to identify the level of "**A Study on the Obstacles Learning of Homophones in English among VIII Standard Students**".

HYPOTHESES TESTING

Analysis is a technique of social research which presents qualitative data in an objective, systematic and quantitative.

The investigator also tests the significance to find out the significant difference between the various groups of demographic variables on *"A Study on the Obstacles Learning of Homophones in English among VIII Standard Students"*.

The following are the Hypotheses to be tested.

HYPOTHESIS: 1

There is no significant difference in the mean scores of Obstacles Learning of Homophones in English among VIII Standard Students in terms of their Gender.

TABLE: 1

The table gave below shows the mean, standard deviation and "t" values of Obstacles Learning of Homophones in English among VIII Standard Students in terms of their **Gender**.

GENDER	N	M	SD	df	't' value	Level of Significance at 0.05
MALE	145	72.59	5.09			
FEMALE	155	74.76	4.26	298	3.99	Significant

INTERPRETATION:

The computed table value of **t = 3.99** is greater than the critical table value at 0.05 level of significance (ie) 1.96 for df = 298, which implies that there is significant difference in the mean scores of Obstacles Learning of Homophones in English among VIII Standard Students in terms of their **Gender**.

RESULT:

Hence the null hypothesis is Rejected.

HYPOTHESIS: 2

There is no significant difference in the mean scores of Obstacles Learning of Homophones in English among VIII Standard Students in terms of their Residential Place.

TABLE: 2

The table gave below shows the mean, standard deviation and "t" values of Obstacles Learning of Homophones in English among VIII Standard Students in terms of their **Residential Place**.

Residential Place	N	M	SD	df	't' value	Level of Significance at 0.05
RURAL	212	73.26	4.69			
URBAN	88	74.78	4.89	298	2.48	Significant

INTERPRETATION:

The computed table value of **t = 2.48** is greater than the critical table value at 0.05 level of significance (ie) 1.96 for df = 298, which implies that there is significant difference in the mean scores of Obstacles Learning of Homophones in English among VIII Standard Students in terms of their **Residential Place**.

RESULT:

Hence the null hypothesis is rejected.

HYPOTHESIS: 3

There is no significant difference in the mean scores of Obstacles Learning of Homophones in English among VIII Standard Students in terms of their school type as Government and Government-Aided.

TABLE: 3

The table gave below shows the mean, standard deviation and "t" values of Obstacles Learning of Homophones in English among VIII Standard Students in terms of their **school type as Government and Aided**.

School Type	N	M	SD	df	't' value	Level of Significance at 0.05
GOVERNMENT	178	72.75	5.02			
GOVERNMENT-AIDED	64	77.28	3.77	240	7.51	Significant

INTERPRETATION:

The computed table value of **t = 7.51** is greater than the critical table value at 0.05 level of significance (ie) 1.96 for df = 240, which implies that there is significant difference in the mean scores of Obstacles Learning of Homophones in English among VIII Standard Students in terms of their **school type as Government and Aided**.

RESULT:

Hence the null hypothesis is rejected.

HYPOTHESIS: 4

There is no significant difference in the mean scores of Obstacles Learning of Homophones in English among VIII Standard Students in terms of their school type as Government-Aided and Un-Aided.

TABLE: 4

The table gave below shows the mean, standard deviation and "t" values of Obstacles Learning of Homophones in English among VIII

Standard Students in terms of their **school type as Aided and Un-Aided**.

School Type	N	M	SD	df	't' value	Level of Significance at 0.05
GOVERMENT AIDED	64	77.28	3.77			
UN-AIDED	58	72.69	2.96	120	7.51	Significant

INTERPRETATION:

The computed table value of **t = 7.51** is greater than the critical table value at 0.05 level of significance (ie) 1.96 for df = 120, which implies that there is significant difference in the mean scores of Obstacles Learning of Homophones in English among VIII Standard Students in terms of their **school type as Aided and Un-Aided**.

RESULT:

Hence the null hypothesis is rejected.

HYPOTHESIS: 5

There is no significant difference in the mean scores of Obstacles Learning of Homophones in English among VIII Standard Students in terms of their school type as Un-Aided and Government.

TABLE: 5

The table given below shows the mean, standard deviation and "t" values of Obstacles Learning of Homophones in English among VIII Standard Students in terms of their **school type as Un-Aided and Government**.

School Type	N	M	SD	df	't' value	Level of Significance at 0.05
UN-AIDED SCHOOL	58	72.69	2.96			
GOVERNMENT SCHOOL	178	72.75	5.02	234	0.12	Not Significant

INTERPRETATION:

The computed table value of **t = 0.12** is lesser than the critical table value at 0.05 level of significance (ie) 1.96 for df = 234, which implies that there is no significant difference in the mean scores of Obstacles Learning of Homophones in English among VIII Standard Students in terms of their **school type as Un-Aided and Government**.

RESULT:

Hence the null hypothesis is accepted.

HYPOTHESIS: 6

There is no significant difference in the mean scores of Obstacles Learning of Homophones in English among VIII Standard Students in terms of their Parent's occupation as Government and Private Job.

TABLE: 6

The table gave below shows the mean, standard deviation and "t" values of Obstacles Learning of Homophones in English among VIII Standard Students in terms of their **Parent's occupation as Government and Private Job**.

Parent's occupation	N	M	SD	df	't' value	Level of Significance at 0.05
GOVERNMENT JOB	170	73.88	4.59			
PRIVATE JOB	130	73.48	5.07	298	0.70	Not Significant

INTERPRETATION:

The computed table value of **t = 0.70** is lesser than the critical table value at 0.05 level of significance (ie) 1.96 for df = 298, which implies that there is no significant difference in the mean scores of Obstacles Learning of Homophones in English among VIII Standard Students in terms of their **Parent's occupation as Government and Private Job**.

RESULT:

Hence the null hypothesis is accepted.

HYPOTHESIS: 7

There is no significant difference in the mean scores of Obstacles Learning of Homophones in English among VIII Standard Students in terms of their Parent's education level as literate and illiterate.

TABLE: 7

The table gave below shows the mean, standard deviation and "t" values of Obstacles Learning of Homophones in English among VIII Standard Students in terms of their **Parent's education level as Literate and Illiterate**.

Parent's Qualification	N	M	SD	df	't' value	Level of Significance at 0.05
LITERATE	212	74.09	4.59			
ILLITERATE	88	72.79	5.19	298	2.04	Significant

INTERPRETATION:

The computed table value of **t = 2.04** is greater than the critical table value at 0.05 level of significance (ie) 1.96 for df = 98, which implies that there is significant difference in the mean scores of Obstacles Learning of Homophones in English among VIII Standard Students in terms of their **Parent's education level as Literate and Illiterate**.

RESULT:

Hence the null hypothesis is rejected.

HYPOTHESIS: 8

There is no significant difference in the mean scores of Obstacles Learning of Homophones in English among VIII Standard Students in terms of their Parent's annual income as Above fifty thousand and Below fifty thousand.

TABLE: 8

The table given below shows the mean, standard deviation and "t" values of Obstacles Learning of Homophones in English among VIII Standard Students in terms of their **Parent's annual income as Above fifty thousand and Below fifty thousand**.

Annual Income	N	M	SD	df	't' value	Level of Significance at 0.05
BELOW 50,000	128	72.89	4.89			
ABOVE 50,000	172	74.31	4.65	298	2.54	Significant

INTERPRETATION:

The computed table value of **t = 2.54** is greater than the critical table value at 0.05 level of significance (ie) 1.96 for df = 98, which implies that there is significant difference in the mean scores of Obstacles Learning of Homophones in English among VIII Standard Students in terms of their **Parent's annual income as Above fifty thousand and Below fifty thousand**.

RESULT:

Hence the null hypothesis is rejected

CONCLUSION

In this chapter the collections of data were tabulated, analyzed and interpreted. The next chapter deals with the summary findings and conclusion of the present investigation on "*A Study on the Obstacles Learning of Homophones in English among VIII Standard Students*".

Chapter - V

Findings and Conclusion

INTRODUCTION

The fifth and concluding chapter of the thesis summarizes the research study and discusses its findings. It also analyses their implications for the Obstacles of Learning Homophones in English among VIII Standard Students. It puts forth suggestions for further research in the area and highlights the limitations of the present study.

The research study was started by formulating a hypothesis. The research tool used in the study to collect the data was chosen. The literature on the research topic was surveyed to understand the existing literature on the research topic. Then the field study was planned and conducted accordingly.

The findings of the study are given below. Data analysis involves analytical thinking. This is done only after collecting all the relevant data and which is always focused on the research problems and the hypotheses and questions arising in the statement of the problem.

Here the investigator has compiled and summarized the results in a logical order in relation to the objectives and hypothesis of the study. The data has been interpreted and presented more clearly with the help of findings representation.

STATEMENT OF THE PROBLEM

The basic problem undertaken for investigation in the present study is to examine the *"A Study on the Obstacles Learning Of Homophones In English Among Viii Standard Students"*.

OBJECTIVES OF THE STUDY

The following are the objectives of the present study

1. To find out the significant difference in the mean scores of Obstacles Learning of Homophones in English among VIII Standard Students in terms of their **Gender**.
2. To find out the significant difference in the mean scores of Obstacles Learning of Homophones in English among VIII Standard Students in terms of their **Residential Place.**
3. To find out the significant difference in the mean scores of Obstacles Learning of Homophones in English among VIII Standard Students in terms of their **school type as Government and Aided.**
4. To find out the significant difference in the mean scores of Obstacles Learning of Homophones in English among VIII Standard Students in terms of their **school type as Aided and Un-Aided.**
5. To find out the significant difference in the mean scores of Obstacles Learning of Homophones in English among VIII Standard Students in terms of their **school type as Un-Aided and Government.**
6. To find out the significant difference in the mean scores of Obstacles Learning of Homophones in English among VIII Standard Students in terms of their **Parent's occupation as Government and Private Job.**
7. To find out the significant difference in the mean scores of Obstacles Learning of Homophones in English among VIII

Standard Students in terms of their **Parent's education level as Literate and Illiterate.**

8. To find out the significant difference in the mean scores of Obstacles Learning of Homophones in English among VIII Standard Students in terms of their **Parent's annual income as Above fifty thousand and Below fifty thousand.**

HYPOTHESIS OF THE STUDY

The following are the hypotheses constructed for the present study

1. There is no significant difference in the mean scores of Obstacles Learning of Homophones in English among VIII Standard Students in terms of their **Gender**.
2. There is no significant difference in the mean scores of Obstacles Learning of Homophones in English among VIII Standard Students in terms of their **Residential Place.**
3. There is no significant difference in the mean scores of Obstacles Learning of Homophones in English among VIII Standard Students in terms of their **school type as Government and Aided.**
4. There is no significant difference in the mean scores of Obstacles Learning of Homophones in English among VIII Standard Students in terms of their **school type as Aided and Un-Aided.**
5. There is no significant difference in the mean scores of Obstacles Learning of Homophones in English among VIII Standard Students in terms of their **school type as Un-Aided and Government.**
6. There is no significant difference in the mean scores of Obstacles Learning of Homophones in English among VIII Standard Students in terms of their **Parent's occupation as Government and Private Job.**
7. There is no significant difference in the mean scores of Obstacles Learning of Homophones in English among VIII Standard Students in terms of their **Parent's education level as literate and illiterate.**

8. There is no significant difference in the mean scores of Obstacles Learning of Homophones in English among VIII Standard Students in terms of their **Parent's annual income as above fifty thousand and below fifty thousand.**

FINDINGS OF THE RESEARCH

The following are the findings for the present study

1. There is significant difference in the mean scores of Obstacles Learning of Homophones in English among VIII Standard Students in terms of their Gender.
2. There is significant difference in the mean scores of Obstacles Learning of Homophones in English among VIII Standard Students in terms of their Residential Place.
3. There is significant difference in the mean scores of Obstacles Learning of Homophones in English among VIII Standard Students in terms of their school type as Government and Aided.
4. There is significant difference in the mean scores of Obstacles Learning of Homophones in English among VIII Standard Students in terms of their school type as aided and Un-Aided.
5. There is no significant difference in the mean scores of Obstacles Learning of Homophones in English among VIII Standard Students in terms of their school type as Un-Aided and Government.
6. There is no significant difference in the mean scores of Obstacles Learning of Homophones in English among VIII Standard Students in terms of their Parent's occupation as Government and Private Job.
7. There is significant difference in the mean scores of Obstacles Learning of Homophones in English among VIII Standard Students in terms of their Parent's education level as Literate and Illiterate.
8. There is significant difference in the mean scores of Obstacles Learning of Homophones in English among VIII Standard Students in terms of their Parent's annual income as Above fifty thousand and Below fifty thousand.

RESEARCH IMPLICATIONS

Learning strategies are useful tools for students because they open up more reliable and less frustrating routes to success in language learning. The obstacles appeared and exist among students helps to criticize the language learning difficulties. The results obtained from the students examines the difficulties arises in learning the homophones.

This overall findings results that there is significant difference in the mean scores of Obstacles of Learning Homophones in English among VIII Standard Students in terms of their Gender, Residential Place, type as Government, and Aided, type as Aided and Un-Aided, Parent education level as Literate and Illiterate, Parent annual income as Above fifty thousand and Below fifty thousand.

This exactly shows that VIII standard students facing obstacles in learning Homophones in English Language.

SUGGESTIONS FOR THE FURTHER RESEARCH

1. This study will conducted among various school level of Tamilnadu Government.
2. This study will conduct among the students of higher secondary level.
3. A comparative study will be conducted among junior secondary and senior secondary students.
4. A comparative study will be conducted among the students of urban and rural area.

RECOMMENDATIONS OF THE STUDY

1. Needs to be introduced for teachers, parents and caregivers at the alternative care settings to develop language skill among the students.
2. Strong educational programmes and system should be established by amending the existing weak clauses.
3. Professional care should utilize their contact with students to screen for this problem and educate them to overcome their learning difficulties.

4. Teacher should take initiative and provide encouragement to the school students regarding their English learning academic development.
5. This study extends and suggests that the teachers shall be encouraged student's behavior attitude and learning capability.
6. Students shall be counseled through regular test and evaluation from their respectful teachers.

CONCLUSION

The present study clearly shows that VIII standard students suffer from serious difficulties with their English Homophones learning, despite the earlier introduction of English in schools. Intensive school practice on the application of learning rules seems to have paid off, however, since the study participants performed at their best on these aspects.

The aspects that the participants are most challenged by have their inter-lingual origin. The most serious problem is learning homophones, especially short ones. The participants have exhibited a great difficulty at representing homophones properly in their speaking.

Hence this study results that most of the students learning in VIII standard facing problems in learning homophones. Thus, the overall findings results that there is significant difference in the mean scores of Obstacles Learning of Homophones in English among VIII Standard Students in terms of their Gender, Residential Place, type as Government, and Aided, type as Aided and Un-Aided, Parent's education level as Literate and Illiterate, Parent's annual income as Above fifty thousand and Below fifty thousand. this exactly shows that VIII standard students facing obstacles in learning Homophones in English Language.

BIBLIOGRAPHY

1. AdyBailey, K. M., *Focus on the Language Classroom: An Introduction to Classroom Research for Language Teachers*, Cambridge University Press, Cambridge, 1991.

2. Bandura, A., *Social Learning Theory*, Prentice-Hall, Englewood Cliffs, NJ, 1977.
3. Berg, B. L., *Qualitative Research Methods for the Social Sciences*, Allyn and Bacon, Needham Heights, Mass., 1995.
4. Bogdan, R. C. & Biklen, S. K., *Qualitative Research for Education: An Introduction to Theory and Methods*, Allyn and Bacon, Boston, 1998.
5. Brown, H. D., *Principles of Language Learning and Teaching*, Longman, New York, 2012.
6. Cangelosi, J. S., *Classroom Management Strategies: Gaining and Maintaining*
7. *Students' Cooperation (5th ed.)*, John Wiley & Sons, New York, 2004.
8. Charles, C. M., *Building Classroom Discipline (7th ed)*. Longman, New York, 2013.
9. Cohen, A. D. & Dörnyei, Z., Focus on the Language Learner: Motivation, Styles and Strategies, In N. Schmitt (Ed.) *An Introduction to Applied Linguistics*, Arnold, London, 2009.
10. Çohen, L & Manion, L., *Research Methods in Education*, Routledge, London, 1996. *Sosyal Bilimler Enstitüsü Dergisi Say : 27 Y l: 2009/ 2 (1-16 s.)*
11. Comish, R., Rader, C. K., W, Daboval, J. & Northam, C., National Impact – A Classroom Trust Inventory. *Psychology*, 33 (1), 1996, 37-40. Cook, V., *Second Language Learning and Language Teaching*, Arnold, London, 2014.
12. Darch, C. B. & Kameenui, E. J., *Instructional Classroom Management: A Proactive Approach to Behavior Management (2nd ed.)*, Longman, White Plains, NY, 2013.
13. Gajendra, V. (Ed.), *Researching Education: Perspectives and Techniques*, Falmer Press, London, 2008.
14. Galloway, V. & Labarca, A., From Student to Learner: Style, Process, and Strategy. Chapter 4 in D. Birckbichler, ed., *New Perspectives and Directions in Foreign language Education. The*

ACTFL Foreign Language Education Series, Lincolnwood, IL: National Textbook Company, 2013.

15. Hadley, A. O., *Teaching Language in Context*, Heinle & Heinle Publishers, Boston, 2013.

16. Jacobson, J., Lapp, D., & Mendez, M. (2003). *Accommodating differences among English language learners: 75 literacy lessons.* Colorado Springs, CO: PEAK Parent Center.

17. Jacobson, J., Moore, K., & Lapp, D. (2007). *Accommodating differences among English language learners: 75 literacy lessons* (2nd ed.). Colorado Springs, CO: PEAK Parent Center.

18. Jones, V. F. & Jones, L. S., *Comprehensive Classroom Management: Creating Communities of Support and Solving Problems*, Allyn and Bacon, Boston, 2012.

19. Rohrkemper, M. M. & Good, T. L., Proactive Teaching. In M. J. Dunkin (Ed.), *The International Encyclopedia of Teaching and Teacher Education*, Pergamon Press, Oxford, 2008.

20. Randall, Mick, and Paul Meara. "How Arabs Read Roman Letters?" *Reading in a Foreign Language* 4/1 (1988): 133-145.

21. Ryan, Ann. "Learning the Orthographical Form of L2 Vocabulary: A Receptive and Productive Process". *Vocabulary: Description, Acquisition and Pedagogy*. Ed. Norbert Schmitt and Michael McCarthy. Cambridge, UK: Cambridge University Press. 1997. 181–198

22. Ryan, Ann, and Paul Meara. "The Case of the Invisible Vowels: Arabic Speakers Reading English Words". *Reading in a Foreign Language* 7 (1991): 531–540.

23. Schlagal, Bob. "Classroom Spelling Instruction: History, Research, and Practice". *Reading Research and Instruction* 4/1 (2002): 44-57.

24. Sitton, Rebecca. *Spelling Sourcebook One*. Portland, OR: Northwest Textbook, 2005.

25. Templeton, Shane, and Darrell Morris. "Questions Teachers Ask about Spelling". *Reading Research Quarterly* 34/1 (1999): 102-136.

26. Treiman, Rebecca, and Marie Cassar. "Spelling Acquisition in English". *Learning to Spell: Research, Theory, and Practice across Languages.* Ed. Charles A. Perfetti, Laurence Rieben, and Michel Fayol. Mahwah, NJ: Erlbaum. 1997. 61-80.

27. Wang, Min, and Esther Geva. "Spelling Performance of Chinese Children Using English as a Second Language: Lexical and Visual-Orthographic Processes". *Applied Psycholinguistics* 24 (2003): 1–25.

28. Salus, P., & Flood, J. (2003). *Language: A user's guide: What we say and why.* Colorado Springs, CO: PEAK Parent Center.

29. Schwartz, R.M., & Raphael, T.E. (1985). Concept of definition: A key to improving students' vocabulary. *The Reading Teacher,* 39, 198–205.

30. Smith, C. (2002). *Building a strong vocabulary: A twelve-week plan for students.* Bloomington, IN: ERIC/EDINFO Press. (ERIC Document Reproduction Service No. ED468896)

31. Strickland, D., Ganske, K., & Monroe, J. (2002). *Supporting struggling readers and writers.* Newark, DE: International Reading Association.

32. Suarez-Rivas, M. (Ed.). (2014). *Latino read-aloud stories.* New York: Blackdog and Leventhal.

33. Spielmann, G. & Radnofsky, M., Learning Language under Tension: New Directions from a Qualitative Study. *The Modern Language Journal,* 85, 2001, 259-278. Stake, R., *The Art of Case Research.* Sage Publications: Thousand Oaks, CA, 1995.

34. Zutell, Jerry, and Virginia Allen. "The English Spelling Strategies of panish-Speaking Bilingual Children". *TESOL Quarterly* 22 (1988): 333–340.

35. Y ld r m, A. & im ek, H., *Sosyal Bilimlerde Nitel Ara t rma Yöntemleri (6.Bask),* Seçkin, Ankara, 2006.

3. Achievement and Effect of Innovative Teaching

Chapter - 1

INTRODUCTION

Education is usually understood as a course of study to acquire a body of knowledge or skills undertaken to enhance one's ability to do a particular job and be able to earn more money. The more liberal definitions of education, where it is understood as development and refinement of one's personality, without necessarily an eye to economic advantage, have been out of use for long, and one finds only scattered instances of the practice of education with such aims. The educational process has been the subject of much comment by academics and writers. Their observations range from praise to cynicism, mostly the latter. Education is an easy target for criticism because its stated aims are often so nobly ambitious that they have little chance of being realized. It should give us pause that so many people who have made their mark in the world of ideas, who have been acknowledged leaders and innovators, have held formal education and educational institutions in low regard. We have collected here a variety of thought-provoking observations on education.

IMPORTANCE OF EDUCATION

Importance has been considered as an instrument of economic, social and political change the ultimate goal education is to develop necessary skills among the people education is to develop necessary skills among the people education for adults in the key element in the rural development endeavor they can run their own affair and to enable them to become self reliance by increasing productivity through their dedication and hard work.

An individual's education starts from birth and extends up to death the process of education can be hastened through study and instruction, an individual is educated not only in the classroom, college and universities, but also in the play fields, place to works and workshop social gathering etc. Education paves way for the development advancement and perpetuation culture.

Education can be regarded as a process. That continues experiences are engaged in by the learners as to develop his innate potentialities Education as a product and attitudes. That result from the learner's participation in learning process. Keeping the importance of "man" to the social well being, educationists contemplated of the education are conservation, communication the young generation, interpretation and innovations of culture of the society.

MEANING OF EDUCATION

Education being a most important social activity, its meanings has been changing through the ages due to changes in social and physical conditions as well as philosophical outlook of people towards life.

DEFINATION OF EDUCATION

Education is the most powerful weapon which you can use to change the world - Nelson Mandela tthe function of education is to teach one to think intensively and to think critically. Intelligence plus character-that is the goal of true education-Martin Luther King, Jr. Education is not preparation for life; education is life itself. One of the few things a person is willing to pay for and not get- William Lowe Bryan The roots of education are bitter, but the fruit is sweet-

Aristotle Education is what remains when we have forgotten all that we have been taught. Education is a progressive discovery of our ignorance- Will Durant Education is the key to unlock the golden door of freedom- George Washington Carver

Need of education

Across countries, education plays a vital role not only in acquiring knowledge but also inculcating social, ethical, moral and spiritual values. In our model, schooling teaches people to interact with others and raises the benefits of civic participation including voting and organizing. Education raises the benefits of civic participation. Education is able to instill in the child a sense of maturity and responsibility in bringing in him the desired changes.

AIMS OF EDUCATION

1. Education for earning purpose
2. Education for lifelong reading
3. Leadership qualities
4. Life skills
5. Good health and Good habits

NEED AND SIGNIFICANCE OF THE STUDY

In this present context, most of the students learn the subject pass the examination and forget the concept, facts, terms and principles when they go out. Unless some intervention is made, the student cannot comprehend the concept in the Food the Medicine. Hence it is the duty of the Tamil teacher to make an instructional design that would support them in realizing and envisaged instructional objectives. So the investigator felt a need to select this topic to improve the easy understanding capacity of the students.

At present, the teacher in Indian schools take more time to complete the classroom instructions by the traditional method of teaching due to over loaded syllabi and lack of time in the classroom situation. Further the teachers are not able to concentrate on the development of all the cognitive skills. The investigator felt that this kind of study is needed particularly for secondary students to improve better understanding and application of their mind in enhancing their knowledge.

SCOPE OF THE STUDY

The main purpose of the present investigation was to enhance the understanding level of the students in learning Food the Medicine at secondary level particularly to IXth standard students. The teaching strategy developed by the investigator can be followed by all Indian classroom situation, whether it is crowded or in multi-graded situation. It gives an opportunity for the teacher to motive the children. The teacher can identify the suitable method of teaching. The teaching strategy can be followed by analyzing the knowledge, understanding and application level competency and appropriate activities can be given to attain the competency in a joyful manner. This teaching approach used in schools to develop a positive attitude towards the Tamil subject and Tamil teachers, though the present study is to the class of IXth standard, the strategy may be adopted to secondary and higher secondary level too. This strategy may be followed in teaching of other subject such as Science etc.

STATEMENT OF THE PROBLEM

The problem of the present investigation is "*A Study on Achievement and Effect of Innovative teaching of the Lesson Food the Medicine among IXth Standard Students*".

FOOD

Good food is a basic need of human body. It is of prime importance in the attainment of normal growth and development. The role of nutrition food cannot be neglected in the promotion of health and prevention of disease. Food is another necessary thing for the body. Nutritious foods help us to maintain good health. Consumption of healthy foods helps us to minimize any health related problems. We all should know, how, when and what to eat.

We should always include a portion of green vegetables, fruits or salads in our meal. Green vegetables are sources of vital nutrients. Our digestive system plays a key role in our overall health. Fiber rich foods such as whole grain wheat, bran rice, etc. help us improve our digestive system.

A balanced and nutritious diet helps the proper growth of the body. But we must remember that we eat to live and not that we live to eat. In India, over-eating causes a large number of deaths. If we eat less, we may live more.

Life today is not like how it was before. Long ago, people ate foods that are very good for their health. They ate foods that do not contain chemicals, preservatives, artificial colors, and artificial flavors. People also had a lot of time to cook their own foods. Therefore those people were not been affected by the food that they ate, because all of the foods that they had were natural foods and healthy. That is why they did not have any problem on their health and they lived longer than now. But these days, everyone is busy and don't have time to cook their own food. People eat foods that are easily cooked or ready cooked. They do not even think of what they eat, and if it can affect their health or not. That is a bad way that most people do because our health depends on what we eat daily. Foods are the building blocks of every cell in the body, are responsible for the proper functioning of the whole body. It is important, for that reason, to know what is good for our body and what is not. Healthy foods are called such because they are good for our health. Healthy food can be found in fruits, vegetables, meat, nuts, seafood and dairy foods. Healthy Food, from the ancient times to modern age, has always been an important part of human life. Man cannot live without it, because it is the basic need of human being. In this modern age, food has become very easy to prepare with the help of technology, and it takes less time to prepare a variety of food than it took in the past. One can easily buy preprocessed food from the market and it saves time. Unfortunately, these canned foods should not replace the healthy food. Healthy food is essential for human being, because it has basic effects on people's life and their behavior.

Healthy food is very important to have a good life and a better communication for many reasons. First of all, people who eat healthy food, they have the ability to do hard work. Second, if a person eats food which has vitamins, proteins, iron and other important nutrients, then he will be free from diseases, and he can enjoy his life. Moreover, everyone definitely likes to meet those who have a good health, so a person who is healthy, he has friends. For example, a person who looks weak and does not live healthy lifestyle will feel lonely, and he will not be happy. Finally, a good mind can be developed if people eat healthy food, and this is necessary for children. Therefore, if you want good physique, intelligent mind and good friends, you should eat healthy food.

Besides having a good life and communication for people at any age, healthy food is the perfect kind of food for children in many ways. First of all, it is very necessary for proper growth and development throughout childhood. Parents can offer a wide variety of fruits, vegetables, whole grains and healthy proteins to make sure that their kids get the nutrients they need to be equal with every physical level of their life. Second, children who eat a healthy, balanced food are less likely to suffer from harmful diseases such as over fatness.

TYPES OF FOOD

HEALTHY AND UNHEALTHY FOOD

Foods can be classified into two types, unhealthy (junk) and healthy food. Some people do not have time to cook what they want to eat or they don't want to spend a lot of time cooking. Therefore, they eat foods that contain little or no nutrients a part of energy. Those foods are called junk foods. There are some advantages and disadvantages of eating junk foods. The advantages of eating junk foods are that they save time. For example, it doesn't take hours to prepare. They can also be cooked easily. The other advantage of unhealthy food is that it is tasty and delicious to eat. Junk food also doesn't cost a lot of money to buy it. For example, in some restaurant, people can buy French fries, sandwiches, and drinks at a cheaper price. The disadvantage of eating unhealthy food that may cause a lot of trouble to our health is that it contains a lot of sugar and salt.

HEALTHY EATING AND LIVING

When we do not eat healthy foods, we will become unhealthy and inactive. If we are aware of our healthy body weight we should eleminate certain food items.

Being healthy means eating right and exercising. To keep a healthy balance diet a person should try to eat daily at least a portion of the six major food groups, and exercise at least three times a week to keep the body fit and reduce the chances of poor health. A wholesome diet and lifestyle can help a person live a long healthy life.

ORGANIC FOOD

The organic food contains more nutrients. The benefits of eating healthy are more evident than ever. Everyday a new study comes out on how a person can maintain a healthy life.

SLEEP AND HEALTHY LIFESTYLE RESEARCH

Sleeping, along with other healthy life habits has arisen awareness in recent years. As it will be stated later, the majority of university undergraduates rarely took healthy living seriously. The research mainly covered the concept of a healthy lifestyle, the sleeping hours. Every day normal sleeping eight hours per day or minimum six hours.

SMART EATING

We all indulge in the activity of eating food because it is a necessity of life, but whether we make the decision to eat healthy or unhealthy foods depends on personal choice and discipline. Smart Eating offers instructions for men, women, athletes, healthy people, and people with weight problems or illnesses.

PHYSICAL EXERCISE AND SPORTS

We know the proverb, **"A sound mind in a sound body"**. In order to keep the body healthy, we need to keep the mind sound. Physical exercises keep us fit. There are different kinds of physical exercises. We may walk a kilometer or two every day. We may take some yogic exercises. At the same, games and sports are very useful for health.

Physical fitness is being healthy. They must eat healthy foods and workout or exercise regularly. One of the first steps to fitness is a healthy diet. It is needed for healthy bones, skin and hair. Simple carbohydrates like common sugar (all sweets, and junk food) provide immediate energy.

PERSONAL FITNESS

Personal Fitness Physical fitness is being healthy. They must eat healthy foods and workout or exercise regularly. It is needed for healthy bones, skin and hair. Proteins can be found in many foods but are more abundant in meat, fish, eggs, milk and dairy products.

FAST FOOD

Fast food is the worst enemy of human health these days. It is of great importance to most health problems of this century worldwide are being caused by the bad nutrition and the high cost of good quality food, a contributor of this is fast food.

It is a fact that fast food is killing people slowly and most people are not even aware of the ill effects of them problems like obesity, cholesterol problems, heart problems and diabetes. These are just few of catastrophe effects that these types of foods are causing.

HEALTHY EATING DISCURSIVE

Healthy Eating My discursive essay is about healthy eating. On the other hand people who eat healthily and who do not eat fatty foods can still die from cancer and other diseases. It aids the release of energy from food and from all including the brain, nerve cells and the muscles. So looking at these points healthy eating food is important.

Humans need a lot of things to survive. **Potassium, Sodium, Fat, Calories, Fiber, and a bunch of vitamins** the large assortments of food give people this. Calories give us energy, which we needed to hunt food thousands of years ago, and what we still need to walk around every day, breath, sit, etc.

Food is needed by the human body for energy, to repair and build cells and to prevent sickness and heal from it.

We eat for life. So food is needed as our nutrient. Nutrient such as crab, protein, fat, vitamin and mineral is important to get a balance diet. so that human can grow up healthy and can get a good brain, healthy body, food is important to humans because when we take food in our body breaks it down to protein which we use for all sorts of activities. It provides protein so we have energy to do things. It gives our body the nutrients we need.

THE IMPORTANCE OF THE FOOD GUIDE PYRAMID

The food guide pyramid plays an important role in the health education of the majority of people in the United States. It is meant to guide the general healthy public in how to eat healthy to stay healthy. It includes a wide variety of foods to provide a healthy range of nutrients that are needed daily. The food guide pyramid is an excellent way to educate the public on how to eat healthy. The new food guide pyramid also includes exercise. This is a way to universally educate people. The food guide pyramid is not a way to cure anything or solve any immediate problems; it is guidelines that help people to understand what they should be eating. The food guide pyramid is meant for people without special health circumstances ages 2 and up. It is a way to promote variety in a diet and to help people understand what is good for them. The food guide pyramid includes foods that do not promote chronic diseases. Foods that cause chronic diseases are avoided in the food guide pyramid. As more research is done the food guide pyramid progresses with it. The dietary guidelines are updated every 5 years; these are what provide all of the information for the food guide pyramid. From the first food guide pyramid, it has improved greatly with the research that has been done. It definitely progresses along with the most up to date information that is available.

NEED OF FOODS

The human body can be compared to a machine, just as an engine burns up coal or oil in order to generate .Its energy, so the human body requires food in order to produce the forces .which keep the heart beating ,the lungs breathing and the limbs moving. But the discovery of vitamins at the turn of the present century has rediscovered the science of nutrition.

Most of us understand that weight management depends upon the energy balance equation; the amount of energy you put into your body food calories versus the amount of energy you expend. But how do you know how many calories your body needs to reach or maintain a certain weight. Understanding your body's energy requirements can help guide you when making nutritional choices.

THE ACCURATE WAY OF HEALTHY FOOD

There are three primary components that make up your body's energy expenditure. Adding these three components together, basal metabolic rate, energy utilized during physical activity, and the thermic effect of food is the most accurate way of determining how many calories your body requires each day.

BASAL METABOLIC RATE (BMR)

Most of the body's energy, about 60-70%, goes to supporting the ongoing metabolic work of the body's cells. This includes such activities as heart beat, respiration and maintaining body temperature. To determine you're BMR:

For adult males - Multiply the body weight by 10; add double the body weight to this value. [i.e., for a 150 lb male, 1,500 + (2 x 150) = 1,800 cal/day BMR].

For adult females - Multiply body weight by 10; add the body weight to this value. [i.e., for a 120 lb female, 1,200 + 120 = 1,320 cal/day BMR].

Thermic Effect of Food

The last component to calculate has to do with your body's management of food. The increase in energy required to digest food is referred to as the Thermic Effect of Food and it's simple to determine:

TEF = total kcals consumed x 10%

[i.e., 2,000 kcals consumed/day x 0.10 = 200 kcals expended for TEF] nutrition important

Nutrition is the supply of materials - food - required by organisms and cells to stay alive. In science and human medicine, nutrition is the science or practice of consuming and utilizing foods.

In hospitals, nutrition may refer to the food requirements of patients, including nutritional solutions delivered via an IV intravenous or IG intragastric tube.

Nutritional science studies how the body breaks food down catabolism and repairs and creates cells and tissue anabolism -

catabolism and anabolism = metabolism. Nutritional science also examines how the body responds to food.

"Nutritional Science investigates the metabolic and physiological responses of the body to food and diet, including the role of nutrients in the cause, treatment, and prevention of disease."

Nutrition also focuses on how diseases, conditions and problems can be prevented or lessened with a healthy diet. *"Let thy food be thy medicine and thy medicine be thy food."*

RECENT NUTRITION DEVELOPMENTS FROM MEDICAL NEWS TODAY

Scientists from Tel Aviv University, Israel, wrote in the journal Obesity that a large breakfast-containing 700 calories - promotes weight loss and lowers the person's risk of developing heart disease, high cholesterol and diabetes.

Prof. Daniela Jakubowicz and colleagues emphasized that when we eat our food has a considerable impact on how our bodies process food.

Antoine Lavoisier (France, 1743-1794) - became known as the father of chemistry and also the father of nutrition.

Major food manufacturers employ nutritionists and food scientists. Nutritionists may also work in journalism, education and research. Many nutritionists work in the field of food science and technology.

There is a lot of overlap between what nutritionists and dietitians do and studied. Some nutritionists work in health care, some dietitians work in the food industry, but a higher percentage of nutritionists work in the food industry and food science and technology, and a higher percentage of dietitians work in health care.

One could very loosely generalize and say that a nutritionist focuses firstly on a food, and then looks at its effects on people, while a dietician looks at the human, and then how that human's health is influenced by food.

If I discovered a new fruit and wanted to find out what it consisted of I would go to a nutritionist. If I found out I had a long-term disease and wanted to know whether I needed to adjust my food intake because of the disease, I would go to a dietician.

Nutrition is present in all processes of life. Right from the very moment the sperm fertilizes an egg, through fetal development in the uterus, to the birth, human growth, maturity, old age, and eventual death. Even after death the human body serves as nutrition for other organisms. Anything that involves life and chemical or biochemical movement has nutrition at its core.

Anything that lives is dependent on energy, which results from the combustion of food.

TYPES OF NUTRITIOUS FOOD

Information on human nutrition and eating nutritious food types including **fruits and vegetables,** nuts, **and** berries to **prevent diseases** including **cancer**. Nutrition is the provision, to cells and organisms, of the materials necessary to support life. Many common health problems can be prevented or alleviated with good nutrition.

Eating a healthy nutritious diet has been shown over and over to prevent a variety of diseases, including cancer. Good nutrition is vital to good health, disease prevention, and essential for healthy growth and development of children and adolescents. A nutrient is a source of nourishment, an ingredient in a food, e.g. protein, carbohydrate, fat, vitamin, mineral, fiber and water.

1. **Carbohydrates** - our main source of energy.
2. **Fats** - one source of energy and important in relation to fat soluble vitamins.
3. **Roughage (Fiber)** - the fibrous indigestible portion of our diet essential to health of the digestive system.
4. **Minerals** - those inorganic elements occurring in the body and which are critical to its normal functions.
5. **Proteins** - essential to growth and repair of muscle and other body tissues.
6. **Vitamins** - water and fat soluble vitamins play important roles in many chemical processes in the body.

Water - essential to normal body function - as a vehicle for carrying other nutrients and because 60% of the human body is water Nutrition

The intake of food, considered in relation to the body's dietary needs. A healthy diet includes preparation of food and storage methods that preserve nutrients from oxidation, heat or leaching, and that reduce risk of food-born illnesses.

SIDDHA SYSTEM OF INDIAN MEDICINE

The system is believed to be developed by the **18 Siddhar's** in the south called siddhar. Siddhar's total nos are eighteen, with **Agathiyar** being the **first Siddhar**.

Siddha system of medicine is one of the oldest medical systems of India existed separately in early times. The system has flourished well in India for many centuries. Although this system has declined in later years, in the wake of changing mode of life and modern medicine, it continues to sustain its influence on the masses because of its incomparable intrinsic merits. Siddha medicine can combat all types of diseases, especially the chronic diseases, which baffles and eludes even the modern sophisticated medicine.

The prevention and the cure of illness is the basic aims of all systems of medicine. **'Nature is man and man is nature'**.

The Siddha system has, in addition, a transcendental motivation, a concern for what might be called the 'IMMORTALITY OF THE BODY'.

The universe consists of five elements. They are solid, fluid, radiance, gas, and ether. All created and evolved matter in the world is it animal, vegetable, or mineral, falls under these categories. The human anatomy and physiology, the causative factor of disease, the materials for the treatment and cure of diseases, the food for the sustenance of the body, all fall within the five elemental categories. This is the working hypothesis.

Health is maintained. The body consists of seven 'dhatus': lymph, blood, muscle, fat, bone, marrow and Sukkilam and Artavam male and female hormones.

The words *'First to find out the disease and then to find out the cause of the disease'* in the ancient text of Thirukural denotes the approach to disease and determination of the etiology of the disease.

FOOD THE MEDICINE

Food are Powerful Medicine and been used centuries to treat wide range of ailments which food to use for relief defects were the pain is located.

A close look at the eating habits of animals and birds reveals they eat food raw and ripe consisting of all the six tastes whereas man eats only food stuff of four tastes, leaving bitter and astringent, which are pre-requisites for healthy circulation of blood. Bitterness fights against bacterial infection and astringency maintains the right blood quality and its constituents. Small quantities of agathi grand flora, bitter gourd, seeds of solanum anthocarpum, flowers of neem eaten now and then in small quantities, ward of many microbiological and bacterial infections.

As a sampler, when excessive smoking causes dizziness, stomach disorders and makes the male suffer from nicotine poison, immediately the lady knows the sure cure for this disorder and gives him Agatha Grand flora leaves, deliciously cooked at regular intervals and thus cures him of his malady, similarly she knows the properties of medicinal food recipes out of edible greens, leaves, barks, berries and other vegetables and the value of pepper, mustard, ginger and a host of other household provisions, rarely men of the past generations were perforce compelled to visit the medical experts and specialists who were scarce and few.

The leafy green mentioned above and several other bitter lasting foods and dishes as in mangos leaves and other plants and medicinal herbs, kill or exterminate the nematodes like thread worm, hookworm and tape worms and similar germs infesting the bowels and alimentary canal.

Beal leaves when followed regularly ensure good health by proper digestion and assimilation of food. It also removes the toxins in the body and is a blood purifier.

Neem leaves proves wonderful disinfectant and germicide. Regular intake of this herb in any kind will be a sure elixir of life.

Grass – 'Doorva' (cynodon dactylon), which has been proven scientifically to possess the power of generating electricity in minute degree. When handling it augment one's personal magnetism. It is of high medicinal value when administered orally. .

Mango leaves taken at regular intervals will cure many bodily illnesses.

'Tulsi leaves' regular intervals will build strong muscles and bones. It is also a wonderful prophylactic drug for many ailments.

Fig leaves and fruits correct blood constituents due to its astringent properties. With a primary knowledge of hundreds of species in vegetable kingdom and the knowledge of physical body, its physiology and anatomy and simple rules of health and hygiene, any layman can lead a healthy life free from diseases.

Taken regular oil bath, giving the person youth, glow and luster. There are many illustrations of Siddhars stating by proper physical exercise and perfect breathing, food habits, evacuation of bowels, many undesirable conditions get eliminated. Siddhars have in daily use are onion, garlic, ginger, lemon, jequirity and turmeric etc.

The ancient Siddhars were capable of describing the use of such things rich in vitamins, minerals, proteins, hormones, electrolytes and other nutrients grouped them as disease preventives for promoting longevity.

"Food is medicine and medicine is food" and "Prevention is better than cure" were the slug lines of Siddhars and their followers.

CANCER AND FOOD MEDICINE

Garlic may help prevent lung cancer - eating raw garlic twice a week could help halve the risk of developing lung cancer, according to a study published in the journal Cancer Prevention Research.

Eating cruciferous vegetables could reduce the risk of prostate cancer - the risk of prostate cancer may be reduced by consuming more than one serving per week of broccoli, cauliflower, and other cruciferous vegetables, according to Yale School of Medicine researchers who reported their findings in reported in the Journal of the National Cancer Institute. Fresh air and sunlight are very important for our health. Fresh air helps us to improve our immune system and overall health. So a morning walk is very useful for health.

Sunlight helps our body to produce **vitamin-D**. A dirty and damp atmosphere causes lots of diseases. Fresh and pure drinking water is also necessary for good health. Impure drinking- water is the cause of several diseases. As per Doctor's advice, every human being should take six glasses of water per day. So, we must take care of these things.

OBJECTIVES OF THE STUDY

1. To find out whether there is any significant difference between the mean scores of boys and girls in pre-test of control group in A Study on Achievement and Effect of Innovative Teaching of the Lesson Food the Medicine among IXth Standard Students.
2. To find out whether there is any significant difference between the mean scores of boys and girls in pre-test of Experimental group in A Study on Achievement and Effect of Innovative Teaching of the Lesson Food the Medicine among IXth Standard Students.
3. To find out whether there is any significant difference between the mean scores of boys in pre-test of control group and Experimental group in A Study on Achievement and Effect of Innovative Teaching of the Lesson Food the Medicine among IXth Standard Students.
4. To find out whether there is any significant difference between the mean scores of boys and girls in post-test of control group in A Study on Achievement and Effect of Innovative Teaching of the Lesson Food the Medicine among IXth Standard Students.
5. To find out whether there is any significant difference between the mean scores of control group and Experimental group of pre-test performance in A Study on Achievement and Effect of

Innovative Teaching of the Lesson Food the Medicine among IXth Standard Students.

6. To find out whether there is any significant difference between the mean scores of control group and Experimental group of post-test performance in A Study on Achievement and Effect of Innovative Teaching of the Lesson Food the Medicine among IXth Standard Students.
7. To find out whether there is any significant difference between the mean scores of control group of post-test and pre-test performance in A Study on Achievement and Effect of Innovative Teaching of the Lesson Food the Medicine among IXth Standard Students.
8. To find out whether there is any significant difference between the mean scores of Experimental group of post-test and pre-test performance in A Study on Achievement and Effect of Innovative Teaching of the Lesson Food the Medicine among IXth Standard Students.

HYPOTHESES OF THE STUDY

1. There is no significant difference between the mean scores of boys and girls in pre-test of control group in A Study on Achievement and Effect of Innovative Teaching of the Lesson Food the Medicine among IXth Standard Students.
2. There is no significant difference between the mean scores of boys and girls in pre-test of Experimental group in A Study on Achievement and Effect of Innovative Teaching of the Lesson Food the Medicine among IXth Standard Students.
3. There is no significant difference between the mean scores of boys in pre-test of Control group and Experimental group in A Study on Achievement and Effect of Innovative Teaching of the Lesson Food the Medicine among IXth Standard Students.
4. There is no significant difference between the mean scores of boys and girls in post-test of control group in A Study on Achievement and Effect of Innovative Teaching of the Lesson Food the Medicine among IXth Standard Students.

5. There is no significant difference between the mean scores of control group and Experimental group of pre-test performance in A Study on Achievement and Effect of Innovative Teaching of the Lesson Food the Medicine among IXth Standard Students.
6. There is no significant difference between the mean scores of control group and Experimental group of post-test performance in A Study on Achievement and Effect of Innovative Teaching of the Lesson Food the Medicine among IXth Standard Students.
7. There is no significant difference between the mean scores of control group of post-test and pre-test performance in A Study on Achievement and Effect of Innovative Teaching of the Lesson Food the Medicine among IXth Standard Students.
8. There is no significant difference between the mean scores of Experimental group of post-test and pre-test performance in A Study on Achievement and Effect of Innovative Teaching of the Lesson Food the Medicine among IXth Standard Students.

LIMITATIONS OF THE STUDY

1. The researcher conducted the experiment only in school located in urban area
2. This study was conducted in one chapter of the Tamil syllabus for secondary school students
3. This study was conducted to IXth standard students particularly in Sri Venkateshwara Matric Higher Secondary School, Thirukogarnam, Pudukkottai.
4. The experimental treatment was given with duration of one month only
5. The sample consists of 50 students

CONCLUSION

In this chapter we discussed about overview of the problem and significance, its needs and objectives of the study. The next chapter deals with the review of related literature.

Chapter - II

Review of The Related Literature

INTRODUCTION

According to **W.R. Borg**, "the literature in any field forms the foundation upon which all future work will be built. It we fail to build the foundation of Knowledge provided by the review of literature our work is likely to be shallow and native and will often duplicate work that has already been done better by someone else".

According to **Charter V.Good,** "the keys to the vast store house of published literature may open doors to sources of significant problems and explanatory hypotheses and provide helpful orientation for definition of the interpretation of results. In order to be creative and original, one must read extensively and critically as a stimulus to thinking".

NEED OF REVIEW OF LITERATURE

The review of literature is essential due to the following reasons.

1. One of the early steps in planning a research work is to review research done previously in the particular area of interest and relevant area quantitative and qualitative analysis of this research usually gives the worker an indication of the direction.

2. It is very essential for ever investigator to be up-to-date in his information about the literature, related to his own problem already done by others.
   It is considered the most important prerequisite to actual planning and conducting the study.
3. It avoids the replication of the study of findings to take an advantage from similar of related literature as regards to methodology, techniques of data collection, procedure adopted and conclusions drawn. He can justify his own Endeavour in the field.
4. It provides as source of problem of study an analogy may be drawn for identifying and selecting his own problem of research. The researcher formulates his hypothesis on the basis of review of literature. It also provides the rationale for the study. The results and findings for the study can also be discussed at length.
5. The review of literature indicates the clear picture of the problem to be solved. The scholarship in the field can be developed by reviewing the literature of the field.

OBJECTIVES OF REVIEW OF LITERATURE

The review of literature serves the following purposes in conducting research work:

1. It provides theories, ideas, explanations' or hypothesis which may prove useful in the formulation of a new problem.
2. It indicates whether the evidence already available solves the problem adequately without requiring further investigation. It avoids the replication.
3. It provides the sources for hypothesis. The researcher can formulate research hypothesis on the basis of available studies.
4. It suggests method, procedure sources of data and statistical techniques appropriate to the solution of the problem.
5. It locates comparative data and findings useful in the interpretation and discussion of results. The conclusions drawn in the related studies may be used as the subject for the findings of the study.

6. It helps in developing experts and general scholarship of the investigator in the area investigated.
7. It contributes towards the accurate knowledge of the evidence or literature in one's area of activity is a good avenue towards making oneself. This knowledge is an assert ever after wards, whether one is employed in an institution of higher learning or a research organization.

PURPOSE OF THE REVIEW OF LITERATURE

Review of the related literature besides, to allow the researcher to acquaint himself with current knowledge in the field or area in which he or she is going to conduct his or her research, serves the following specific purposes.

1. The review of related literature enables the researcher to define the limits of the field. It helps the researcher to delimit and define his problem. The knowledge of related literature brings the researcher up to data on the work which others have done and them to state the objectives clearly and concisely
2. By reviewing the related literature the researchers can avoid unfruitful and useless problem areas. He can select those areas in which positive findings are likely to result and his Endeavour's would be likely to add to the knowledge in a meaningful way.
3. Through the review of related literature the researcher can avoid unintentional duplication of well established findings. It is no use of replicate a study when the study when the stability and validity of its result have been clearly established.
4. The review of related literature gives the researcher an understanding of the research methodology which refers to the way the study is to be conducted. It help the researcher to know about the tools and instruments which proved to be useful and promising the previous studies. The advantage of the related literature is also to provide insight into statistical methods through which validity of results is to be established.
5. The final and important specific reason for reviewing the related literature to know about the recommendations of previous

researcher for further research which they have listed in their studies.

Bruce W.Tuckman (1978) has enumerated the following purposes of the review.

1. Discovering important variable.
2. Distinguishing what has done from what needs to be done.
3. Synthesizing the available studies to have perspective
4. Determining meanings relevance of the study and relationship with the study and its deviation from the available studies.

Edward 1. Vockell (1983) has pointed out the following two purposes:

1. The main purpose of this review is to put the hypothesis to be examined in the research report into its proper context.
2. Secondary purposes of this part of the report are to provide readers with guidelines regarding where they can look to find more information and to establish the author's credential by letting readers know that the researcher is aware of what has been giving on with regard to the current and related topics.

The review of literature provides some insight regarding strong points and limitations of the previous studies. It enables him to improve his own investigation.

STUDIES CONDUCTED IN INDIA

Dr. MV. Varatharasan (Tamil Nadu 1965) reveals from Thirumoolar that everyone should practice yoga everyday to maintain a prosperous living.

Dr. Stephen (INDIA, 1843) an agricultural chemist. He is known for his Babcock test which determines dairy butterfat in milk and cheese processing. He is also known for the *single-grain experiment* that eventually led to the development of nutrition as a science.

Babcock had the idea of feeding dairy cattle with just one food source, either all corn plant or all wheat plant. He placed two heifers on either diet However, when one of his animals died they were ail taken away and he was not allowed to continue researching.

A succession of discoveries eventually found that something in the fat soluble portion of the corn affected reproduction. The scientists called this factor A - What we know today as Vitamin A.

Agathiyalingam (Tamil Nadu, 1967)

As research evolved and further active properties were found, the water soluble ones were vitamin B. Reported in 1949 isolated the active ingredient, a cobalamin. It could also be injected straight into muscle as a treatment for pernicious (potentially fatal) anemia.

Vitamin was clarified thanks to research carried out with guinea pigs. Very few animals, including humans, guinea pigs, primates, some bats, some birds, and some reptiles require vitamin C from food -all other animals are able to synthesize it internally produce it themselves.

Dr. Pamela, (Tamil Nadu). She is a naturopathic doctor who uses lifestyle medicine, and more specifically plant-based nutrition, to prevent and reverse many of the chronic diseases ailing her patients. She has appeared in the blockbuster documentary Forks Over Knives and is an internationally recognized speaker and expert in the field of nutrition, medicine, and health.

STUDIES CONDUCTED IN ABROAD

The Bible, Book of Daniel Daniel was captured by the King of Babylon and had to serve in the King's court. Daniel objected to being fed fine foods and wine, saying he preferred vegetables, pulses and water. The chief steward reluctantly agreed to a trial, comparing Daniel's dietary preference to those of the court of the King of Babylon. For ten days Daniel and his men had their **vegetarian** diet, while the King's men had theirs. The trial revealed that Daniel and his men were healthier and fitter, so they were allowed to carry on with their diet.

Hippocrates (Greece, ca460BC - ca370BC), one nutrient theory - according to Hippocrates everybody is the same, no matter what they have been eating, or where they have lived. He concluded that every food must contain one nutrient which makes us the way we are. This one-nutrient myth continued for thousands of years.

Hippocrates is also famous for having said ***"Let thy food be thy medicine and thy medicine be thy food."***

Antoine Lavoisier (France, 1743-1794) became known as the father of chemistry and also the father of nutrition. He became famous for the statement ***"Life is a chemical process".*** He also designed the "calorimeter", a device which measured heat produced by the body from work and consumption from different amounts and types of foods. At the age of 24 he became a member of the French Academy of Science. In 1794, during the French Revolution, he was beheaded.

Christiaan Eijkman (Holland, 1858-1930) a famous physician and pathologist (doctor who identifies diseases by studying cells and tissues under a microscope). He noticed that some of the people in Java developed Beriberi, a disease which leads to heart problems and paralysis. When he fed chickens a diet consisting mainly of white rice they also developed Beriberi type symptoms, but the chickens fed unprocessed brown rice did not. White rice has the outer bran removed, while brown rice does not. When he fed brown rice to patients with Beriberi they were cured. Many years later it was found that the outer husks (outer bran) in rice contain thiamine, or **vitamin** B1. Together with Sir Frederick Hopkins, he received the Nobel Prize for Physiology/Medicine.

Dr. James Lind (Scotland, 1716-1794) a pioneer on hygiene in the Scottish and Royal (British) navies. He stressed the importance of good ventilation, cleanliness of sailor's bodies, clean bedding, below deck fumigation, fresh water by distilling sea water, and the consumption of citrus fruits to prevent and cure **scurvy.** He is well respected today for his work in improving practices in preventive medicine and improved nutrition. He published his *Treatise on Scurvy.* Many decades later British sailors were known as Limeys because they regularly consumed lime juice and enjoyed better health and vigor than sailors in most other navies.

Dr. William Beaumont (USA, 1785-1853) a surgeon in the US Army. He became known as the *Father of gastric physiology for* his research on human digestion. Beaumont met Alexio St. Martin, a French trapper who was shot in the stomach. Beaumont treated him but was unable to close the hole in his stomach, which healed with an opening to the outside (a fistula). St. Martin allowed Beaumont to make observations periodically, even allowing him to fiddle around with his innards, which must have been painful.

CONCLUSION

The review gave lot of insight to the investigator in selecting the research problem and suitable methodology. The research gap was also identified on the basis of the review. The methodology adopted by the researcher in this study was discussed in the chapter upcoming.

Chapter - III

Methodology

INTRODUCTION

Parallel Group experimental Design was adopted of find out a study on achievement and the lesson food the medicine among IXth standard students. Research methodology is a way to systematically solve the research problem. It may be understood as a science of studying now research is done scientifically. This chapter explained the methods adopted to conduct this study. The entire chapter has been discussed under various sub-headings such as, need and significance of the study, statement of the problem, objectives framed hypotheses, formulated operationlisation and measurement of variable, sampling procedure, and techniques of data collection and statically techniques.

In order that the research should be conducted successfully, a suitable methodology with specific operational steps and constructed tools are necessary. In the present study, the investigator aims at finding the relationship between the school environment and the achievement of students in their academic subjects. The details of various steps followed in the investigation are discussed in the chapter.

METHOD OF THE STUDY

The investigator adopted Parallel Group experimental design for the present study.

STATEMENT OF THE PROBLEM

The problem of the present investigation is "*A Study on Achievement and Effect of Innovative Teaching of the Lesson Food the Medicine among IXth Standard Students*".

OBJECTIVES OF THE STUDY

1. To find out whether there is any significant difference between the mean scores of boys and girls in pre-test of control group in A Study on Achievement and Effect of Innovative Teaching of the Lesson Food the Medicine among IXth Standard Students.
2. To find out whether there is any significant difference between the mean scores of boys and girls in pre-test of Experimental group in A Study on Achievement and Effect of Innovative Teaching of the Lesson Food the Medicine among IXth Standard Students.
3. To find out whether there is any significant difference between the mean scores of boys in pre-test of control group and Experimental group in A Study on Achievement and Effect of Innovative Teaching of the Lesson Food the Medicine among IXth Standard Students.
4. To find out whether there is any significant difference between the mean scores of boys and girls in post-test of control group in A Study on Achievement and Effect of Innovative Teaching of the Lesson Food the Medicine among IXth Standard Students.
5. To find out whether there is any significant difference between the mean scores of control group and Experimental group of pre-test performance in A Study on Achievement and Effect of Innovative Teaching of the Lesson Food the Medicine among IXth Standard Students.
6. To find out whether there is any significant difference between the mean scores of control group and Experimental group of

post-test performance in A Study on Achievement and Effect of Innovative Teaching of the Lesson Food the Medicine among IXth Standard Students.

7. To find out whether there is any significant difference between the mean scores of control group of post-test and pre-test performance in A Study on Achievement and Effect of Innovative Teaching of the Lesson Food the Medicine among IXth Standard Students.

8. To find out whether there is any significant difference between the mean scores of Experimental group of post-test and pre-test performance in A Study on Achievement and Effect of Innovative Teaching of the Lesson Food the Medicine among IXth Standard Students.

HYPOTHESES

1. There is no significant difference between the mean scores of boys and girls in pre-test of control group in A Study on Achievement and Effect of Innovative Teaching of the Lesson Food the Medicine among IXth Standard Students.
2. There is no significant difference between the mean scores of boys and girls in pre-test of Experimental group in A Study on Achievement and Effect of Innovative Teaching of the Lesson Food the Medicine among IXth Standard Students.
3. There is no significant difference between the mean scores of boys in pre-test of Control group and Experimental group in A Study on Achievement and Effect of Innovative Teaching of the Lesson Food the Medicine among IXth Standard Students.
4. There is no significant difference between the mean scores of boys and girls in post-test of control group in A Study on Achievement and Effect of Innovative Teaching of the Lesson Food the Medicine among IXth Standard Students.
5. There is no significant difference between the mean scores of control group and Experimental group of pre-test performance in A Study on Achievement and Effect of Innovative Teaching of the Lesson Food the Medicine among IXth Standard Students.

6. There is no significant difference between the mean scores of control group and Experimental group of post-test performance in A Study on Achievement and Effect of Innovative Teaching of the Lesson Food the Medicine among IXth Standard Students.
7. There is no significant difference between the mean scores of control group of post-test and pre-test performance in A Study on Achievement and Effect of Innovative Teaching of the Lesson Food the Medicine among IXth Standard Students.
8. There is no significant difference between the mean scores of Experimental group of post-test and pre-test performance in A Study on Achievement and Effect of Innovative Teaching of the Lesson Food the Medicine among IXth Standard Students.

LIMITATIONS OF THE STUDY

1. The researcher conducted the experiment only in school located in urban area
2. This study was conducted in one chapter of the Tamil syllabus for secondary school students
3. This study was conducted to IXth standard students particularly in Sri Venkateshwara Matric Higher Secondary School, Thirukogarnam, Pudukkottai.
4. The experimental treatment was given with duration of one month only
5. The sample consists of 50 students

RESEARCH METHODS

The researcher adopted Experimental method for this research. The researcher conducted the experiment for IX standard students in Sri Venkateshwara Matric Higher Secondary School, Thirugokarnam, Pudukkottai.

TOOLS OF THE STUDY

A criterion – referenced test was constructed in consultation with the available Tamil teachers and experts and also based on the text book .Since the study focused in Food and Medicine on only one topic that is, integral calculus and criterion – referenced test was constructed.

RESEARCH TOOL

The investigator himself developed a research tool which is indicated below.

A questionnaire on Tamil was taken by the researcher. The researcher conducted pre-test at the beginning of the study and Post-test after providing a suitable teaching learning experience.

Construction of Research Tool

The pattern of the test is same as the control and Experimental group. The test consists of fifty marks. All the Questions are questionnaire type. The question paper consists of four levels. There are one mark, two marks, three marks and five marks levels. In this study control and experimental group of the students are treated equally, without any partially based on the understanding the concept of the topic.

Description of the research tool and scoring procedure

The researcher has taken only questionnaire type questions. The test paper consist of choose, fill ups, match the following. Each question carries one mark, two marks, three marks and five marks.

Samples of the study

50 students of male and female studying in class IX STD of Sri Venkateshwara Matric. Higher Secondary School, Thirugokarnam, Pudukkottai District were taken as the sample for analysis. This consists of 25 students in controlled group Section - A and 25 students in experimental group Section– B.

PILOT STUDY

A pilot study is an initial investigation to give information that will be necessary when designing a future trial or study. For example a pilot may be used to:

1. Assess the time required to examine each patient,

2. To determine the quality of a proposed questionnaire
3. To estimate the variability of key variables.

Hence the investigator conducted the pilot study in the experiment to determine the quality of the question paper.

VALIDATION OF THE TOOL

VALIDITY

For construction of the tool books and experts were consulted and hence the criterion referenced test has content validity.

The items of the test were analyzed based on-the expert in relation to its objectivity and suitability on the basic of the expert's opinion two items were changed in the tool. Thus the tool has content validity and expert validity.

RELIABILITY

The reliability of the test was found by Experimental method. The investigator found that this is suitable method to find out the reliability of the study.

The study was conducted for 50 students in Pre-test stage. After two weeks the same test was conducted to the experimental group at post-test stage. The reliability co-efficient was computed using spearman's rank difference method.

SAMPLING TECHNIQUE USED

50 students have been taken as sample for present study IXth standard A section boys and girls are Control groups. And B section IXth standard students boys and girls are Experimental groups. Each section consists of 25 students.

COLLECTION OF DATA

The investigator collected the data from the selected control group and experimental group. The pre-test and post-test were conducted using the criterion test. The investigator himself taught Tamil lesson to the control group by using traditional method. The experimental method was taught through (i) CD approach (ii) by entertaining a

Siddha Doctor for demonstration (iii) by demonstrating the usefulness of Natural Medicine Siddha herbals in Tamil concepts in Sri Venkateshwara Matric Hr.Sec.School, Thirugokarnam, Pudukkottai. After completion of the treatment the post-test was conducted to measure the understanding ability of learning in various concepts of the Tamil in both groups. Thus all the data were collected systematically for the analysis in the present study.

ANALYSIS OF THE DATA

In the present study, the relevant data obtained from the test scores in the pre-test and the post-test were analyzed using different statistical techniques.

Descriptive Analysis

It provides information about the nature of a particular group of individuals. Mean and standard deviation were calculated to determine the central tendencies and dispersion variables to describe the properties of the sample.

Differential Analysis

It provides inference involving determination of statistical significance of difference between groups with reference to the selected variables. To compare the difference between the mean scores of the sample can be calculated by using the T" test.

Relational Analysis

Correlation refers to the relationship between two or more paired variables or more sets of data. The degree of relationship is measured and represented by co-efficient of correlation. This coefficient may be identified either the letter.

STATISTICAL TECHNIQUES USED

Standard Deviation

Standard deviation is the average or mean of all the averages for multiple sets of data. Scientists and statisticians use the standard deviation to determine how closely sets of data are to the mean of all the sets. Standard deviation is an easy calculation to perform.

T test

A't'-**test** is any statistical hypothesis test in which the test statistic follows a student's't' distribution if the null hypothesis is supported. It can be used to determine if two sets of data are significantly different from each other, and is most commonly applied when the test statistic would follow a normal distribution if the value of a scaling term in the test statistic were known. When the scaling term is unknown and is replaced by an estimate based on the data, the test statistic (under certain conditions) follows a Student's *t* distribution.

CONCLUSION

Selection of control group and experimental group, limitations of the study, research method, construction of research tool and technique of data analysis are discussed in this chapter. Methodology of the study is given in the third chapter the next chapter deals with the analysis and interpretation of Data.

Chapter - IV

Analysis and Interpretation of Data

INTRODUCTION

The most essential work in any research problem is used and application of statistical tools in analyzing and interpreting the research data. This chapter deals with the statistical analysis of the Data. Interpretation with relevant tables and diagrams Thus interpretation is the careful, Logical and critical examination of the result analysis. This is useful in making statement about what the results analysis indicate.

In this chapter, the classified data presented in tables are statistically analyzed, a brief interpretation follows each table data are described in terms of mean and standard deviation with respect to Gender control group and experimental group pre test and post test Food the Medicine. A detailed study was done by the investigator was explained throughout this chapter.

SYSTEM OF DATA ANALYSIS

The purpose of the present study is to find out the impact on CD approach in teaching concepts of Food the Medicine at secondary level. In this Study, the test of significance (t-test) was used to test the Research Hypothesis and the computation of t-value was identified by the investigator using the Mean and Standard Deviation. Since the total number of students selected for the present study is fifty, the investigator used the formula of t-test related to correlated and un-correlated group.

HYPOTHESES TESTING

Hypotheses – 1

There is no significant difference between the mean scores of boys and girls in pre-test of control group in A Study on Achievement and Effect of Innovative Teaching of the Lesson Food the Medicine among IXth Standard Students.

Table 1

S. No	Gender	N	Mean	Standard Deviation	t–value	Level of significance at 0.05 level
1	Boys	11	11.27	3.90		
2	Girls	14	10.57	3.76	0.45	Not significant

Interpretation

Since our obtained 't' – value (0.45) is less than the table value (2.07), with degree of freedom 23, there is no significance difference between the mean scores of boys and girls in pre-test of control group.

Finding

Hence the Null Hypothesis is **accepted**.

Hypotheses – 2

There is no significant difference between the mean scores of boys and girls in pre-test of Experimental group in A Study on Achievement and Effect of Innovative Teaching of the Lesson Food the Medicine among IXth Standard Students.

Table 2

S. No	Gender	N	Mean	Standard Deviation	t–value	Level of significance at 0.05 level
1	Boys	11	10.36	3.54		
2	Girls	14	9.21	3.34	0.83	Not significant

Interpretation

Since our obtained 't' – value (0.83) is less than the table value (2.07), with degree of freedom 23, there is no significance difference between the mean scores of boys and girls in pre-test of Experimental group.

Finding

Hence the Null Hypothesis is **accepted**.

Hypotheses – 3

There is no significant difference between the mean scores of boys and girls in post-test of Control group in A Study on Achievement and Effect of Innovative Teaching of the Lesson Food the Medicine among IXth Standard Students.

Table 3

S. No	Gender	N	Mean	Standard Deviation	t–value	Level of significance at 0.05 level
1	Boys	11	22	3.38		
2	Girls	14	21.5	3.63	0.35	Not significant

Interpretation

Since our obtained 't' – value (0.35) is less than the table value (2.07), with degree of freedom 23, there is no significance difference between the mean scores of boys and girls in post-test of control group.

Finding

Hence the Null Hypothesis is **accepted**.

Hypotheses – 4

There is no significant difference between the mean scores of boys in pre-test of Control and Experimental group in A Study on Achievement and Effect of Innovative Teaching of the Lesson Food the Medicine among IXth Standard Students.

Table 4

S. No	Gender	N	Mean	Standard Deviation	t–value	Level of significance at 0.05 level
1	Control Group	11	11.27	3.90		
2	Experimental Group	11	10.36	3.54	0.57	Not significant

Interpretation

Since our obtained 't' – value (0.57) is less than the table value (2.09), with degree of freedom 20, there is no significance difference between the mean scores of boys in pre-test of control and experimental group.

Finding

Hence the Null Hypothesis is **accepted**.

Hypotheses – 5

There is no significant difference between the mean scores of Control and Experimental group of pre-test in A Study on Achievement and Effect of Innovative Teaching of the Lesson Food the Medicine among IXth Standard Students.

Table 5

S. No	Gender	N	Mean	Standard Deviation	t–value	Level of significance at 0.05 level
1	Control Group	25	10.84	3.80	1.08	Not significant
2	Experimental Group	25	9.72	3.54		

Interpretation

Since our obtained 't' – value (1.08) is less than the table value (2.01), with degree of freedom 48, there is no significance difference between the mean scores of pre-test in control and experimental group.

Finding

Hence the Null Hypothesis is **accepted**.

Hypotheses – 6

There is no significant difference between the mean scores of post-test in Experimental group and Control group in A Study on Achievement and Effect of Innovative Teaching of the Lesson Food the Medicine among IXth Standard Students.

Table 6

S. No	Gender	N	Mean	Standard Deviation	t–value	Level of significance at 0.05 level
1	Experimental Group	25	25.32	3.45		
2	Control Group	25	21.64	3.52	3.72	Significant

Interpretation

Since our obtained 't' – value (3.72) is greater than the table value (2.01) with degree of freedom 25, Hence there is significance difference between the mean scores of post-test of experimental and control group.

Finding

Hence the Null Hypothesis is **rejected**.

Hypotheses – 7

There is no significant difference between the mean scores of Control group of post-test and pre-test in A Study on Achievement and Effect of Innovative Teaching of the Lesson Food the Medicine among IXth Standard Students.

Table 7

S. No	Gender	N	Mean	Standard Deviation	t–value	Level of significance at 0.05 level
1	Post-test	25	21.64	3.52		
2	Pre-test	25	10.84	3.80	10.38	significant

Interpretation

Since our obtained 't' – value (10.38) is greater than the table value (2.01) with degree of freedom 48, Hence there is significance difference between the mean scores of post-test and pre-test of control group.

Finding

Hence the Null Hypothesis is **rejected**.

Hypotheses – 8

There is no significant difference between the mean scores of Experimental group of post-test and pre-test in A Study on Achievement and Effect of Innovative Teaching of the Lesson Food the Medicine among IXth Standard Students.

Table 8

S. No	Gender	N	Mean	Standard Deviation	t–value	Level of significance at 0.05 level
1	Post-test	25	25.32	3.45		
2	Pre-test	25	9.72	3.54	16.08	significant

Interpretation

Since our obtained 't' – value (16.08) is greater than the table value (2.01) with degree of freedom 48, Hence there is significance difference between the mean scores of post-test and pre-test of Experimental group.

Finding

Hence the Null Hypothesis is **rejected**.

CONCLUTION

In this chapter various data collected from the IXth standard students have been analyzed and interpretations. The next Chapter deals with summary of the findings and conclusion.

Chapter - V

Summary, Findings and Conclusion

INTRODUCTION

Research methods are utmost importance in a research process. They describe the various steps of the plan of attack to be adopted in solving problems. The present problem comes under experimental research as the study deals with the existing or present condition of IX th standard students.

Though the data are valid, reliable and adequate, they do not serve any useful purpose unless. They are carefully processed, systematically classified and tabulated, scientifically analyzed, intelligently interpreted and rationally included.

According to Best (1977), "statistical data describe group behaviours or group characteristics abstracted from a number of individual observation which are combined to make generalization possible. The data after collection have to be processed*and analyzed in accordance with the outline lid down for the purpose at the time of developing the research plan, analysis of data is thus considered as an important awareness of any type of research. It needs high level of Judgment Skill, thought knowledge and technical ability of generalization.

Interpretation of data is an extremely important and useful branch of Important and useful branch of science of statistics. Statistical facts by themselves have no utility, but interpretation makes it possible to utilize the collected data in various fields of activity. The usefulness of collected data lies in its proper Interpretation.

STATEMENT OF THE PROBLEM

"A Study on Achievement and Effect of Innovative Teaching of the Lesson Food the Medicine among IXth Standard Students".

OBJECTIVES OF THE STUDY:-

1. To find out whether there is any significant difference between the mean scores of boys and girls in pre-test of control group in A Study on the Achievement and Effect of Innovative Teaching of Lesson Food, the Medicine among IXth Standard Students.
2. To find out whether there is any significant difference between the mean scores of boys and girls in pre-test of Experimental group in A Study on Achievement and Effect of Innovative Teaching of Lesson Food, the Medicine among IXth Standard Students.
3. To find out whether there is any significant difference between the mean scores of boys in pre-test of control group and Experimental group in A Study on the Achievement and Effect of Innovative Teaching of Lesson Food, the Medicine among IXth Standard Students.
4. To find out whether there is any significant difference between the mean scores of boys and girls in post-test of control group in A Study on the Achievement and Effect of Innovative Teaching of Lesson Food, the Medicine among IXth Standard Students.
5. To find out whether there is any significant difference between the mean scores of control group and Experimental group of pre-test performance in A Study on the Achievement and Effect of Innovative Teaching of Lesson Food, the Medicine among IXth Standard Students.
6. To find out whether there is any significant difference between the mean scores of control group and Experimental group of

post-test performance in A Study on the Achievement and Effect of Innovative Teaching of Lesson Food, the Medicine among IXth Standard Students.

7. To find out whether there is any significant difference between the mean scores of control group of pre-test and post-test performance in A Study on the Achievement and Effect of Innovative Teaching of Lesson Food, the Medicine among IXth Standard Students.
8. To find out whether there is any significant difference between the mean scores of Experimental group of pre-test and post-test performance in A Study on the Achievement and Effect of Innovative Teaching of Lesson Food, the Medicine among IXth Standard Students.

HYPOTHESES OF THE STUDY

Based on the objectives the following null hypothesis is formulated for Testing.

1. There is no significant difference between the mean scores of boys and girls in pre-test of control group in A Study on Achievement and Effect of Innovative Teaching of the Lesson Food the Medicine among IXth Standard Students.
2. There is no significant difference between the mean scores of boys and girls in pre-test of Experimental group in A Study on Achievement and Effect of Innovative Teaching of the Lesson Food the Medicine among IXth Standard Students.
3. There is no significant difference between the mean scores of boys in pre-test of Control group and Experimental group in A Study on Achievement and Effect of Innovative Teaching of the Lesson Food the Medicine among IXth Standard Students.
4. There is no significant difference between the mean scores of boys and girls in post-test of control group in A Study on Achievement and Effect of Innovative Teaching of the Lesson Food the Medicine among IXth Standard Students.
5. There is no significant difference between the mean scores of control group and Experimental group of pre-test performance

in A Study on Achievement and Effect of Innovative Teaching of the Lesson Food the Medicine among IXth Standard Students.

6. There is no significant difference between the mean scores of control group and Experimental group of post-test performance in A Study on Achievement and Effect of Innovative Teaching of the Lesson Food the Medicine among IXth Standard Students.
7. There is no significant difference between the mean scores of control group of post-test and pre-test performance in A Study on Achievement and Effect of Innovative Teaching of the Lesson Food the Medicine among IXth Standard Students.
8. There is no significant difference between the mean scores of Experimental group of post-test and pre-test performance in A Study on Achievement and Effect of Innovative Teaching of the Lesson Food the Medicine among IXth Standard Students.

VARIABLES

THE VARIABLES IN THE STUDY

Food the Medicine is the variable taken for the present study.

METHODOLOGY IN BRIEF

The investigator followed the "Experimental method" for the present study. The following tool was developed and administered to IXth standard students. The IXth standard students have responded to the questionnaire. The dada thus collected were put in to appropriate statistical analysis.

TOOLS USED

Food the Medicine Tamil Exam type Questionnaire was developed, validated and used by the investigator.

STATISTICAL TECHNIQUES USED

The following statistical techniques were used in the study. Descriptive and inferential analysis - mean, standard Deviation and t-test.

FINDINGS

1. There is no significant difference between the mean scores of boys and girls in pre-test performance in control group. **(Accepted)**
2. There is no significant difference between the mean scores of boys and girls in pre-test performance in Experimental group. **(Accepted)**
3. There is no significant difference between the mean scores of boys and girls in post-test performance in control group. **(Accepted)**
4. There is no significant difference between the mean scores of boys in pre-test performance in control group and Experimental group. **(Accepted)**
5. There is no significant difference between the mean scores of pre-test performance in control group and Experimental group. **(Accepted)**
6. There is no significant difference between the mean scores of post-test performance in Experimental group and control group.**(Rejected)**
7. There is no significant difference between the mean scores of post-test and pre-test performance in control group. **(Rejected)**
8. There is no significant difference between the mean scores of post-test and pre-test performance in experimental group.**(Rejected)**

LIMITATION OF THE STUDY

1. The present study was confined to 50 IXth standard students of Sri Venkateshwara Matric. Hr. Sec. School, Thirukogarnam, Pudukkottai.
2. The chapter of Food the Medicine was only taken by the investigator for the research.

RESEARCH IMPLICATIONS

The findings of this experimental study show that, the 3 Dimensional approaches in Tamil subject can be practiced in the classroom situation in order to attain better understanding by the students.

SUGGESTION FOR FURTHER RESEARCH

1. It can be replicated with other science subject.
2. The present study was conducted among IXth standard students only.
3. Therefore it is suggested that it may be conducted among the pupils if other classes also.
4. The Researcher conducted the Research in the urban area school. Hence it is suggested that this research also be implemented to rural area school for the development of the pupils.

CONCLUSION

The researcher carried out the study of "A Study on Achievement and Effect of Innovative Teaching of the Lesson Food the Medicine among IXth Standard Students". This study revealed that the effectiveness of students understanding Food the Medicine is improved with the help of CD approach concept. The pre test performance of the control group and experimental group level is minimum, when compared to the post test performance of control and experimental group. The experimental group having high level of performance in post test, when introducing the CD approach in Tamil teaching. Both boys and girls performance better in experimental group of the post-test. The present research revealed that teacher should always teach certain competencies in Tamil concept by using novel method of CD approach for easy understanding of Food the Medicine.

BIBILIOGRAPHY

1. Adolf Otto Reinhold Windaus **(1927)** - synthesized **VitaminD,** for which he won the Nobel Prize in Chemistry.

2. Albert Szent-Gydrgyi **(1928)** - isolated ascorbic acid (VitaminC). In 1932 he proved that it was Vitamin C by preventing scurvy. In 1937 he synthesized Vitamin C and won the Nobel Prize.

3. Edwin B. Hart **(1925)** - discovered that trace amounts of copper are essential for iron absorptt n.

4. Eric John Underwood and Hedley Marston **(1935)** - discovered the necessity of cobalt. They were not working together - the discoveries were made independently.

5. Elsie Widdowson (**1940)** - drew up the nutritional principles for rationing which took place in the United Kingdom during and after World War II. Widdowson also oversaw the government mandated addition of vitamins to food during World War II and some post-war years. Widdowson and Robert McCance coauthored *The Chemical Composition of Foods* in 1940, which became the basis for modern nutritional thinking.

6. Eugene Floyd Dubois **(1936) -** demonstrated that school and work performance are linked to caloric intake.

7. Erhard Ferhnholz **(1938) -** discovered the structure of Vitamin E, which was later synthesized by Paul Karrer.

8. Linus Pauling (**1968)** - coined the term *orthomolecular nutrition.* He proposed that by giving the body the right molecules in the right concentration - optimum nutrition - these nutrients would be better utilized and provide superior health and contribute towards longer lives. Pauling's work was the basis for future research which eventually led to large intravenous doses of Vitamin C for improving survival times and quality of life of some terminal **cancer** patients. Pauling was awarded the Nobel Prize in Chemistry.

9. The National Research Council (USA) **(1941)** - set up the first RDAs (Recommended Dietary Allowances).

10. The Department of Agriculture (USA) (**1992) -** set up the *Food Guide Pyramid,* which was to be subsequently criticized by nutritionists throughout the world for different reasons.

11. William Cumming Rose **(1930s)** identified essential amino acids which the body cannot synthesize, but which are necessary protein components.

12. 2002 - a link between violent behavior and nutrition was revealed in a *Natural Justice* study (USA).**2005** - Researchers found that the adenovirus is a cause of **obesity,** as well as bad nutrition.

4. Error Committed By Mathematics Students in Higher Secondary

Chapter - I

INTRODUCTION

Research on understanding more completely what a mathematics disability means? And what we can do about it in school has lagged behind similar work being done in the area of reading disabilities. Compared to the research base in early reading difficulties, early difficulties in mathematics and the identification of mathematics disability in later years are less researched and understood.

Fortunately, attention is now being directed to helping students who struggle learning basic mathematics skills, mastering more advance mathematics e.g., measurement and solving mathematics problems. This explain in detail what a mathematics disability is the sources that cause such a disability and how a mathematics disability impacts students in making calculation related problems at Higher secondary school level.

Education is the process of developing the capacities and potentials of the individual so as to prepare that individual to be successful in a specific society or culture. From this perspective, education is serving primary as an individual development function.

Education begins at birth and continues throughout life. It is constant and ongoing. The quality of a nation depends upon the quality of its citizens. The quality of citizens depends on the quality of their education and quality of mathematics education besides other factors depends upon study habits and study attitude of the learners. Quality of education is reflected through the function of Motivational Factors and study attitude of the students. Thus to enhance the quality of education, it is necessary to improve the study habituation using motivational factors and study attitudes of the students in mathematics.

MEANING OF MATHEMATICS

Mathematics should be visualized as the vehicle to train a child to think reason, analyze, and articulate, logically. Apart from being a specific subject it should be treated as a concomitant to any subject involving analysis and meaning.

According to a new English Dictionary, "Mathematics"-in strict sense –is the abstract science which investigates deductively the conclusions implicit in the elementary conception of spatial and numerical relations.

On the basis of above definitions we can say of conclude that

1. Mathematics is the science of measurement, quantity and magnitude.
2. Mathematics is the systematized, organized and exact branch of science.
3. Mathematics is the science of calculation.
4. Mathematics is the science of measurement, quantity and magnitude.
5. It deals with quantitative facts and relationships.
6. It is the abstract form of science.
7. It is a science of logical reasoning.
8. It settles in the minds habit of reasoning.
9. It is an inductive and experimental science.
10. Mathematics is the science, which draws necessary conclusions.

TEACHING OF MATHEMATICS:

Mathematics is the language in which God has written the universe. Mathematics is the pivot of all civilizations. It enters every walk of life. Our entire civilization depends on the intellectual penetration and utilization of nature, which has its real foundation in the mathematical Science.

Roger Bacon has rightly remarked, "Mathematics is the gate and key of the Sciences... Neglect of mathematics works injury to all knowledge, since he who is ignorant of it cannot know the other sciences or the things of the world. And, what is worse, men who thus ignorant are unable to perceive their own ignorance and so do not seek a remedy".

National Policy on Education (1986) highlighted, "Mathematics should be visualized as the vehicle to train a child to think, reason, analyse, and articulate logically. Apart from being a specific subject it should be treated as a concomitant to any subject involving analysis and meaning".

Mathematical form of today has more and more new applications for day to day life and the rapid growth of desired applications help to develop more and more new fields of mathematics. Today, mathematics holds an important place in schools. Mathematics has its own disciplinary values. In fact, mathematics is an expression of the human mind, and it reflects the active will, the contemplative reason, and the desire for aesthetic perfection. Its basic elements are logic and intuition, analysis and construction, and generality and individuality.

Mathematics is a creative process, deriving ideas and suggestions from real problems, idealizing and formulating the relevant concepts, posing questions, intuitively deriving possible conclusions and then and only then, proving the hunch or the intuited argument deductively. Mathematics is the only subject whose knowledge develops the habit of hard work, concentration, well organized personality and clarity in the students.

Locke has remarked, "Mathematics is a way to settle in the minds of children, a habit of reasoning". The power of critical thinking, logical reasoning, process of induction, and generalization, and establishment of relationship between different components can be developed through the teaching of mathematics. Generally while teaching mathematics the following principles are to be followed:

i. Make Mathematics realistic and interesting.

ii. Consider the student's prior knowledge.

iii. Make the Mathematics curriculum socially interactive.

iv. Frame innovative Mathematics projects.

PLACE OF MATHEMATICS IN SCHOOL CURRICULUM

Mathematics occupies an important place in the school curriculum. It has been its important part ever since the beginning of formal education and it continues to be so.

Realising its social relevance, **Kothari Education Commission** (1964–66) suggested, "Science and mathematics should be taught on a compulsory basis to all pupils as a part of general education during first ten years of schooling". Also the commission recommended that, "Proper foundation in the knowledge of mathematics should be laid at the school".

According to the commission the advent of automation and cybernetics in this country marks the beginning of the new scientific industrial revolution and makes it the entire imperative to devote special attention to the study of mathematics. Modern developments in science and technology require a new habit of original and critical thinking and the foundations of such a habit have to be laid in school mathematics.

Teaching higher secondary school mathematics should reflect the chief characteristics such as abstractness, precision, generality and logical nature. The following are the reasons for keeping mathematics in the school curriculum:

(i) It is the basis of all sciences.

(ii) It is correlated to other subjects and human life.

(iii) It generates logical attitude.

(iv) It provides a definite way of thinking.

(v) It provides opportunity to develop mental abilities of the child.

Objectives of Teaching Mathematics at Higher Secondary Level

National Policy on Education (1986) put forth the following objectives of teaching mathematics at Higher secondary level:

i. To develop understanding about the inter-relationship of mathematical facts, formula, principles and processes.

ii. To develop understanding of the theoretical and abstract aspects of mathematics.

iii. To develop skill in solving the same problem by various possible methods.

iv. To learn the application of mathematics in man's day-to-day, social, vocational, occupational, and recreational life.

v. To gain confidence and competence in the learning of mathematics.

vi. To develop logical thinking, reasoning power, analytical thinking and critical thinking.

vii. To develop skill in using higher geometrical instruments and field work.

viii. To provide, thorough Mathematical ideas, aesthetic and intellectual enjoyment and satisfaction and to give an opportunity for creative expression.

MATHEMATICS AND PROBLEM SOLVING ABILITY

Problem solving is an important component of mathematics because students would be able to achieve all the three values namely functional, logical and aesthetic. The main objective of teaching mathematics is to train up the students in the art of problem solving. Problem solving in mathematics is helpful in the proper development of one's mental powers. Every problem in mathematics trains an individual in scientific method of reasoning and thinking.

The habit of thinking and problem solving developed by the study of mathematics helps in establishing an intelligent and good understanding of our surroundings and in the development of some common abilities like arithmetic reasoning, numerical ability and logical reasoning which are very much essential for the day to day life situations.

Mathematics is an essential discipline because of its practical role to the individual and society. Presenting a problem and developing the skills needed to solve that problem is more motivational than teaching the skills without a context.

The National Council of Teachers of Mathematics (NCTM, 2000) has recommended that the Mathematics curriculum should focus on the following:

i. Developing skills and applying these skills to handle real life problems.

ii. Gathering, organizing, interpreting and communicating information.

iii. Developing curiosity, confidence and open mindedness.

iv. Formulating key questions, analyzing and conceptualizing problems, defining problems and goals, discovering patterns and similarities, seeking out appropriate data, experimenting transferring skills and strategies to new situations.

APPROACHES OF TEACHING MATHEMATICS

An approach is a way of arriving at a solution by the use of logical reasoning. It is precisely what it indicates. It is a means of working through a situation, be that a programme, project, issue, risk or pretty much anything. This may involve the use of methodologies either individually, grouped or cherry picked. There are various approaches of teaching Mathematics. Broadly speaking they are teacher centered and learner centered.

Fischer and Fischer (1987) have identified seven styles of teaching Mathematics. They are as follows:

i. Student centered style: Here the teacher provides a structure and the students pursue it according to their interests and liking.

ii. Teacher centered style: In this, the teacher plays a dominant role. The teaching learning process is determined by the teacher. Learners are passive listeners.

iii. Subject Centered style: Here, the main focus of the teacher is on the organized contents of the subject matter to be presented to the learners.

iv. Task Centered Style: The teacher prescribes the material to be learnt by the learners and then he expects specific performance on the part of the students. Here learning is seen on individual bases.

v. Learning Centered Style: Unlike child centered and subject centered styles, here the emphasis is on the learners and their learning irrespective of their abilities and disabilities.

vi. Co-operative Planner Style: Means and ends of instructions are prepared by the teacher in cooperation with the learners. Here the teacher encourages and supports the learners in every way.

vii. Emotional Involvement Style: In this style of teaching the teacher is emotionally involved. He enters the teaching learning process with zeal and dedication and thus he succeeds in producing good class room environment.

HISTORY OF MATHEMATICS

Mathematics has been the backbone of our civilization. It is exaggeration to say that history of mathematics is the no history of civilization. Mathematics has led to the development of various subjects, vocations and technology.

In the history of mathematics there have been some very remarkable developments in the form of discovery and evolution of certain ideas and processes. These ideas and processes claim special status and significance in the overall progress of mathematical knowledge.

AIMS OF TEACHING MATHEMATICS

It is a scientific world; the credit of all the technical progress in science goes to mathematics progress of science has taken place side-by side with the progress of mathematics. That is way mathematics is known as the "mother of science". If we look at the syllabus of mathematics of developed countries we see that the level of mathematical subject material is very progressive at primary level.

Mathematics could be said 'soul' of science. Without mathematics, science will be incapable to save its existence. Today's world is world of science and therefore foundation of this world is based on mathematics. These aims pertain to the entire school stage. Apart from the enabling of student to acquire essential mathematics knowledge, skill, interest and attitudes. The teaching of mathematics has to help them in many ways.

1. Utilitarian aim.
2. Disciplinary aim.
3. Cultural aim.
4. Adjustment aim.
5. Social aim.
6. Moral aim.
7. Aesthetic aim.
8. Inter-disciplinary aim.
9. Self-education aim.
10. Education preparation aim.
11. Development of powers aim.

PREPARATION FOR LIFE

Preparation for the life means giving the knowledge, which has got same utility in life and its vocations. Utility of Mathematics is more to be dealt with, life world remain incomplete without good knowledge of Mathematics. So, preparation for life "is one of the significant aims of teaching Mathematics in schools.

ROLE OF MATHEMATICS AND ITS IMPORTANCE

Mathematics has got as honored place among the science, it is the most powerful tool ever developed by man. Its contribution to the development of science. The place it occupies in contemporary society as an indispensable working tool of common man, its vital role in the affairs of man are given it a position of pre – eminence among the different areas of knowledge.

Express the goals of elementary school Mathematics in the following way.

1. Development of computational facility
2. Development of physical understanding
3. Development of rational power
4. Development of positive attitude towards Mathematics.

Ability to perform necessary computations, accuracy, precision, speed, neatness, etc. ability to represent verbal statements by diagrams and symbols, ability of logical thinking, ability to estimate measurements and conceive approximation to answers, ability to solve common problems related with home and social life, ability to develop interest in some vocations.

1. To enable the learner to know and understand various Mathematics symbols, theories etc.
2. To enable the learner to solve problems in day to day life.
3. To prepare the learner for economic, purposeful, productive, creative and consecutive living.
4. To develop the power of thinking and reasoning.
5. To develop scientific and realistic attitude towards life.
6. To develop interest in Mathematics learning.
7. To develop skill in computation.

Learners of Mathematics many times have to solve problems that involve symbolic calculations by performing appropriate sequences of steps. These steps involve the manipulation of mathematical formula obtained from the ones that appears. There are courses on specific subjects, like Integral and Equations, in which a high percentage of the work of the students is devoted to learning different methods of problem resolution of the above kind and learning when these methods are successful. For instance, a typical course on Ordinary Equations can include methods for the solution of linear equations, solution of equations by separation of variables, homogeneous equations, etc. Similarly, a course where basic integration methods are explained will include integration-by-parts and specific methods for the integration of rational functions, among others; all these methods are processes that consist of steps to be applied to the integrand. In general Algebra is the particularly suitable to this approach, as calculations and predefined steps are necessary for the resolution of particular types of problems, although other considerations are also needed such as applicability conditions for certain steps.

DYSCALCULIA

Dyscalculia is a term that has been used for many years when talking about a math disability. Dyscalculia means "a severe or complete inability to calculate". Some people use the term dyscalculia to describe a child who has problems learning mathematics skills and concepts. However, the terms learning disabilities in mathematics and mathematics disability are used more widely today.

CHARACTERISTICS OF DYSCALCULIA

DYSCALCULIA IS A LEARNING DISABILITY IN MATHEMATICS

Dyscalculia is a broad term for severe difficulties in mathematics. It includes all types of mathematics problems ranging from inability to understand the meaning of numbers to inability to apply mathematics principles to solve problems. Dyscalculia is one type of learning disability that can be served in special education programs.

CAUSES OF DYSCALCULIA AND MATHEMATICS DISABILITIES

As with other types of learning disabilities, dyscalculia is believed to involve the language and visual processing centers of the brain. Evidence suggests learning disabilities such as dyscalculia may be inherited or can be caused by problems with brain development. Exposure to prenatal or environmental toxins (such as lead paint) may also play a role.

CHARACTERISTICS OF DYSCALCULIA AND MATHEMATICS DISABILITIES

Dyscalculia includes a wide range of mathematics difficulty. Dyscalculia involves inability to understand the meaning of numbers their quantities. Students with Dyscalculia cannot understand basic operations of addition and subtraction. They may not understand complex problems such as multiplication, division, and more abstract problems. Because they do not understand mathematics concepts, they do not remember and cannot build on them to master more complex problems.

ASSESSMENT AND INDIVIDUAL EDUCATION PROGRAMS

If students have dyscalculia, a referral assessment to determine and diagnosis occurs. Most likely, the school will evaluate to determine the student has a learning disability in mathematics rather than using the term dyscalculia. This will require an evaluation to identify the specific types of errors each individual student makes. If they qualify for special education, teachers will develop an individual education program. Typical strategies focus on developing mathematics vocabulary and comprehension of mathematics concepts and operations.

MISCONCEPTIONS ABOUT DYSCALCULIA

People with learning disabilities such as dyscalculia are at-risk for being seen as less capable than they are. However, they have general ability to learn that is comparable to or higher than many of their peers. They simply have specific skill weaknesses in some areas. In many ways, students with learning disabilities have creative problem solving skills and can achieve well with appropriate specially designed instruction.

LEARNING DIFFICULTIES IN MATHEMATICS

Some assessments are specifically marketed as dyscalculia tests. It is possible, however, for evaluators to determine if a student has dyscalculia and learning disabilities in mathematics through general types of diagnostic mathematics assessments, reviews of student work, and cognitive assessments. Whatever assessment is used, it is most important that evaluators identify the specific deficits affecting the student's mathematics abilities to enable teachers to develop appropriate instruction to address those problems.

WHAT SUSPECT IF THE STUDENT HAS DYSCALCULIA

If the student has dyscalculia and may be learning disabled, contact school principal or counselor for information on how to request assessment for the student. For students in college and vocational programs, the school advising office can assist with finding appropriate resources.

DYSCALCULIA IS A TERM NOT TYPICALLY USED IN SCHOOLS

Students in school may not use the term dyscalculia, but it can still appropriately evaluate your student's learning disability. Typically public schools use the labels and language from federal IDEA regulations. Dyscalculia is a diagnostic term found in psychiatric diagnostic systems. Schools consider it one of several types of mathematics disorders they can serve under the label, learning disability.

LEARNING DISABILITY IN ARITHMETIC

1. Difficulty in analyzing and solving mathematics problems of various complexity (one or multiple step), including those involving probability
2. Difficulty in associating the spoken form with the correct printed material
3. Difficulty in learning the cardinal and ordinal system of counting
4. Difficulty in understanding the meaning of the process sign
5. Difficulty in understanding the arrangement of numbers on a page
6. Inability to follow and remember the sequence of steps used in various mathematical operations
7. Difficulty with concepts of space, time, size, distance, quantity and/or linear measurement

BASE FOR THE STUDENT'S MATHEMATICAL DEVELOPMENT

Mathematics calculation related problems can arise at nearly any stage of a student scholastic development. While very little is known about the neurobiological or environmental causes of these problems, many experts attribute them to deficits in one or more of five different skill types. These deficits can exist independently of one another or can occur in combination.

INCOMPLETE MASTERY OF NUMBER FACTS

Number facts are the basic computations (9 + 3 = 12 or 2 x 4 = 8) students are required to memorize in the earliest grades of elementary school. Recalling these facts efficiently is critical because it allows a student to approach more advanced mathematical thinking without being bogged down by simple calculations.

COMPUTATIONAL WEAKNESS

Many students, despite a good understanding of mathematical concepts, are inconsistent at computing. They make errors because they misread signs or carry numbers incorrectly, or may not write numerals clearly enough or in the correct column. These students often struggle, especially in school, where basic computation and "right answers" are stressed often they end up in remedial classes, even though they might have a high level of potential for higher-level mathematical thinking.

DIFFICULTY TRANSFERRING KNOWLEDGE

One fairly common difficulty experienced by people with mathematics problems is the inability to easily connect the abstract or conceptual aspects of math with reality. Understanding what symbols represent in the physical world is important to how well and how easily a student will remember a concept. Holding and inspecting an equilateral triangle, for example, will be much more meaningful to a child than simply being told that the triangle is equilateral because it has three equal sides. With this problem find connections such as these painstaking at best.

DIFFICULTY COMPREHENDING THE VISUAL AND SPATIAL ASPECTS AND PERCEPTUAL DIFFICULTIES

A far less common problem and probably the most severe is the inability to effectively visualize mathematics concepts. Students who have this problem may be unable to judge the relative size among three dissimilar objects. This disorder has obvious disadvantages, as it requires that a student rely almost entirely on rote memorization of verbal or written descriptions of mathematics concepts that most people take for granted. Some mathematical problems also require students to combine higher-order cognition with perceptual skills, for instance, to determine what shape will result when a complex 3-D figure is rotated.

SIGNS OF MATHEMATICS DIFFICULTIES

OUTPUT DIFFICULTIES

A student with problems in output may

1. be unable to recall basic mathematics facts, procedures, rules, or formulas
2. be very slow to retrieve facts or pursue procedures
3. have difficulties maintaining precision during mathematical work
4. have difficulties with handwriting that slow down written work or make it hard to read later
5. have difficulty remembering previously encountered patterns
6. forget what he or she is doing in the middle of a mathematics problem

ORGANIZATIONAL DIFFICULTIES

A student with problems in organization may

1. have difficulties sequencing multiple steps
2. become entangled in multiple steps or elements of a problem
3. lose appreciation of the final goal and over emphasize individual elements of a problem
4. not be able to identify salient aspects of a mathematical situation, particularly in word problems or other problem solving situations where some information is not relevant
5. be unable to appreciate the appropriateness or reasonableness of solutions generated

LANGUAGE DIFFICULTIES

A student with language problems in mathematics may

1. have difficulty with the vocabulary of mathematics
2. be confused by language in word problems
3. not know when irrelevant information is included or when information is given out of sequence.
4. have trouble learning or recalling abstract terms
5. have difficulty understanding directions
6. have difficulty explaining and communicating about mathematics, including asking and answering questions
7. have difficulty reading texts to direct their own learning
8. have difficulty remembering assigned values or definitions in specific problems

ATTENTION DIFFICULTIES

A student with attention problems in mathematics may

1. be distracted or fidgety during mathematics tasks
2. lose his or her place while working on a mathematics problem
3. appear mentally fatigued or overly tired when doing mathematics

VISUAL SPATIAL OR ORDERING DIFFICULTIES

A student with problems in visual, spatial, or sequential aspects of mathematics may

1. be confused when learning multi-step procedures
2. have trouble ordering the steps used to solve a problem
3. feel overloaded when faced with a worksheet full of mathematics exercises
4. not be able to copy problems correctly
5. may have difficulties reading the hands on an analog clock
6. may have difficulties interpreting and manipulating geometric configurations

7. may have difficulties appreciating changes in objects as they are moved in space

DIFFICULTIES WITH MULTIPLE TASKS

A student with problems managing and/or merging different tasks in mathematics may

1. find it difficult to switch between multiple demands in a complex mathematics problem
2. find it difficult to tell when tasks can be grouped or merged and when they must be separated in a multi-step mathematics problem
3. cannot manage all the demands of a complex problem, such as a word problem, even thought he or she may know component facts and procedures.

SEVERAL SOURCES OF MATHEMATICS CALCULATION PROBLEMS

When a student is identified as having a mathematics disability, his difficulty may stem from problems in one or more of the following areas memory, cognitive development, and visual-spatial ability.

MEMORY

Memory problems may affect a student's mathematics performance in several ways. A student might have memory problems that interfere with his ability to retrieve (remember) basic arithmetic facts quickly. In the upper grades, memory problems may influence a student's ability to recall the steps needed remember what specific symbols (e.g., å, s, ð, e") mean. While helping student with mathematics homework, the difficulty remembering how to perform a problem that was taught at school that day.

LEARNING DIFFICULTIES IN MATHEMATICS

Student identified as manifesting Learning Difficulties in mathematics can demonstrate deficits in arithmetic calculation, mathematics reasoning or both. In general, authorities agree that approximately 6% of the school population have difficulties in mathematics that cannot be attributed to low intelligence, sensory deficits, or economic deprivation. While the data are sparse at this time, it appears that deficits in arithmetic calculation skills are more frequently identified than deficits in arithmetic reasoning.

However, common sense would suggest that attempts to reason mathematically would be constrained by limitations in calculations skills. Unfortunately, a major difficulty in identifying mathematics learning disabilities accurately is that, like learning to read, learning mathematics concepts is dependent upon the teacher's knowledge of the concepts and ability to present them The breadth and complexity of the field of mathematics make the identification and study of the cognitive phenotypes that define mathematics learning disabilities a formidable endeavor. Learning disability can result from deficits in the ability to represent or process information in one or all of the many mathematical domains (e.g., geometry) or in one or a set of individual competencies within each domain. The goal is further complicated by the task of distinguishing poor achievement due to inadequate instruction from poor achievement due to an actual cognitive disability.

NEED OF THE STUDY

The role of Mathematics is very important in our day-to-day life. Avoiding the errors while doing the mathematics and improving the level of underachievers in Mathematics is a must. The investigation is aimed at first identifying the error committed by mathematics in higher secondary level and find out the role of study in determining their achievement.

Learning is possible only by hard work. So a systematic scheme for learning is very essential. The amount of learning of a person depends upon the habit of study of that person. Formation of good study habits is an important aspect of the learning process in mathematics. Pupils should be helped to evaluate critically their own study habits. So, that they may discover weaknesses and try to improve their study efficiency.

In every class, there are three types of students namely.

1. Those who perform very well
2. Those who never perform well
3. Those can perform well; but don't fare well, in Mathematics.

The pupils of the third category may have the general intelligence to do well. But owing to several factors they do not fare well in Mathematics, special attentions will help the pupils of this category to bring out their abilities in full. If third is not, done in schools, the society may have to lose eminent Mathematicians and great Mathematics.

The influence of the teacher on the self- concepts has been studied both with reference to the effect on the self - concepts as well as academic achievement, a students self concept is a functional limiting a fascinating factor in academic achievement. Therefore it was through fit to analyze error committed by mathematics in higher secondary level students and their influence in achievement levels in school situation.

There is general criticism that the generation of higher secondary school boys and girls in our schools has some problems in doing mathematics. Hence the study focuses to identify the error committed by mathematics in higher secondary level at Sivagangai Educational District.

SCOPE OF THE STUDY

The ultimate aim of education is to help students to Identifying the learning difficulties in Mathematics with their under achievements have important implication in learning. By knowing the level of higher secondary students the study focuses. The educationist can adopt suitable methods to subdue the effect on them on the student's behavior in mathematics.

The ability to compute, problem solve and apply concepts and skills in mathematics influences multiple decisions in our lives. The National Research Council reported that mathematics is especially evident in our technology-rich society, where number sense and problem solving skills have increased the importance and demands of advanced levels of proficiency.

However, mathematics is often challenging for students with and without disabilities to master. This describes the changing context and expectations of mathematics standards and curriculum, given the specific characteristics of students with disabilities.

Arithmetic ability is important in a modern society and mathematical skill prior to school entry is one of the best predictors of educational success. Problem-based learning is particularly suitable in fields like Mathematics. It is quite usual to find solution of solving methods to express mathematical knowledge and doing Calculations without error.

However, these happen to be somewhat hard for students. For instance, when a learner faces the integration-by-parts method, one possibility is to try to understand the general formula, while on the other hand another possible scenario is to learn by watching particular examples. Both approaches are complementary and in fact, teachers usually move back and forth in order to manage their students to understand the underlying concepts.

Thus it is that, however successful a course may appear to be, there are students who begin to struggle and who will need appropriate help to be able to pursue mathematics further. The aim of the present study was to investigate the ***Error Committed by Mathematics Students in Higher Secondary Level at Sivagangai Educational District***.

STATEMENT OF THE PROBLEM

The aim of mathematical education is surely success for all pupils, yet it seems to be a fact of life that whilst a few prosper in mathematics, a much greater calculation finds mathematics difficult.

It is associated problem, so that the student learners will have the knowledge, skill, attitudes, motivation and commitment to work individually and collectively towards finding the solutions for their learning problems without commit error.

Thus the present investigation has the need to identify "*A Study on the Error Committed by Mathematics Students in Higher Secondary Level at Sivagangai Educational District*".

OBJECTIVES OF THE STUDY

The Objectives of the study are as follows

1. To find out the significant difference in the Error Committed by Mathematics students in Higher Secondary Level in terms of their **Gender**.

2. To find out the significant difference in the Error Committed by Mathematics students in Higher Secondary Level in terms of their **Locality**.
3. To find out the significant difference in the Error Committed by Mathematics students in Higher Secondary Level in terms of their **Type of School**.
4. To find out the significant difference in the Error Committed by Mathematics students in Higher Secondary Level in terms of their **Type of School Management**.
5. To find out the significant difference in the Error Committed by Mathematics students in Higher Secondary Level in terms of their **Medium of Instruction**.
6. To find out the significant difference in the Error Committed by Mathematics students in Higher Secondary Level in terms of their **Father's Occupation**.
7. To find out the significant difference in the Error Committed by Mathematics students in Higher Secondary Level in terms of their **Father's Educational Status**.
8. To find out the significant difference in the Error Committed by Mathematics students in Higher Secondary Level in terms of their **Parent's Income.**

HYPOTHESES OF THE STUDY

The Hypotheses of the Study are as Follows

1. There is no significant difference in the Error Committed by Mathematics students in Higher Secondary Level in terms of their **Gender**.
2. There is no significant difference in the Error Committed by Mathematics students in Higher Secondary Level in terms of their **Locality**.
3. There is no significant difference in the Error Committed by Mathematics students in Higher Secondary Level in terms of their **Type of School**.

4. There is no significant difference in the Error Committed by Mathematics students in Higher Secondary Level in terms of their **Type of School Management**.
5. There is no significant difference in the Error Committed by Mathematics students in Higher Secondary Level in terms of their **Medium of Instruction**.
6. There is no significant difference in the Error Committed by Mathematics students in Higher Secondary Level in terms of their **Father's Occupation**.
7. There is no significant difference in the Error Committed by Mathematics students in Higher Secondary Level in terms of their **Father's Educational Status**.
8. There is no significant difference in the Error Committed by Mathematics students in Higher Secondary Level in terms of their **Parent's Income.**

LIMITATIONS OF THE STUDY

The error committed in learning Mathematics students at higher secondary stages of education by pupils with different intellectual capacities and interests are very vast and varied. So the present investigation is confined to pupils of Higher Secondary School Level.

The present study is confined only to Three hundred Higher secondary school students in Sivagangai District.

1. The present study is limited only Five Schools Student.
2. The present study Gender, Locality of School, Type of School, Type of School Management, Medium of Instruction, Father's occupation, Father's Educational Status, Parent's income perceived error committed by mathematics chosen.
3. This study was conducted in the year 2014-2015 only.

CONCLUSION

Thus the chapter has need, scope, limitation objective, hypothesis of the study. The next chapter deals with the Review of Related Literature.

Chapter - II

Review of Related Literature

INTRODUCTION

Review of related literature helps researches to define his positions not only with reference to the problem that he wishes to tackle but also relating to the field. It is and indispensable step for researches as it gives him a deeper insight and in understanding of his problems.

By examining what is already done about the problem the investigator becomes familiar with varies trends and phases in research in his area.

Review of the literature ensures the avoidance of the unnecessary duplications.

The present chapter summarizes the research studies related to the problem under investigation.

Review of research studies is of fundamental importance to prove insight into the problem, to familiarize the researcher with the studies previously done, to make the researcher adopt suitable design and to ensure perfection in the study to be made.

With this view, the researcher has attempted to review numerous relevant and pertinent studies that have been undertaken by the educational researchers.

THE PURPOSE OF THE REVIEW OF LITERATURE

The review of literature is essential due to the following reasons:

1 One of the early steps in planning a research work is to review research done previously in the particular area of interest and relevant are quantitative and analysis of this the research usually gives the worker an indication of the direction.

2 It is very essential for very investigator to be up-to-date in his information about the literature related to his own problem already done by others. It is considered the most important per-requisite to actual planning and conducting the study.

3 It avoids the replication of the study of finding to take an advantage from similar or related literature as regards to methodology, techniques of data collection procedure adopted and conclusion drawn. He can justify his own Endeavour in this field.

4 It provides as source of problem of study, an analog may be drawn for identifying and selecting have own problem of research. The researcher formulates his hypotheses on the basis of review of literature. It also provides the relation for the study, the result and finding of the study, as also discussed at length. The review of literature indicates the clear picture of the problems to be solved. The scholarship in the field can be developed by reviewing the literature of the field.

STUDIES CONDUCTED IN INDIA

Price and Ansari (2014), has suggested a division between higher secondary and secondary level. Student with primary are those with the most severe form of mathematical difficulties that are caused by a developmental impairment of the neurological foundations of numerical magnitude processing. Student who do not suffer from primary level but still have difficulties due to other factors, such as working memory deficits, poor schooling, behavioral attention problems, etc., are labeled as having secondary level.

The National Mathematics Advisory Panel (2013), was reported that mathematics is the invisible culture of our age and emphasizes that mathematics is embedded in our lives in many ways: practical, civic, professional, recreational, and cultural. This is especially evident in our technology-rich society. Number sense and problem-solving skills have increasing importance, as technology (e.g., calculators, computers, software programs, etc.) enhances both the opportunities for, as well as the demands of, advanced levels of proficiency in mathematics.

Lange (2012), has stated learning difficulties in calculation in mathematics are a social construction. The socio-cultural significance of mathematics constitutes low achievement in mathematics as a socio-educational problem on a social level and as a problem beyond the control of the affected student at an individual level. Mathematics learning has a serious impact on student's perceptions of themselves not only as mathematics learners, but also as members of school community and society in general. The learning or non-learning of mathematics was also a construction of identity and this has an effect on students' foregrounds.

Kalaivanan.K (2010), was studied the assessment of learning difficulties of under achievers in mathematics among higher secondary students. The major findings of the study revealed that there was no significant gender difference among high, average in achievement

Yakesh & Pandey.Y (2008), has studied adjustment of high achievers and underachievers in Mathematics for a sample of 480 students. The findings were (1) There is negative and significant relationship between adjustment problems and achievement in Mathematics (2) underachievers and overachievers differ significantly in their adjustment. No significant difference was found between boys and girls in their adjustment (4) Poor adjustment was the cause of low achievement in mathematics among pre university students.

Thangamani (2005), has studied of self concept and attitude towards mathematics of the underachievers in mathematics. The sample consists of 290 students. The major findings were.

(1) Gender has no significant influence on self – concept of the students.

(2) The percentage of underachievers is considerably higher in Government school than in Government aided school.

(3) The academic underachievement varied significantly with sex. Girls in comparison with boys had higher achievement.

Johnson (2005), has Characterized of Students with Disabilities Initially, students who demonstrate poor skills in numerical calculation abilities were described as students with dyscalculia and were eligible to receive special educational services if the instructional needs met the criteria . Presently, it is estimated that between four and seven percent of the school-age population experience some form of mathematics-focused disability. Approximately, one fourth of the students identified with learning disabilities were identified because they underperformed in mathematics. It has been found that students with learning disabilities in mathematics perform several grade levels below their general education peers, struggle in basic mathematics skills and have difficulty in problem-solving situations. Difficulties in mathematics are part of a larger educational concern. Students who exhibit deficits in mathematics skills also show evidence of social deficits such as deficiencies in self-help skills and poor organization. In addition, students with learning disabilities are frequently characterized as having perceptual and neurological concerns that impact learning. Students with difficulties in mathematics often have other related difficulties, such as in memory, poor calculation skills, number reversals and difficulty understanding conceptual and/or procedural processes, especially as represented through symbols and signs

Gowrisha (2004), has carried out a study of under achievement in relation to study habits and attitude. The findings are the 98.7% of the under achievers tend to possess unfavorable attitude towards teacher and needed guidance 92.5% of underachievers indicated deficiency in school and home environment, 24.6% in attitude towards education, 100% in study habits, 72.8% faced mental conflicts, 97.5% had poor concentration, 70.3% had problems related to home assignments, 72.8% were Low in self confidence and 96.2% lacked proper attitude towards examination.

STUDIES CONDUCTED IN ABROAD

Gray and Tall (2014), has gave evidence of younger student performing arithmetic which shows that when taught arithmetic procedures, the less able seek security in carrying out the process whilst the more able soon develop a more flexible kind of thinking in which notation is used to mean either a process to give a result or a concept to be manipulated at a higher level. A precept is defined to be the amalgam of process and concept which is represented by the same symbolism, thus 2+3 represents the process of addition of 2 and 3, and the result of the process (5), 2+3x represents both the process of adding 2 to 3 times x and the resulting expression, sin x=opposite/hypotenuse represents both the process of calculating the sine as a ratio of lengths and also the value of the sine as the result of the calculation. It is hypothesized that less successful students have greater difficulties with the processes and concentrate on the lesser target of being able to carry them out satisfactorily whilst more successful students develop a more flexible method of handling notation, being able to see it either as a process to calculate a needed result or as an object to be manipulated as part of a more complex piece of symbolism. In other words success comes from flexible perceptual thinking whilst short-term success but long-term failure comes from procedural thinking. Here we are concerned with the performance of students transferring to the Universiti Teknologi Malaysia at 16+ who find difficulty with the mathematics that is pre-requisite for courses in engineering and other sciences. The students attending this university are in the 50th to 90th percentile of the ability range for the whole population and therefore represent a broader ability band than that normally attending university in many countries. It therefore increases the perceived gap in ability between the most and least able and, if there is a qualitative difference in thinking processes to be observed, then it is likely to be seen here.

Anderson (2012), has studied the learning difficulty in applying notion of vector in mathematics among "A" level students in Singapore the study aimed at: developing instructional material for Linking the notion of vectors, especially composition of vector and resolution of a vector, with the real mathematics world. The exploring the effectiveness of the use of the Prediction Demonstration Explanation method in helping students grasp the notion of vectors. The sample consisted of 94 Junior college students, who were taught by the method, showed a better improvement in performance on the tests than students in the control group.

Bryant, Hartman, & Kim, (2012), has stated several factors that may interfere with learning and subsequent mastery of concepts and skills in mathematics by students with disabilities,

1. **Perceptual skills:** By definition, students with learning disabilities have difficulty with spatial relationships, distances, and sequencing. These difficulties may interfere with the acquisition of and demonstration of mathematics concepts and skills, such as estimating size and distance, and problem solving.

2. **Language:** Vocabulary and language of mathematical concepts is not only varied, but also abstract. Students with difficulties and/ or disabilities in the area of language may also have difficulties with understanding such mathematical concepts as first, second, greater than, less than, as well as associated vocabulary terms such as vertex, complimentary, acute, etc. For students who have deficits in both reading and mathematics, the difficulty with word-problem solving is accentuated.

3. **Reasoning:** Students with disabilities may not possess with abstract reasoning skills necessary for higher level math skills development. These skills in reasoning may also present difficulties if instruction in mathematics is at the conceptual, abstract level.

4. **Memory**: Many students with learning and behavioral problems have difficulties remembering information that was presented. This is especially evident with the abstract symbols used in mathematics (e.g., minus, greater than, less than, etc.). Considerations for Instruction in Mathematics Current legislation, reforms and revised curriculum standards in mathematics focus attention on research-based instruction for all students. Difficulties with learning mathematics occur in one or more domains and on a continuum of needs, from temporary to severe problems, which may manifest at different points in a child's learning. Multiple instructional approaches and interventions may be necessary, since difficulties may be encountered at different ages and in different mathematical

domains. Various researches based instructional approaches and Meta cognitive strategies both enhance and scaffold instruction for student mastery of abstract concepts especially within inclusive mathematics classes.

Tymoczko, Ernest, (2011), has explained Mathematics was a human activity involving the solution of problematic situations. In finding the responses or solutions to these external and internal problems, mathematical objects progressively emerge and evolve. According to constructivist theories, people's acts must be considered the genetic source of mathematical conceptualization.

b) Mathematical problems and their solutions are shared in specific institutions or collectives involved in studying such problems. Thus, mathematical objects are socially shared cultural entities.

c) Mathematics was a symbolic language in which problem-situations and the solutions found are expressed. The systems of mathematical symbols have a communicative function and an instrumental role.

d) Mathematics is a logically organized conceptual system. Once a mathematical object has been accepted as a part of this system, it can also be considered as a textual reality and a component of the global structure. It may be handled as a whole to create new mathematical objects, widening the range of mathematical tools and, at the same time, introducing new restrictions in mathematical work and language.

To build our model, we take the notion of problem-situation as a primitive idea. Problems do not appear in isolation; the systematic variation of the variables intervening in problem-situations yields different fields of problems, sharing similar representations, solutions, etc.

The subject performs different types of practices, or actions intended to solve a mathematical problem, to communicate the solution to other people or to validate or generalize that solution to other settings and problems. The genesis of a subject's knowledge arises as a consequence of that subject's.

Lange (2009), has carried out the study as learning difficulties in mathematics were seen as a social construction within the social practice of school mathematics education and therefore closely related to the socio-cultural significance attributed to mathematics in Western societies. Consequently, the learning or non-learning of mathematics seriously affected student's perceptions of themselves and therefore their construction of identity. Many different disabilities can affect student's mathematics learning and performance, but none more than disabilities that affect cognition mental retardation, traumatic brain injury, attention-deficit/hyperactivity disorder, and learning disabilities, to name a few. Several specific areas of disability are clearly connected to math learning difficulties. Visual processing, visual memory, and visual-spatial relationships all impact math proficiency in that they are threads in the fabric of conceptual understanding and procedural fluency. Specific math learning difficulties also can affect a student's ability to formulate, represent and solve math problems.

Mathematical learning disability was understudied compared to reading disorder or dyslexia. A search of the Psych database for articles published between 2006 and 2012 using the search terms "reading disorder", "reading disability", and dyslexia resulted in 1873 articles in peer-reviewed journals. When a dyscalculia, "mathematics disorder", "mathematics disability", "mathematics difficulties", "arithmetic disorders" and "mathematics disorders" were used as search terms, 182 articles were found. For every article that was published in the field of MLD, roughly 10 articles about reading disability were published.

Accommodations for Students, who are Gifted and Learning Disabled in Mathematics (2009).

1. Student will require extended test time in the area of mathematics.
2. Student will require flexible scheduling to allow for small-group or individual instruction in math, and small-group or individual advisement in the area of Advanced Educational Services.
3. Student will require higher order thinking curriculum across his or her curriculum areas.

4. Student will require compacted or differentiated curriculum in his or her areas of giftedness.
5. Student should be helped to "visualize" mathematics problems, i.e. they can draw visual aids, and utilize all visual aids available within the assignment.
6. Allow problems to be read out loud, possibly multiple times to utilize student's auditory strengths.
7. Use real-learning to teach mathematics.
8. Use rhythm and music to teach basic mathematics facts.
9. Allow for assistive technology, i.e. calculators, color-coding.

Characteristics of Students who are Gifted and Learning Disabled in Mathematics

1. Student will benefit from an individualized educational plan that emphasizes his or her gifts, i.e. acceleration or enrichment in his or her area of giftedness, higher order thinking assignments in areas of high potential.
2. Student will benefit from social emotional support from an individual advisor; and in the form of a support group that includes other twice exceptional learners.
3. Student should be assigned case management by staff trained in his or her learning disability.
4. Student may require small group instruction in mathematics, reduced work load in mathematics, mathematics instruction delivered in a wide variety of forms, and extended test time in the area of mathematics.
5. Student should be trained in how to utilize his or her unique gifts to in part compensate for his or her disability in the area of mathematics.
6. Assignments across the curriculum could be "layered"
7. Student should be encouraged to engage activities that include higher order thinking/application of skills across all curriculums, including mathematics once basic skills are obtained.

8. While student may require instruction in multiple forms for mathematics, he or she may require reduced instruction time in other areas; thus allowing for higher order- thinking time.

Learning disability is not a single disorder, but is a general category of special education composed of disabilities in any of seven specific areas:

(1) receptive language,

(2) expressive language,

(3) basic reading skills,

(4) reading comprehension,

(5) mathematics calculation and

(6) mathematical reasoning.

Wilson and Dehaene (2007), has listed three potential subtypes of mathematics disabilities with specific neurological origins. The first subtype was referred to as a deficit in verbal symbolic representation; people with this subtype have problems learning and retrieving arithmetic facts and may have problems with counting sequence. The brain areas that are relevant for this subtype are the left frontal and/or temporal language areas and the left basal ganglia and angular gyros. The second subtype involves a deficit in executive functions that originates from frontal lobe dysfunction and results in problems with procedural usage, strategy and arithmetic fact retrieval. The third subtype involves a deficit in spatial attention and is related to posterior superior parietal dysfunction and the object file or object tracking system; thus, subsidizing should be affected in people with this subtype. The third subtype is perhaps most difficult to separate from number sense deficit (which has been proposed to the core deficit of because of the connection between numerical and spatial representations).

The book by Sierpinska (2006), represents an important step forward, when discerning between understanding acts and processes and when relating "good understanding" of a mathematical situation (concept, theory, problem) to the sequence of acts of overcoming obstacles specific to this situation. Through the historic-empirical approach it is possible to identify meaningful acts for understanding a concept. Nevertheless, we think that taking the notion of object as primitive and deriving meaning from understanding cause some difficulties in analyzing the processes of assessing students' understanding. From our point of view, a theory of conceptual understanding useful for mathematics education should not be limited to saying, for example, that understanding the concept of function was a person's mental experience assigning some object to the term 'function'. A cultural entity, a very complex, not ostensive object is designated with the term 'function'. The problem of understanding is, consequently, closely linked to how the nature of mathematical knowledge is conceived.

National Mathematics Advisory Panel Report (2005), has stated that further investigates for mathematical calculation teaching strategies and provides additional support for the research results. According to those studies, four methods of instruction show the most promise. They were:

Systematic and explicit instruction, a detailed instructional approach in which teachers guide students through a defined instructional sequence. Within systematic and explicit instruction students learn to regularly apply strategies that effective learners use as a fundamental part of mastering concepts.

1. Self-instruction, through which students learn to manage their own learning with specific prompting or solution-oriented questions.
2. Peer tutoring, an approach that involves pairing students together to learn or practice an academic task.
3. Visual representation, which uses manipulative, pictures, number lines, and graphs of functions and relationships to teach mathematical concepts.
4. On that, to make use of this information, an educator would need to know much more about each approach. So let's take a closer look.

Freudenthal, (2003), has stated that flexible, crystallized concept can be mentally manipulated and used for higher level thinking. For instance 2+3x can be part of a more complex expression such as

(2+3x)2–15x(2+3x). The more able faced with the problem of factorization may chunk this sub-expression as a single entity and see the factorization (2+3x–15x)(2+3x) = (2–13x)(2+3x).

Tall & Thomas (2000), has gave an initial meaning can be given to the symbolism which enables it to be manipulated in a coherent way. Initial experiences might therefore concentrate on:

1. Interpreting information and translating it into an appropriate symbolism,
2. Understanding the conventions of mathematics and the choice of symbolism in different contexts,
3. Being able both to give initial meaning to symbols and also eventually to manipulate them in a reutilized and efficient manner. Once procedures have become reutilized, attention can be turned to the more complex actions that cause remedial students difficulties (and which surfaced clearly in the Diagnostic Test).
4. Coordinating two or more processes,
5. Reversing or undoing a process,
6. Coping with singular cases (exceptional ones which seem not to follow the general pattern and so require special treatment). Attention needs to be focused on the important idea that so many symbols, e.g. 2+3, 3x+4y, –3, sine=opposite/hypotenuse, f(x), lim etc, represent both a process of calculation and the result of that calculation:
7. Focusing on the fact that same symbolism represents both the process to get a result and the result itself.
8. Crystallizing processes into concepts (by the simple process of meaningfully using the same notation for both). Knowing that the less able are more likely to want to operate procedurally, the task of focusing on coordinating procedures and manipulating them as concepts needs to be done in contexts where the more powerful methods of operation clearly lead to easier ways of doing the mathematics. Students need to also be aware of.

a. using different representations of the same concept (e.g. graphical, numerical, symbolic),

b. transferring between different representations, to use whichever is easier for a given task.

It cannot be expected that the less able will, by some magical process, be brought to a position where they operate indistinguishably from the more able, desirable though this may be. But, cognizant of the different qualities of thinking processes between those who succeed and those who fail, we hypothesize that a plausible way in which students may become more successful is to become consciously aware of more successful thinking strategies and that this must be done in a context designed to impose less cognitive strain. The implementation of such a remediation strategy is now the subject of ongoing research

Begium Gagné (2000), postulates that there are four phases of learning: the apprehending phase, the acquisition phase, the storage phase and the retrieval phase. This might suggest that the more able can reach these four phases but, for the less able, the last phase may be of a problem. Perhaps the mind of the less able is like a flawed computer diskette. Sometimes, it will respond well to some mathematics problems (usually the easier ones) and it will 'blank out' to more difficult ones.

Steen (2000), was suggested, "...Teachers normally act as if each student's mind is a blank slate - or an empty computer disk - on which effective teachers can record whatever information they like. Research in cognitive science suggests otherwise: each student's mind is more like a computer program than a computer disk. Each student brings to the mathematics classroom a rich set of prior mathematical experiences that provide a unique mental framework in which the student creates new patterns derived from new experiences. Learning occurs not in the act of remembering, but in the gradual development of mental frameworks unique to each individual. In other words, students learn by modifying their mind's program, not by storing new data in their mind's memory".

Gill (1994) in her article indicated that middle school and higher secondary school girls have positive attitudes towards school but negative attitudes towards mathematics. It focussed on the gendering, the separation of boys and girls of Australian schools through the study of 7th, 8th and 10th graders in co-educational programmes as well as girls school only. The results indicated that even when girls are taught in all girls schools, they still have negative attitudes towards mathematics.

Stipek and Granlinski (1991) in their article indicated that girls have lower expectations for themselves in math than boys, and that girls believe they do not have mathematical ability. When girls do poorly in mathematics, they attribute their poor performance to their inability to do mathematics. It is suggested that girls should be encouraged to have higher expectations for them in mathematics.

Jain (1989) designed a study to find out the mathematical interest of four hundred 9th grade students (male and female) from the high/higher secondary schools of rural and urban schools of Bathinda District in relation to their residential background, sex, achievement motivation and academic achievement. Two groups of students on the basis of residential background, sex achievement motivation and academic achievement were formed. It is concluded that the residential background is significantly related to mathematical interest of students. Sex has significant influence on the development of mathematical interest of students. It is concluded that the measures of residential background, sex and achievement motivation are contributing individually but for academic achievement which does not influence the development of mathematical interest of the students.

CONCLUSION

The review of studies conducted in India and abroad in this area helped the investigator to a greater extent in revising some of the procedures involved in this study. On the whole, the literature review was of immense use to the investigator in understanding the problem under study from different angles. The next chapter deals with research methodology.

Chapter - III

Research Methodology

INTRODUCTION

Research methodology involves systematic procedures starting from the initial identification of the problem to its final conclusions. Its role is to carry on the research work in a scientific and valid manner. It provides the tools and techniques by which the research problem is attacked. It consists of procedures and techniques for conducting a study. It is of little value unless used properly. Proper use must be learnt by the researcher. It involves such general activities as identifying problems, review of the literature, formulating hypotheses, procedure for testing hypotheses, measurement, data collection and analysis of data, interpreting results and drawing conclusions. Thus, it consists of all general and specific activities of research. Mastery in it enhances understanding of the research activities. Thus, research design and methodology have the identical meaning of mapping strategy of research.

RESEARCH DESIGN

This chapter presents details regarding the following

1. Selection of Dependent variables and Categorical variables.

2. Construction of tools to measure the ***Error Committed by Mathematics students in Higher Secondary Level.***
3. Methods of establishing the reliability, validity of the tools constructed.
4. Sampling procedure adopted in this study.
5. Scheduling the survey and collecting the data.

STATEMENT OF THE PROBLEM

The aim of mathematical education is surely success for all pupils, yet it seems to be a fact of life that whilst a few prosper in mathematics, a much greater calculation finds mathematics difficult.

It is associated problem, so that the student learners will have the knowledge, skill, attitudes, motivation and commitment to work individually and collectively towards finding the solutions for their learning problems without commit error.

Thus the present investigation has the need to identify "*A Study on the Error Committed by Mathematics Students in Higher Secondary Level at Sivagangai Educational District*".

OBJECTIVES OF THE STUDY

The objective of this present study will gives the detailed analysis of the research on "*A study on the error committed by mathematics students in higher secondary level at Sivagangai Educational District*". The present study will helpful in understanding the Learning difficulties in Calculation and over all Mathematics to be tested.

The Objectives of the study are as follows

1. To find out the significant difference in the Error Committed by Mathematics students in Higher Secondary Level in terms of their **Gender**.
2. To find out the significant difference in the Error Committed by Mathematics students in Higher Secondary Level in terms of their **Locality**.
3. To find out the significant difference in the Error Committed by

Mathematics students in Higher Secondary Level in terms of their **Type of School**.

4. To find out the significant difference in the Error Committed by Mathematics students in Higher Secondary Level in terms of their **Type of School Management**.
5. To find out the significant difference in the Error Committed by Mathematics students in Higher Secondary Level in terms of their **Medium of Instruction**.
6. To find out the significant difference in the Error Committed by Mathematics students in Higher Secondary Level in terms of their **Father's Occupation**.
7. To find out the significant difference in the Error Committed by Mathematics students in Higher Secondary Level in terms of their **Father's Educational Status**.
8. To find out the significant difference in the Error Committed by Mathematics students in Higher Secondary Level in terms of their **Parent's Income**.

HYPOTHESES OF THE STUDY

According to Bruce, 'A hypothesis could be defined as an expectation about event based on generalization of the assumed relationship between variable'.

Hypothesis means subject to the verification and statement about solution of the problem.

The Hypotheses should be framed according to the Variables chosen to find the significance of ***Error committed by mathematics students in higher secondary level at Sivagangai Educational District***.

1. There is no significant difference in the Error Committed by Mathematics students in Higher Secondary Level in terms of their **Gender**.
2. There is no significant difference in the Error Committed by Mathematics students in Higher Secondary Level in terms of their **Locality**.

3. There is no significant difference in the Error Committed by Mathematics students in Higher Secondary Level in terms of their **Type of School**.
4. There is no significant difference in the Error Committed by Mathematics students in Higher Secondary Level in terms of their **Type of School Management**.
5. There is no significant difference in the Error Committed by Mathematics students in Higher Secondary Level in terms of their **Medium of Instruction**.
6. There is no significant difference in the Error Committed by Mathematics students in Higher Secondary Level in terms of their **Father's Occupation**.
7. There is no significant difference in the Error Committed by Mathematics students in Higher Secondary Level in terms of their **Father's Educational Status**.
8. There is no significant difference in the Error Committed by Mathematics students in Higher Secondary Level in terms of their **Parent's Income**.

DELIMITATIONS OF THE STUDY

The error committed in learning Mathematics students at higher secondary stages of education by pupils with different intellectual capacities and interests are very vast and varied. So the present investigation is confined to pupils of Higher Secondary School Level.

The present study is confined only to Three hundred higher secondary school students in Sivagangai District.

1. The present study is limited only Five Schools, Student.
2. The present study Gender, Locality of School, Type of School, Type of school Management, Medium of instruction. Father's occupation, Father's Educational Status, Parents income perceived error committed by mathematics chosen.
3. This study was conducted in the year 2014-2015 only.

RESEARCH METHOD

The investigator preferred "Normative Survey Method" for the present study. In this study, the investigator used survey method to collect data and to identify the *Study on the error committed by mathematics students in higher secondary level at Sivagangai Educational District.*

RESEARCH TOOLS

W. Best observes that the questionnaire is the most important tools in collecting both quantitative and qualities information, for the present study questionnaire was prepared with view to gather information in details regarding on the *Error committed by mathematics students in higher secondary level at Sivagangai Educational District.*

The word 'tool' is defined a means to collect evidence. In the present study the investigator selected questionnaire as tool for the most important collecting data because it is used increasingly to enquire the current conditions, opinions and response of a groups.

CONSTRUCTION OF RESEARCH TOOLS

The research tool on "A study on the error committed by mathematics students in higher secondary level at Sivagangai District" was constructed and standardized by the researcher and also the personal data sheet was constructed by the investigator for this present study. The responded who respond the correct answers were given scores and these score were considered for data analysis.

ADMINISTRATION OF THE RESEARCH TOOL AND SCORING PROCEDURE

Before administering the test necessary instruction and directions were given to the students. No time limit is given to the students were asked to complete the inventory as early as possible. It is a five scale of opinion types of tool with 30 numbers of Questions. Scoring was done as per the scoring scheme. The scores obtained in all questionnaires along with the personal data are consolidated and tabulated on consolidation sheet for the purpose of analysis. Each subject was given a specific number, the concerned with teachers was entered in the specific line.

SAMPLES OF THE STUDY

After finalizing the variables of present study, the Stratified Random Sampling method is used consideration was given to whether the entire population is to be made the subject for data collection or a particular group is to be selected as representative of the whole population. The entire population here refers to all the students studying in higher secondary school at Sivagangai District.

PILOT STUDY

Wiersma (1991), defined a pilot study as A study conducted prior to the major research study that in some way is a small-scale model of the major study conducted for the purpose of gaining additional information by which the major study can be improved for example, an exploratory use of the measurement instrument with a small group for the purpose of refining the instrument.

The pilot study concerned with refining the items collected. The collected items were presented before the expert with a request to offer their considered opinion regarding the suitability objectivity clarity and relevancy of the statement collected from different sources.

The opinion of the experts was taken into consideration. The pilot study is an initial study which is conducted by the investigator to know more about the research problem in various aspects.

Based on the pilot study, the main study was conducted by the investigator while administering the research in the pilot study, some doubts were raised by the school students and the investigator clarified all of their doubts and difficulties.

Based on that, the investigator gave the instructions. Further, the investigator obtained some ideas from the experts and modified the irrelevant Item that is coming in the present study. After getting response from the respondents, the investigator gave frequencies for the correct response and these frequencies were converted into scores and those scores were used to Analysis and interpretation of data.

The pilot study for this present study was conducted in Government Higher Secondary School- Sivagangai with 30 numbers of questions. Before the collection of data instructions were given to the students.

VALIDITY OF THE TOOL

In validation process, the investigator used two measures in order to establish validation of tools. The first measure of validation is called reliability. The second measure of validation process is called validity.

The investigator established content validity. To find out the validity of research tool, the investigator discussed each and every item of the questionnaire with the experts in the relevant of Calculation oriented errors faced by the students in Mathematics among the higher secondary school level. Based on the opinion of the experts, the objectivity and worthiness of the items of the questionnaire were arranged.

RELIABILITY OF THE TOOL

The reliability of questionnaire on indentifying error committed in Learning Calculation in Mathematics among Higher School Students was established by making Split Half method. The reliability of the tool refers to the internal consistency observed in measurement of reliability. And the tool has the sufficient reliability value as **'R'** is equals to **0.88** consistencies.

The reliability test has been calculated by using the *Spearman-Brown formula.*

$$R=\frac{2xr^{oe}}{1+r^{oe}}$$

$$=\frac{2x0.79}{1+0.79}$$

$$R=0.88$$

Such it is conclude the Questionnaire as highly Reliable and the method was employed to evaluate the stability of the measurement.

SAMPLING TECHNIQUE USED

Stratified Random Sampling method was adopted for this purpose.

In this method of sampling every individual in the population has an equal and independent chance of being chosen for the samples.

After finalizing the variables of present study, consideration was given to whether the entire population is to be made the subject for data collection or a particular group is to be selected as representative of the whole population. The entire population here refers to all the under high school students studying in Sivagangai District.

Of the above techniques, the selection of a group as a representative of the whole population was found to be more convenient and suitable. This technique leads to a considerable save of time, effort and finance. The number of students selected will be small and so it is possible to make a detailed and intensive study. This generally leads to more accurate and reliable results. As this sampling technique has many advantages, it was selected for the collection of data.

In any behavioral research, various methods are utilized for selection and drawing of samples. After a detailed study of all these methods and considering the variables selected for the research work, the Stratified Random sampling method was found to be most suitable.

In this method, the entire population will be divided into smaller homogenous groups or strata, and then a sample is selected within each group. Every sampling unit in the population is placed in one of the strata prior to the selection of the sample so that the sum of the strata is identical with the population.

COLLECTION OF DATA

The investigator himself met each and every school students who are studying in various schools located at Sivagangai District. Before going to administer the research tool, the investigator revealed the purpose of the present study to the higher secondary school students and then asked them to give their responses for each and every item that are given in the questionnaire. The responses of the school students were recorded.

Table showing Schools Selected for the Study

S.No.	Schools Selected for the Study	Male	Female	Total
1.	Alagappa Model Higher Secondary School, Karaikudi	43	17	60
2.	Muthukaruppan Visalakshi Government Higher Secondary School, Karaikudi	35	25	60
3.	Government Higher Secondary School, Ariyakudi.	37	23	60
4.	Alagappa Matriculation Higher Secondary School, Karaikudi.	60	-	60
5.	Chittal Achi Memorial Higher Secondary school, Kandanur	30	30	60
6	Total	205	95	300

ANALISIS OF DATA

The term analysis refers to the compilation of certain measures along with searching for pattern and relationship that among groups. For the present study the investigator collected the data from higher secondary school students using the tool developed to find out questionnaire of sample with the ***Error Committed by Mathematics students*** of higher secondary school learners with reference to atmosphere and learning conditions.

This involves computing measures of central tendency like Mean and the measures of variability like Standard deviation. The computed values are used to describe the property of the particular sample and description of data to manageable size.

STATISTICAL TECHNIQUES USED

Statistical Techniques serves the fundamental purpose of the description and inferential analysis. It is concerned with numerical description of a particular group observed. Any similarity to those outside the group cannot be taken for granted.

The data describe one group only. Simple educational research involves descriptive statistics and provides valuable information about the nature of a particular group or class.

Data collected from tests have little meaning or significance until they have been classified or rearranged in a systematic way.

Descriptive statistics were used to describe the sample with reference to the variables taken for the study. In the differential analysis the significant difference between the groups using t – test was done to find out.

The following Statistical Techniques were used in this study.

1. Mean (M)

2. Standard Deviation (S.D.)

3. 't' – test for determine the significance of difference between means of two sub-groups.

ARITHMETIC MEAN

Sometimes it is more convenient to desire mean from a frequency distribution. An additional column may be opened to record the products of frequency distribution. The total of this frequency distribution will be divided by the total (i.e.) N to get mean.

$$M = A + x\ CI$$

Where, A - Assumed mean value

CI - Class Interval

N - Total number of scores

THE STANDARD DEVIATION

Standard deviation most widely used measure of dispersion of a series and is commonly denoted by the symbol sigma standard deviation is defined as the square root of the average of squares of deviations when such deviations for the values of individual items in a series are obtained from the arithmetic average.

$$= \sum fd^2 \text{ - } fd\ ^2 \times Ci$$

N N

= Standard Deviation

$\sum fd^2$ = The Squared Sum of the Scores

$\sum fd$ = The Sum of the Score of the distribution

N = Number of Scores

CI = Class Interval

't'- TEST

The test of significance of the difference between two mean is known as't'- test. It involves the computation of the ratio between experimental variance (observed difference between two sample means) and error variance (the sampling error factor). The t- critical values necessary for rejection of a null hypothesis are higher for the samples of a given level of significances. Each t - critical value for rejection is based upon the appropriate number of degrees of freedom.

N1 = No. of students in first Group

N2 = No. of Students in Second Group

CONCLUSION

In this chapter the methodology of the study was explained clearly. Each and every step was carefully planned and executed. The research strategies and the collection procedures have been explained. The next chapter deals with the analysis and interpretation of data.

Chapter-IV

Analysis and Interpretation of Data

INTRODUCTION

In the general process of analysis of research data, statistical method has contributed a great deal. It finds a place in almost any research study dealing with large or even small groups of individuals. Complex statistical computations form the basis of many types of research.

Statistics is the body of mathematical techniques or processes for gathering, describing, organizing and interpreting numerical data. It is a basic tool of measurement and research. It is concerned with more than the manipulation of data. It goes back to fundamental purposes of analysis.

In order to achieve results from facts gathered through the methods, several techniques are utilized. Analysis is one of them. In order to arrive at results from the collected data, it is necessary to classify it. Analysis is the reduction of data into categories.

ANALYSIS OF DATA

Analysis of data means studying the tabulated materials in orders to determine inherent facts of meanings. It involves the breaking down of the existing complex faders into simple parts and putting them together in a now arrangement for the purpose of interpretation.

According to Berelson "Analysis is a research technique for objective, systematic and quantitative description of the manifest content of communication". Analysis is a technique of social research which presents qualitative data in an objective, systematic and quantitative form.

According to Kaplan, "Analysis attempts to characterize the meaning in a given body to discourse in a systematic and quantitative fashion.

According Barr and Others "Analysis is an important phase of the classification and summation of data into a summary".

According to Wolfe, "The discovery of order in the phenomena of nature, not withstanding their complexity and apparent confusion is rendered possible by the process of analysis and synthesis which are foundation stone of all scientific methods"

After, collecting the data from the respondents, the investigator gave frequencies for the correct responses and these frequencies were converted into scores. The scores were used to identify "*A study on the error committed by mathematics students in higher secondary level at Sivagangai Educational District*".

HYPOTHESES TESTING

Hypothesis means subject to the verification and statement about solution of the problem. According to *Bruce W. Tuckman,* 'A hypothesis could be defined as an expectation about event based on generalization of the assumed relationship between variable'. The Hypothesis of the present study is to find the "A study on the error committed by mathematics in higher secondary level at Sivagangai Educational District". The Hypotheses should be framed according to the Variables chosen to find the errors committed Mathematics among Students.

HYPOTHESIS: 1

THERE IS NO SIGNIFICANT DIFFERENCE IN THE ERROR COMMITTED BY MATHEMATICS STUDENTS IN HIGHER SECONDARY LEVEL IN TERMS OF THEIR **GENDER.**

Table 1

The table shows the 't' value of Error Committed by Mathematics in Higher Secondary Level in terms of their **Gender**.

Gender	N	Mean	S.D.	df	't' value	Level of significance at (0.05)
Male	205	105.38	10.13			
Female	95	109.46	10.89	298	3.086	Significant

INTERPRETATION

The above table shows that the computed 't' value 3.086 is greater than the critical value 1.96 at 0.05 level of significance. It is inferred that there is **significant** difference in the Error Committed by Mathematics in Higher Secondary Level in terms of their **Gender**. And hence the null hypothesis is **rejected**.

HYPOTHESIS: 2

THERE IS NO SIGNIFICANT DIFFERENCE IN THE ERROR COMMITTED BY MATHEMATICS STUDENTS IN HIGHER SECONDARY LEVEL IN TERMS OF THEIR **LOCALITY.**

Table-2

The table shows the 't' value of Error Committed by Mathematics Students in Higher Secondary Level in terms of their **Locality**.

Locality	N	Mean	S.D.	df	't' value	Level of significance at (0.05)
Rural	207	106.67	11.67			
Urban	93	106.54	7.45	298	0.116	Not Significant

INTERPRETATION

The above table shows that the computed 't' value 0.116 is smaller than the critical value 1.96 at 0.05 level of significance. It is inferred that there is **no significant** difference in the Error Committed by Mathematics students in Higher Secondary Level in terms of their **Locality**. And hence, the null hypothesis is **accepted**.

HYPOTHESIS: 3

THERE IS NO SIGNIFICANT DIFFERENCE IN THE ERROR COMMITTED BY MATHEMATICS STUDENTS IN HIGHER SECONDARY LEVEL IN TERMS OF THEIR **TYPE OF SCHOOL.**

Table-3

The table shows the 't' value of Error Committed by Mathematics students in Higher Secondary Level in terms of their **Type of School**.

Type of School	N	Mean	S.D.	df	't' value	Level of significance at (0.05)
Boy's School	100	106.32	7.56	298	0.472	Not Significant
Co-Education School	200	106.85	11.76			

INTERPRETATION

The above table shows that the computed 't' value 0.472 is smaller than the critical value 1.96 at 0.05 level of significance. It is inferred that there is **no significant** difference in the Error Committed by Mathematics students in Higher Secondary Level in terms of their **Type of School**. And hence the null hypothesis is **accepted**.

HYPOTHESIS: 4

THERE IS NO SIGNIFICANT DIFFERENCE IN THE ERROR COMMITTED BY MATHEMATICS STUDENTS IN HIGHER SECONDARY LEVEL IN TERMS OF THEIR **TYPE OF SCHOOL MANAGEMENT.**

Table-4

The table shows the 'F' values of Error Committed by Mathematics students in Higher Secondary Level in terms of their **Type of School Management**.

Source Of Variance	df	SUM OF SQUARES	MEAN SUM OF SQUARES	'F' RATIO
Between Means	(3–1)	391.02	195.51	1.77

	2		
Within Groups	(N - 3) 297	32783.31	110.40
Total	299	33180.33	

INTERPRETATION

The calculated 'F' value **1.77** is smaller than the critical table value of 2.99 at 0.05 level of significance, with the degree of freedom 2 & 297. It is inferred that, there is **no significant** difference in the mean scores of Error Committed by Mathematics students in Higher Secondary Level in terms of their **Type of School Management**. Hence the null hypothesis is **accepted**.

HYPOTHESIS: 5

THERE IS NO SIGNIFICANT DIFFERENCE IN THE ERROR COMMITTED BY MATHEMATICS STUDENTS IN HIGHER SECONDARY LEVEL IN TERMS OF THEIR **MEDIUM OF INSTRUCTION.**

Table-5

The table shows the 't' value of Error Committed by Mathematics students in Higher Secondary Level in terms of their **Medium of Instruction**.

Medium of Instruction	N	Mean	S.D.	df	't' value	Level of significance at (0.05)
Tamil	193	105.48	10.71			
English	107	108.82	9.90	298	2.718	Significant

INTERPRETATION

The above table shows that the computed 't' value 2.718 is greater than the critical value 1.96 at 0.05 level of significance. It is inferred that there is **significant** difference in the Error Committed by Mathematics students in Higher Secondary Level in terms of their **Medium of Instruction**. And hence the null hypothesis is **rejected**.

HYPOTHESIS: 6

THERE IS NO SIGNIFICANT DIFFERENCE IN THE ERROR COMMITTED BY MATHEMATICS STUDENTS IN HIGHER SECONDARY LEVEL IN TERMS OF THEIR **FATHER'S OCCUPATION.**

Table-6

The table shows the 'F' values of Error Committed by Mathematics students in Higher Secondary Level in terms of their **Father's Occupation**.

Source Of Variance	df	SUM OF SQUARES	MEAN SUM OF SQUARES	'F' RATIO
Between Means	(3–1)2	111.86	55.93	
Within Groups	(N - 3) 297	33168.47	111.68	0.50
Total	299	33180.33		

INTERPRETATION

The calculated 'F' value 0.**50** is smaller than the critical table value of 2.99 at 0.05 level of significance, with the degree of freedom 2 & 297. It is inferred that, there is **no significant** difference in the mean scores of Error Committed by Mathematics students in Higher Secondary Level in terms of their **Father's Occupation**. Hence the null hypothesis is **accepted**.

HYPOTHESIS: 7

THERE IS NO SIGNIFICANT DIFFERENCE IN THE ERROR COMMITTED BY MATHEMATICS STUDENTS IN HIGHER SECONDARY LEVEL IN TERMS OF THEIR **FATHER'S EDUCATIONAL STATUS.**

Table-7

The table shows the 't' value of Error Committed by Mathematics students in Higher Secondary Level in terms of their **Father's Educational Status**.

Medium of Instruction	N	Mean	S.D.	df	't' value	Level of significance at (0.05)
Educated	196	107.56	10.27			
Uneducated	104	104.99	10.87	298	1.986	Significant

INTERPRETATION

The above table shows that the computed 't' value 1.986 is greater than the critical value 1.96 at 0.05 level of significance. It is inferred that there is **significant** difference in the Error Committed by Mathematics students in Higher Secondary Level in terms of their **Father's Educational Status**. And hence the null hypothesis is **rejected**.

HYPOTHESIS: 8

THERE IS NO SIGNIFICANT DIFFERENCE IN THE ERROR COMMITTED BY MATHEMATICS STUDENTS IN HIGHER SECONDARY LEVEL IN TERMS OF THEIR **PARENT'S INCOME.**

Table-8

The table shows the 't' value of Error Committed by Mathematics students in Higher Secondary Level in terms of their **Parent's Income**.

Medium of Instruction	N	Mean	S.D.	df	't'	Level of significance at (0.05)
< 15000	99	106.45	7.73			
> 15000	201	106.78	11.69	298	0.291	Not Significant

INTERPRETATION

The above table shows that the computed 't' value 0.291 is smaller than the critical value 1.96 at 0.05 level of significance. It is inferred that there is **no significant** difference in the Error Committed by Mathematics students in Higher Secondary Level in terms of their **Parent's Income**. And hence the null hypothesis is **accepted**.

CONCLUSION

This chapter deals with analysis and interpretation of data and the next chapter has the findings and conclusion of the present study *On The Error Committed By Mathematics Students In Higher Secondary Level At Sivagangai Educational District*".

Chapter - V

Findings and Conclusion

INTRODUCTION

Mathematics is particularly the domains of number and measurement, originated in efforts to quantify the world. Number and measurement, which receive substantial attention in kindergarten through tenth, are foundational for high school mathematics; without problem solving skills in these areas, students will be limited in their reasoning in other areas of mathematics.

Key elements of reasoning and sense making with number and measurement includes.

1. Reasonableness of answers and measurements. Judging whether a given answer or measurement has an appropriate order of magnitude, and whether it is expressed in appropriate units.
2. Approximations and error. Realizing that all real-world measurements are approximations and that unsuitably accurate values should not be used for real-world quantities; recognizing the role of error in subsequent computations with measurements.
3. Number systems. Understanding number-system properties deeply; extending number system properties to algebraic situations.

4. Counting, recognizing when enumeration would be a productive approach to solving a problem, and then using principles and techniques of counting to find a solution.
5. Higher secondary school can monitor equity by paying focused attention to phenomena that pose potential barriers to engaging every student in reasoning and sense making.

NEED AND SIGNIFICANCE OF THE STUDY

The role of Mathematics is very important in our day-to-day life. Avoiding the errors while doing the mathematics and improving the level of underachievers in Mathematics is a must. The investigation is aimed at first identifying the error committed by mathematics in higher secondary level and find out the role of study in determining their achievement.

Learning is possible only by hard work. So a systematic scheme for learning is very essential. The amount of learning of a person depends upon the habit of study of that person. Formation of good study habits is an important aspect of the learning process in mathematics. Pupils should be helped to evaluate critically their own study habits. So, that they may discover weaknesses and try to improve their study efficiency.

In every class, there are three types of students namely.

1. Those who perform very well
2. Those who never perform well
3. Those can perform well; but don't fare well, in Mathematics.

The pupils of the third category may have the general intelligence to do well. But owing to several factors they do not fare well in Mathematics, special attentions will help the pupils of this category to bring out their abilities in full. If third is not, done in schools, the society may have to lose eminent Mathematicians and great Mathematics.

The influence of the teacher on the self – concepts has been studied both with reference to the effect on the self – concepts as well as academic achievement, a student's self concept is a functional limiting a fascinating factor in academic achievement. Therefore it was through fit to analyze error committed by mathematics in higher secondary level students and their influence in achievement levels in school situation.

There is general criticism that the generation of higher secondary school boys and girls in our schools has some problems in doing mathematics. Hence the study focuses to identify the error committed by mathematics students in higher secondary level in Sivagangai Educational District.

STATEMENT OF THE PROBLEM

The aim of mathematical education is surely success for all pupils, yet it seems to be a fact of life that whilst a few prosper in mathematics, a much greater calculation finds mathematics difficult.

It is associated problem, so that the student learners will have the knowledge, skill, attitudes, motivation and commitment to work individually and collectively towards finding the solutions for their learning problems without commit error.

Thus the present investigation has the need to identify *"A study on the error committed by mathematics students in higher secondary level at Sivagangai Educational District"*.

OBJECTIVES OF THE STUDY

The Objectives of the study are as follows;

1. To find out the significant difference in the Error Committed by Mathematics students in Higher Secondary Level in terms of their **Gender**.
2. To find out the significant difference in the Error Committed by Mathematics students in Higher Secondary Level in terms of their **Locality**.
3. To find out the significant difference in the Error Committed by Mathematics students in Higher Secondary Level in terms of their **Type of School**.
4. To find out the significant difference in the Error Committed by Mathematics students in Higher Secondary Level in terms of their **Type of School Management**.

5. To find out the significant difference in the Error Committed by Mathematics students in Higher Secondary Level in terms of their **Medium of Instruction**.
6. To find out the significant difference in the Error Committed by Mathematics students in Higher Secondary Level in terms of their **Father's Occupation**.
7. To find out the significant difference in the Error Committed by Mathematics students in Higher Secondary Level in terms of their **Father's Educational Status**.
8. To find out the significant difference in the Error Committed by Mathematics students in Higher Secondary Level in terms of their **Parent's Income**.

HYPOTHESES OF THE STUDY

The following are the Hypothesis constructed for the present research studies;

1. There is no significant difference in the Error Committed by Mathematics students in Higher Secondary Level in terms of their **Gender**.
2. There is no significant difference in the Error Committed by Mathematics students in Higher Secondary Level in terms of their **Locality**.
3. There is no significant difference in the Error Committed by Mathematics students in Higher Secondary Level in terms of their **Type of School**.
4. There is no significant difference in the Error Committed by Mathematics students in Higher Secondary Level in terms of their **Type of School Management**.
5. There is no significant difference in the Error Committed by Mathematics students in Higher Secondary Level in terms of their **Medium of Instruction**.
6. There is no significant difference in the Error Committed by Mathematics students in Higher Secondary Level in terms of their **Father's Occupation**.

7. There is no significant difference in the Error Committed by Mathematics students in Higher Secondary Level in terms of their **Father's Educational Status**.

8. There is no significant difference in the Error Committed by Mathematics students in Higher Secondary Level in terms of their **Parent's Income**

FINDINGS OF THE STUDY

The following are the findings for the present research studies;

1. There is **significant** difference in the Error Committed by Mathematics students in Higher Secondary Level in terms of their **Gender**. And hence the null hypothesis is **rejected**.

2. There is **no significant** difference in the Error Committed by Mathematics students in Higher Secondary Level in terms of their **Locality**. And hence, the null hypothesis is **accepted**.

3. There is **no significant** difference in the Error Committed by Mathematics students in Higher Secondary Level in terms of their **Type of School**. And hence the null hypothesis is **accepted**.

4. There is **no significant** difference in the mean scores of Error Committed by Mathematics students in Higher Secondary Level in terms of their **Type of School Management**. Hence the null hypothesis is **accepted**.

5. There is **significant** difference in the Error Committed by Mathematics students in Higher Secondary Level in terms of their **Medium of Instruction**. And hence the null hypothesis is **rejected**.

6. There is **no significant** difference in the mean scores of Error Committed by Mathematics students in Higher Secondary Level in terms of their **Father's Occupation**. Hence the null hypothesis is **accepted**.

7. There is **significant** difference in the Error Committed by Mathematics students in Higher Secondary Level in terms of their **Father's Educational Status**. And hence the null hypothesis is **rejected**.

8. There is **no significant** difference in the Error Committed by Mathematics students in Higher Secondary Level in terms of their **Parent's Income**. And hence the null hypothesis is **accepted**.

SUGGESTIONS FOR FURTHER RESEARCH

1. This present study may be taken up the assessment of the Error Committed by Mathematics students in Higher Secondary Level at Sivagangai Educational District in both the medium of instruction. Also this study may be taken up to assess XI student (or) higher school students (or) elementary school students.
2. Comparative studies may be taken up between the high school level state board and matriculation school students in more than are district.
3. Comparative studies may be taken up between the higher secondary school level state board and matriculation school students in more than are district.
4. This study may be taken up at the state level secondary school (or) higher secondary school students to check out their Error Committed by Mathematics students in Higher Secondary Level. This may take to Professionals and publics as Educational Survey.

RECOMMENDATION OF THE STUDY

The continuing development of Error Committed by Mathematics students in Higher Secondary Level should be a priority in the school classroom. The following is a preliminary list of tips for developing these habits.

1. Provide tasks that require students to figure things out for themselves.
2. Ask students to restate the problem in their own words, including any assumptions they have made.
3. Give students time to analyze a problem intuitively, explore the problem further by using models, and then proceed to a more formal approach.
4. Resist the urge to tell students how to solve a problem when they become frustrated; find other ways to support students as they think and work.

5. Provide adequate wait time after a question for students to formulate their own reasoning.
6. Encourage students to ask probing questions of themselves and one another.
7. Expect students to communicate their reasoning to their classmates and the teacher, orally and in writing, through using proper mathematical vocabulary.
8. Highlight exemplary explanations, and have students reflect on what makes them effective.
9. Establish a classroom climate in which students feel comfortable sharing their mathematical arguments and critiquing the arguments of others in a productive manner.

CONCLUSION

This study has focused on students perspectives on the Error Committed by Mathematics students in Higher Secondary Level. The research about difficulties has taken the spotlight within the field of mathematics. Many students struggle with mathematics at various points in their education. Finding ways to pinpoint those areas of weakness can provide with valuable information to provide effective instruction when and how it's needed. Mathematical difficulties represent a broad spectrum of disabilities present in children who struggle with math. Butterworth (2012), suggest that math difficulties stem from slower processing of numerical information, specifically in the areas of estimation and comparison. In the last decade has revealed three main areas that can be used to diagnose and discover learning deficiencies in mathematics calculation estimation, computation and comparison. Tests based on these tasks can be used to quickly pinpoint students who are at risk and intervene with appropriate instructional strategies to prevent or eliminate the learning gap. Provide an understanding of how changes can be made. It suggests three places to intervene to better support students who are in Error Committed by Mathematics students. These concern the type of learning activities that form the lived experiences, the valorizations in the discursive field pervading mathematics education including discourses on difficulties and immigrants and their students and the class room and home environment that interpret as their foreground. The study result obtained was there is **significant** difference in the Error Committed by Mathematics students in Higher Secondary Level in terms of their **Gender, Medium of Instruction** and in terms of their **Father's Educational Status**. And hence the null hypothesis is **rejected**. Also, the research reveals that there is **no significant** difference in the Error Committed by Mathematics students in Higher Secondary Level in terms of their **Locality,** Type **of School, Father's Occupation** and in terms of their **Parent's Income**. And hence the null hypothesis is **accepted**.

BIBLIOGRAPHY

1. Berkas, N., & Pattison, C. (2007, November). Manipulative: More than a special education intervention. *NCTM News Bulletin.* Retrieved March 20, 2008, from the National Council of Teachers of Mathematics.
2. Browder, D. M., Spooner, F., Ahlgrim-Delzell, L., Harris, A., & Wakeman, S. Y., (2008). A meta-analysis on teaching mathematics to students with significant cognitive disabilities. *Exceptional Children, 74*(4), 407-432.
3. Butler, F. M., Miller, S. P., Crehan, K., Babbitt, B., & Pierce, T. (2003). Fraction instruction for students with mathematics disabilities: Comparing two teaching sequences. *Learning Disabilities Research & Practice, 18*(2), 99-111.
4. Fuchs, L. S., & Fuchs, D. (2002). Mathematical problem-solving profiles of students with mathematics disabilities with and without co-morbid reading disabilities. *Journal of Learning Disabilities, 35*(6), 563–573.
5. Garnett, K. (1998). *Math learning disabilities.*
6. Geary, D. C. (2001). *Mathematical disabilities: What we know and don't know.*
7. Geary, D. C. (2004). Mathematics and learning disabilities. *Journal of Learning Disabilities, 37*(1), 4–15.
8. Gersten, R., Ferrini-Mundy, J., Benbow, C., Clements, D., Loveless, T., Williams, V., Arispe, I., & Banfield, M. (2008). *Report*

of the task group on instructional practices (National Mathematics Advisory Panel).

9. Graham, S., Harris, K. R., & Reid, R. (1992). Developing self-regulated learners. *Focus on Exceptional Children, 24*(6), 1-16.

10. Kilpatrick, J., Swafford, J., & Findell, B. (Eds.). (2001). *Adding it up: Helping children learn mathematics.*

11. Kroesbergen, E. H., & Van Luit, J. E. H. (2003). Mathematics interventions for children with special educational needs. *Remedial and Special Education, 24*(2), 97–114.

12. Kunsch, C., Jitendra, A., & Sood, S. (2007). The effects of peer-mediated instruction in mathematics for students with learning problems: A research synthesis. *Learning Disabilities Research & Practice, 22*(1), 1-12.

13. Lee, J., Grigg, W., & Dion, G. (2007). *The nation's report card: Mathematics 2007* (NCES 2007–494).

14. Lenz, B. K., Ellis, E. S., & Scanlon, D. (1996). *Teaching learning strategies to adolescents and adults with learning disabilities.* Austin, TX: Pro-Ed.

15. Maccini, P., & Gagnon, J. (2000). *Mathematics strategy instruction (SI) for middle school students with learning disabilities.*

16. Manalo, E., Bunnell, J. K., & Stillman, J. A. (2000). The use of process mnemonics in teaching students with mathematics learning disabilities. *Learning Disability Quarterly, 23*(2), 137–156.

17. Mazzocco, M. M. M., & Thompson, R. E. (2005). Kindergarten predictors of math learning disability. *Learning Disabilities Research & Practice, 20*(3), 142–145.

18. Montague, M. (2004). *Math problem solving for middle school students with disabilities.*

19. Montague, M. (2007). Self-regulation and mathematics instruction. *Learning Disabilities Research & Practice, 22*(1), 75-83.

20. Morin, V. A., & Miller, S. P. (1998). Teaching multiplication to middle school students with mental retardation. *Education and Treatment of Children, 21*, 22–36.

21. National Commission on Mathematics and Science Teaching for the 21st Century. (2000). *Before it's too late: A report to the nation from the National Commission on Mathematics and Science Teaching for the 21st Century.*

22. National Mathematics Advisory Panel. (2008). *Foundations for success: The final report of the National Mathematics Advisory Panel.*

23. RAND Mathematics Study Panel. (2003). *Mathematical proficiency for all students: Toward a strategic research and development program in mathematics education.*

24. Reid, R. (2006). *Strategy instruction for students with learning disabilities.* New York: Guilford Press.

25. Spear-Swerling, L. (2005). *Components of effective mathematics instruction.*

26. Swanson, H. L. (1999). Instructional components that predict treatment outcomes for students with learning disabilities: Support for a combined strategy and direct instruction model. *Learning Disabilities Research & Practice, 14*(3), 129-140.

27. Swanson, H. L. (2001). Searching for the best model for instructing students with learning disabilities. *Focus on Exceptional Children, 34*(2), 1-15.

28. U.S. Department of Education. (2007). *Twenty-seventh annual report to Congress on the implementation of the Individuals with Disabilities Education Act, 2005.* Retrieved March 20, 2008, from the U.S. Department of Education

29. U.S. Government Accountability Office. (2005, October). *Federal science, technology, engineering, and mathematics programs and related trends* [GAO-06-114].

30. Walker, D. W., & Poteet, J. A. (1989). A comparison of two methods of teaching mathematics story problem-solving with

learning disabled students. *National Forum of Special Education Journal, 1*, 44–51.

31. Witzel, B. S., Mercer, C. D., & Miller, M. D. (2003). Teaching algebra to students with learning difficulties: An investigation of an explicit instruction model. *Learning Disabilities Research & Practice, 18*(2), 121–131.

32. Xin, Y. P., & Jitendra, A. K. (1999). The effect of instruction in solving mathematical word problems for students with learning problems: A meta-analysis. *The Journal of Special Education, 32*(4), 207–225.

5. Problems Faced in Teaching For Disabled Children

Chapter - I

INTRODUCTION

Teacher should make hundreds of decisions every day - decisions about what should be taught, why it should be taught, when it should be taught, how it should be taught, why it should be taught, and to whom it should be taught. Teacher makes decision that affect the learning of individual students and groups of students. Teacher should make decisions that affect students' future learning and academic progress. All of these important decisions will be based on your knowledge, understanding, experience, purposes, values, attitudes, and beliefs.

As the most significant resource in schools, teachers are critical to raise education standards. Improving the efficiency and equity of schooling depends, in large measure, on ensuring that teachers are highly skilled, well resourced, and motivated to perform at their best.

Teaching children with learning disabilities is a big challenge to most parents and teachers. Most people know, or are taught at an early age, how to process information and develop an organized plan or strategy when confronted with a problem. It should not matter whether that problem is social, academic, or job related. Others find

Such cognitive processes quite difficult. Learning disabilities have only recently been recognized as disabilities. This neurological disorder causes difficulty in organizing information received, remembering it, and expressing information, and therefore, affects a person's basic functions such as reading, writing, comprehension, and reasoning. However, children with learning disabilities can be taught effective learning strategies that will help them approach tasks more effectively.

Learning disabilities are professionally diagnosed difficulties with reading, writing, speaking, listening, spelling, reasoning or doing mathematics. People with learning disabilities have trouble taking in information through their senses and processing that information accurately to the brain-Usually they will receive scrambling information like a distorted radio signal or fuzzy television picture.

A child with Learning Disability appears to exhibit emotional problems due to adjustment difficulties resulting from academic failure. Sometimes kids have trouble expressing their feelings, calming themselves down, and reading nonverbal cues, which can lead to difficulty in the classroom and with their peers. Students with undetected learning disabilities might demonstrate undesirable behavior for a variety of reasons.

They might feel angry, sad, lonely, frustrated, or hopeless as a result of focusing on their difficulties. Special needs students are deprived of a suitable education when they are taught at a mismatched level with students how are significantly above their level. Children with learning disabilities may have problems with Academics, social, home and emotional aspects. These problems they may over come through attending special education classes and parental attention. There is a need for special education for children with learning disability and conduct awareness programs regarding learning disability and their common problems.

The conceptual framework for Teacher Education is "The Teacher as a Reflective Responsive Professional - A Partner in Learning."

Teacher education graduates are known for distinctive abilities that reflect the four knowledge bases that compose this conceptual framework: inquiry, partnership, conceptualism, and professionalism.

As Figure 1 indicates, the four elements of the conceptual framework are related and emanate from our common beliefs about learners and the teaching-learning process. They guide the design of program elements, e.g., program outcomes, instructional strategies and activities in courses, and program evaluation. Inquiry, Conceptualism, and Partnership are encircled by the concept of Professionalism.

The conceptual framework assumes that Professionalism is not a plateau but rather a career-long process of reflection and growth, an ongoing process whereby teachers constantly enhance their understanding of how Inquiry, Conceptualism, and Partnership relate to the teaching-learning process. At the very center of the conceptual framework is the learner. CSU teacher education graduates take seriously their role in implementing and adapting the conceptual framework to a variety of instructional environments, urban and suburban, where learner diversity- measured in terms of gender, race, ethnicity, socio-economic status, and exceptionality- is often in high profile. This contextual approach accounts for the unique challenges facing educators today.

Finally the application of inquiry, partnership, and conceptualism builds upon an arts and sciences foundation and occurs within the framework of a career long continuum of professional development, from initial entry or induction into the profession through various stages of career growth, promotion and developed in the four knowledge bases depends on whether a teacher is entering the profession or has achieved the status of a master teacher. The interrelationships of these components will become more evident in the application of the conceptual framework to the program.

Inquiry

Inquiry is a recursive process of teaching and learning that incorporates aspects of constructivism, reflective practice, and a sociocultural perspective. Constructivism may take various forms.

Reflective practice involves teachers who review, reconstruct, reenact, and critically analyze their classroom teaching and learning often through dialogue with colleagues. In addition, reflective teachers become both "consumers and producers of knowledge about teaching — both teachers and students of Classroom life". The sociocultural view of teacher inquiry, as articulated, sees reflection as an individual act set within the larger cultural system of the school and the community beyond. Moreover, as students participate in the inquiry process, they also review, critically analyze, and self-evaluate their learning and become producers of knowledge within the social context of the classroom.

Partnership

The concept of partnership has a dual meaning as a key element in the teacher education conceptual framework. First, it encompasses the notion of individuals working together to learn as students in cooperative and/ or cohort groups, or as students and their teacher(s) learning with and from each other. Second, partnership refers to the notion of individuals, organizations, or social structures collaborating to facilitate and enhance the achievement of learning outcomes. Such partnerships include teachers working with colleagues, parent and community involvement in schools, and business/school and university/ school collaborations.

Conceptualism

Teaching and learning do not occur in isolation. Context as a conceptual framework includes the entire range of influences surrounding and infusing the teaching-learning process. One important context is the individual learner and the background she or he brings to the classroom. It is an acknowledgement that children and adolescents come to the learning situation with prior knowledge and understandings and that the teacher's capacity to build these prior experiences is an essential element in successful teaching. In this connection the idea of diversity is of central significance, particularly in urban settings where issues surrounding race, multiculturalism, socio-economic status, and exceptionality are in higher focus than in the larger society. Then, too, understanding the various contexts of education means understanding multiple ways in which broad historical, social, economic, political, and technological forces shape - for better or worse - educational priorities and policies at the national, state, and local level.

Professionalism

Broadly defined as the distinguishing features of an occupation that generally requires advanced knowledge or training, the concept of professionalism presupposes the existence of a clearly defined knowledge base that has been codified and is, therefore, accessible to guide and support informed decision making and practice. Hence, as manifest in this conceptual framework, professionalism is viewed as an overarching construct which further assumes that teachers can and should assume greater collective responsibility for defining, transmitting, and enforcing standards of professional practice so that their clients or students are well served.

NEED AND SIGNIFICANCE OF THE STUDY

Class studies have been defined as follows: "Studies of actual classes for devising contrivances and improvements in conducting classes." If a class study is viewed along a time axis, a progression from the preparation and review of curriculum guidance plan to conduct a class with class observation followed by holding a discussion at a review meeting after the class seems to be the most common pattern. The objective of class studies is to obtain information for class improvement. The information obtained is fed back to each teacher who participated in the class study. This raises the teacher's skill at guidance and ability to understand the schoolchildren and hence leads to lesson improvement.

If classes are considered a purposeful activity conducted as part of the overall school life, however, the essence of class studies for schoolchildren with intellectual disability is not to obtain information for class improvement but to "provide daily classes and school life better suited to the children.

In education for schoolchildren with intellectual disability, it can be said that the principles of guidance are learning through natural and necessary concrete experience with learning focused on practical and specific activities linked to daily life. To put it plainly, providing daily classes and school life better suited to the children suggests a need to validate whether the classes indeed improve the quality of school life and truly nurture life skills by questioning "whether there is practical and specific activity" and "whether the children are learning through natural and necessary concrete experience.

SCOPE OF THE STUDY

Conventionally, the provision of education and care for children with special educational needs in teacher education has been primarily the responsibility of non-governmental organizations, churches and individuals, sometimes with financial support from private sources and donor agencies. It was not until the 1980s that the Ministry of Education took an active interest in the efforts to reach children with special educational needs.

In the light of new strategies to reach children with special needs. Most of these special schools were residential, providing long term-care. Teacher education argued that these long-term care centers violates the caretaking tradition of the extended Basotho family system. She further showed that the long-term care is expensive, and disrupts family life. It also has the potential of causing emotional and psychological deprivation, resulting in alienation from the child's extended family and ultimately from society. Recommending every effort to undertake the following:

1. Preserve the traditional caretaking, fostering function of the extended family and locate relations to care for orphaned and abandoned children wherever possible.
2. Integrate children with disabilities into regular schools in their own community with special education support, thereby guaranteeing the right of disabled children to grow up with their parents, siblings, and extended families.
3. Change the philosophy and ensuring practice of long-term care to short-term specialized care and education and provide it for children who need it most: the young sensorial deprived children.
4. Formulate a philosophy, policy and guidelines to assist special centers to fit within the overall special education plans of the Ministry of Education. For this purpose channel international

funding and direct it to the areas of the greatest need and prevent inadequate programs to emerge or to continue.

5. Make programs for children with disabilities self-supporting to a large extent to protect them from disintegrating if and when foreign funding is withdrawn.
6. Upgrade teachers already trained, to increase their number and direct their efforts to educate young sensorial handicapped children.
7. Train teachers for the mentally retarded and generalists for special education by bringing in instructors to prepare teachers in these areas.
8. Give assistance to teachers in the regular classroom and to children with disabilities in the regular classroom by providing training to Itinerant Special Education Teams who will provide help and support to both the teacher and the child with special needs.
9. Encourage families to send their children with disabilities to school where special help will be made available.
10. Conduct an information campaign about the needs and problems of the disabled child.
11. Provide teachers and pre-school teachers with in-service training with course work in special education as part of the basic teacher preparation program.
12. Include in the information campaign on behalf of the disabled, information about ways of preventing the risk of disabilities.
13. Conduct immediately a Lesotho National Campaign to Reach Disabled Children.
14. Establish early infant stimulation programs to assist parents to become teachers of their young children.
15. Admit children with disabilities into pre-schools.
16. Facilitate liaison, hasten decision making. For this purpose an inter-ministerial committee should be created consisting of senior Ministry officials in a decision making position.

17. Need to promote the integration of children with special educational needs into regular school system at all levels.
18. In an attempt to implement this policy, the Unit of Special Education developed the following strategies to reach out to children with special needs, their parents, as well as the whole community:
19. Providing special education to all children who need it.
20. Creating awareness to the whole society about children with special needs and the services available.
21. Conducting a study to determine the feasibility of integration as well as to identify children with special educational needs in the regular primary schools.

STATEMENT OF PROLEM

Problem of the present study is as follows: *"Problems Faced In Teaching for Disabled Children in Elementary Schools at Sivagangai Educational District".*

OPERATIONAL DEFINITION OF KEY TERMS USED:

"Problems Faced In Teaching for Disabled Children in Elementary Schools at Sivagangai Educational District."

Problem

Teachers play a role in the classroom problems when they do not make their objectives clear, and when they do not plan their teaching methods earlier. When teachers follow traditional methods in teaching, this leads to students getting bored, and stressed. This triggers the probability of classroom management problems. A teacher who insists on a classroom full of activity, and quietness' by keeping the students busy, working all the time without any break or any changes in the activities, lead to humiliation working and activity for the students will make the probability of classroom problems due to classroom discipline.

Special education teachers have a higher rate of burnout than is found in most other professions. The burnout rate is the result of a number of issues that often culminate in these teachers leaving their jobs. It is estimated that 75 percent of those who teach special needs students will leave their job within 10 years of starting. The result of this turnover rate is a shortage of special education teachers and a lack of quality programs for the students they serve. While a special education teacher may start their career with the intention of helping disabled students become productive members of society, they face several challenges that make the task extremely difficult. The challenges of the special education teacher include:

The Widespread Misperception That Teaching is Easy: Teaching is a uniquely difficult job, one that comes with a set of huge responsibilities; however, many people fail to recognize the teacher's role. The various disabilities of the students with whom special education teachers work multiplies the job's difficulty. Special education teachers are largely unrecognized and unsupported by the public.

Non-Instructional Responsibilities: Many teachers are trained and willing to teach but find themselves burdened with responsibilities that remove them from the classroom. Special education teachers often find themselves being required to go to meetings, conducting assessments and dealing with loads of paperwork.

Lack of Support: At a time when many large school districts are experiencing high levels of growth, special education teachers are being asked to do more with less. Salaries are being cut in many districts, and there is often very little in the way of technical assistance provided by school administrations.

Dealing with Multiple Disabilities: A special education teacher's classes may have students with various disabilities. Since each student is a unique case, the teacher must modify their lessons to suit each disabled learner by providing individualized education programs.

Handling the Problems of an Inclusive Classroom: The concept of having classrooms that contain both special needs students and students who are developing typically is becoming a popular one. This type of education poses new challenges for a special education teacher. For example, many students who have no disabilities are unaccustomed to dealing with those who do. Teachers in these classes are charged with eliminating cruelty and insensitivity from among their students and ensuring that those with special needs are treated with respect.

Professional Isolation*:* The nature of a special education teacher's work is very different from that of traditional teachers; the result of this is that standard classroom teachers may not view them as colleagues. There may be a professional stigma attached to the work of teaching "slow" students. Special education teachers often work with smaller groups and may focus on skills rather than content, thereby leading to the perception that their work is easier or less important.

Lack of Support From Parents*:* Some parents of special needs children are disinterested in the welfare of their children and fail to provide them with adequate care. Alternatively, they may be overly protective. Both can be problematic for the child and for their teacher. Disinterested parents may have no involvement with their child's education or interaction with their teachers, whereas overprotective parents may have unrealistic expectations from the child and the child's teachers. Both attitudes can shape children in negative ways. Parental disinterest may make special needs students less motivated and parents who are overprotective often diminish their child's confidence and make it harder for them to learn.

The Difficulty of Discipline in a Special Needs Classroom: Disabled children may have behavioral issues including restlessness and moodiness. They may also exhibit problems like a short attention span or an inability to understand what is being taught. Special education teachers have to learn how to deal with these problems as well as how to take appropriate disciplinary measures.

Budget Problems: Across the nation, special education programs are facing increasing enrollment and decreasing budgets. The result is that there are fewer teacher assistants available, which results in a greater workload for special education teachers.

Any one of these challenges would make the work of a special education teacher incredibly difficult; as a group, they turn the job into a set of arduous tasks. Unfortunately, the result of the pressures placed on teachers is that the students suffer. Anyone seeking to go into this area of teaching should be aware of what they will face and have the mental and emotional fortitude to overcome the challenges in order to improve the prospects of their students.

Children"Children with disabilities" or "students with disabilities" means children or students who require special education because of: autism; communication disorders; deaf blindness; emotional disturbances; hearing impairments, including deafness; intellectual disability; orthopedic impairments; other health impairments; specific learning disabilities; traumatic brain injuries; or visual impairments, including blindness.

Autism" means a developmental disability significantly affecting verbal and nonverbal communication and social interaction that adversely affects a child's educational performance. Other characteristics that may be associated with autism are engagement in repetitive activities and stereotyped movements, resistance to environmental change or change in daily routines, and unusual responses to sensory experiences. Essential features are typically but not necessarily manifested before age three. Autism may include autism spectrum disorders such as but not limited to autistic disorder, pervasive developmental disorder, not otherwise specified, and Asperger's syndrome. The term does not apply if a child's educational performance is adversely affected primarily because the child has an emotional disturbance. However, a child who qualifies for special education under the category of autism may also have an emotional disturbance as a secondary disability if the child meets the criteria under emotional disturbance.

Communication Disorder" means the impairment of speech articulation, voice, fluency, or the impairment or deviant development of language comprehension and/or expression, or the impairment of the use of a spoken or other symbol system that adversely affects educational performance. The language impairment may be manifested by one or more of the following components of language: morphology, syntax, semantics, phonology, and pragmatics.

"Deaf blindness" means having both hearing and visual impairments, the combination of which causes such severe communication and other developmental and educational problems that the child cannot be accommodated in special education programs designed solely for students having hearing or visual impairments

"Emotional Disturbance" means a condition exhibiting one or more of the following characteristics over a long period of time and to a marked degree that adversely affects a child's educational performance:

1. An inability to learn that cannot be explained by intellectual, sensory, or health factors;
2. An inability to build or maintain satisfactory interpersonal relationships with peers and teachers;
3. Inappropriate types of behavior or feelings under normal circumstances;
4. A general pervasive mood of unhappiness or depression; or
5. A tendency to develop physical symptoms or fears associated with personal or school problems;
6. The term includes schizophrenia but does not apply to children who are socially maladjusted, unless it is determined that they have an emotional disturbance.

"Hearing Impairment" means a hearing condition, whether permanent or fluctuating, that adversely affects a child's educational performance. The term includes those children who are hard of hearing or deaf.

"Intellectual Disability" means significantly sub average general intellectual functioning, and includes a student whose intelligence test score is two or more standard deviations below the norm on a standardized individual intelligence test, existing concurrently with deficits in adaptive behavior and manifested during the developmental period, and that adversely affects a child's educational performance.

"Orthopedic Impairment" means a motor disability that adversely affects the child's educational performance. The term includes impairments caused by an anomaly, disease or other conditions (e.g., cerebral palsy, spinal bifida, muscular dystrophy or traumatic injury).

"Other Health Impairment" means limited strength, vitality, or alertness, including a heightened alertness to environmental stimuli that results in limited alertness with respect to the educational environment, that:

1. Is due to chronic or acute health problems (e.g. a heart condition, tuberculosis, rheumatic fever, nephritis, asthma, sickle cell anemia, hemophilia, epilepsy, lead poisoning, attention deficit disorder, attention deficit hyperactivity disorder, leukemia, Tourette's syndrome or diabetes); and
2. Adversely affects a child's educational performance.

"Specific Learning Disability" means a disorder in one or more of the basic psychological processes involved in understanding or in using language, spoken or written, which may manifest itself in an imperfect ability to listen, think, speak, read, write, spell or do mathematical calculations. Specific learning disability includes conditions such as perceptual disabilities, brain injury, dyslexia, minimal brain dysfunction, and developmental aphasia. The term does not include learning problems that are primarily the result of visual, hearing, or motor disabilities, intellectual disability, emotional disturbance, or environmental, cultural, or economic disadvantage.

Traumatic Brain Injury" means an acquired injury to the brain caused by an external physical force resulting in total or partial functional disability or psychosocial impairment, or both, that adversely affects a child's educational performance. The term includes open or closed head injuries resulting in impairments in one or more areas, including cognition; language; memory; attention; reasoning; abstract thinking; judgment; problem-solving; sensory, perceptual, and motor abilities; psychosocial behavior; physical functions; information processing; and speech. The term does not include brain injuries that are congenital or degenerative, or brain injuries induced by birth trauma.

"Visual Impairment" means a visual impairment that, even with correction, adversely affects a child's educational performance. The term includes those children who are partially sighted or blind.

Teaching for Disabled Children Learning disability is a classification that includes several areas of functioning in which a person has difficulty learning in a typical manner, usually caused by an unknown factor or factors. While learning disability, learning disorder and learning difficulty are often used interchangeably, they differ in many ways. Disorder refers to significant learning problems in an academic area. These problems, however, are not enough to warrant an official diagnosis. Learning disability on the other hand, is an official clinical diagnosis, whereby the individual meets certain criteria, as determined by a professional (psychologist, pediatrician etc.). The difference is in degree, frequency, and intensity of reported symptoms and problems, and thus the two should not be confused. When the term "learning disorder" is used, it describes a group of disorders characterized by inadequate development of specific academic, language, and speech skills.

The impairments are generally life-long. However, their effects may be expressed differently over time, depending on the match between the demands of the environment and the individual's characteristics. Some impairment may be noted during the pre-school years, while others may not become evident until much later. During the school years, learning disabilities are suggested by unexpectedly low academic achievement or achievement that is sustainable only by extremely high levels of effort and support.

Learning disabilities are due to genetic, other congenital and/or acquired neuro-biological factors. They are not caused by factors such as cultural or language differences, inadequate or inappropriate instruction, socio-economic status or lack of motivation, although any one of these and other factors may compound the impact of learning disabilities. Frequently learning disabilities co-exist with other conditions, including attentional, behavioral and emotional disorders, sensory impairments or other medical conditions.

Elementary School

SSA is the major time bound intervention for Universalization of Elementary Education in India being implemented from 2001 onwards on a mission mode with Central and State Government funding. Since SSA framework stresses the micro level planning and also gives much importance of the quality of data, large child population data base and school data base have been created in

Tamilnadu. Since NUPEA has been entrusted to create and update the school database at National level it has initiated PES on DISE data to improve the quality of school database.

OBJECTIVES OF THE STUDY

The present study has the following objectives,

6. To find out the difference between the mean score of **Male and Female** teachers in respect of a study on basis of problems faced in teaching disabled children in Elementary Schools.
7. To find out the difference between the mean score of **Rural and Urban** area in respect of a study on basis of problem faced in teaching disabled children in Elementary Schools.
8. To find out the difference between the mean score of **Government and Private** school in respect of a study on basis of problems faced in teaching disabled children in Elementary Schools.
9. To find out the difference between the mean score of **B.Ed., and D.TEd** in respect of a study on basis of problem faced in teaching disabled children in Elementary Schools.
10. To find out the difference between the mean score of **Tamil and English** medium in respect of a study on basis of problem faced in teaching disabled children in Elementary Schools.
11. To find out the difference between the mean score of **Trained and Untrained** teachers area in respect of a study on basis of problems faced in teaching disabled children in Elementary Schools.

HYPOTHESES OF THE STUDY

1. There is significant difference between the mean scores of **Male and Female** teachers in respect of a study on basis of problems faced in teaching disabled children in Elementary Schools.
2. There is significant difference between the mean scores of **Rural and Urban** area teachers in respect of a study on basis of problems faced in teaching disabled children in Elementary Schools.
3. There is a significant difference between the mean scores of **Government and Private** school teachers in respect of a study

on basis of problems faced in teaching disabled children in Elementary Schools.

4. There is a significant difference between the mean scores of **B.Ed., and DT.Ed** qualified teachers in respect of a study on basis of problems faced in teaching disabled children in Elementary Schools.
5. There is a significant difference between the mean scores of **Tamil and English** medium school teachers in respect of a study on basis of problems faced in teaching disabled children in Elementary Schools.
6. There is a significant difference between the mean scores of **trained** teachers in Special Education and **Untrained** teachers in Special Education in respect of a study on basis of problems faced in teaching disabled children in Elementary Schools.

LIMITATIONS OF THE STUDY

This study is limited to the Elementary Teachers in Sivagangai District. Teachers is 1 to 5th standard have been taken for the present study. Only 250 samples have been taken for this research.

CONCLUSION

The problems in the classroom, and schools in general, are considered one of the most serious factors facing the component of the educational process, such as parents, teachers, educational administrators, and supervisors, also vandalism, theft, destruction of property, failure in the school, poor study accomplishment, lack of educational facilities such as equipment and technology, the physical environment, and the violence against teachers and students. All these issues could threaten the whole educational process. The results of this study show that the level of the classroom problems of the Educational District of Sivagangai province was medium, from the teachers point of view, there was no statistically significant difference, in the academic problems domain, while there was a statistically significant difference, in the behavioral problems, due to the interaction variables, Gender, Locality, Type of school, Teachers qualification, Medium of instruction and Trained teachers.

Chapter - II

Review of Related Literature

INTRODUCTION

Review of literature is an essential aspect of investigations related to the research study. Related literature acts as the backbone for researcher. Most research work involves substantial use of published literature, indeed the ability to ferret out obscure facts is often seen as the primary activity of the researcher and the regulations for research degrees always contain a requirement that the candidate should demonstrate the ability to make proper critical use of relevant literature.

PURPOSE/IMPORTANCE / SIGNIFICANCE OF LITERATURE REVIEW

For any worthwhile study in any field of knowledge, the research worker needs an adequate familiarity with the work, which has already been done in the area of his choice. "The survey of related studies implies locating, studying and evaluating reports of relevant researches." In the review of literature, previous research studies are abstracted and significant writing of authorities in the area under study is reviewed.

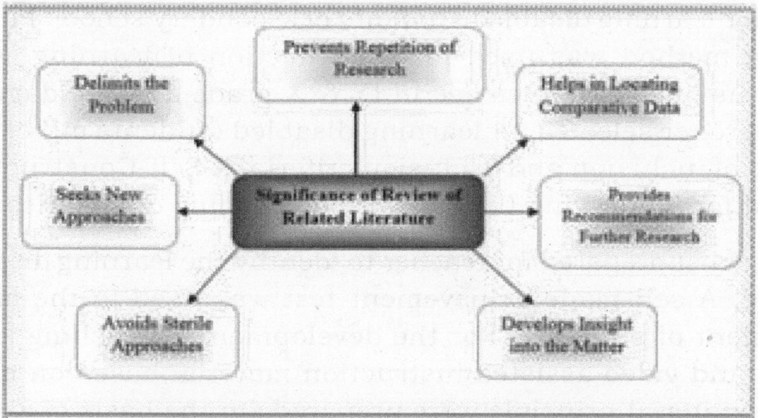

Fig. 2.1 Significance of Review of Related Literature

The term 'Learning Disabilities (LDs)' emerged from a need to identify and serve learning disabled children. The term learning disability was first coined by Samual Kirk in 1963 to describe children who have serious problems in schools but do not fall under other categories of handicap. The researcher has presented an exhaustive survey of researches with regard to learning disability and instructional material. The chapter in hand endeavors to review studies conducted by earlier researchers to give insight into the concept of learning disabilities. This has also helped in identifying the factors influencing it. The present chapter has been organized under the following under the following heads:

1. Studies Conducted in Indian
2. Studies Conducted Abroad

STUDIES CONDUCTED IN INDIA

The various research studies conducted in relation to learning disabilities in Indian conditions are presented as follows:

RANI and **KAPOOR** (2012) conducted a study on development of teaching learning material for Home Science students with learning disabilities. The objectives of the study are: (i) to identify learning disabled students in secondary school (ii) to study the achievement of learning disabled in Home Science. (ii) to develop teaching learning material in Home Science for learning disabled students of secondary school (iv) to evaluate the efficacy of developed material in Home

Science for learning disabled students of secondary school. Purposive sampling method was used for the selection of learning disabled children having Home Science in IX & X grade at secondary stage. The researcher selected 14 learning disabled students out of 300 on the basis of inclusion and exclusion criteria. A Self-Constructed tool was used for identifying the category of learning disabilities.

A checklist prepared for teacher to identify the learning disabilities was used. A self-made achievement test was used to the measure achievement of students. For the development of teaching learning material and video assisted instruction material based on program learning material principle were prepared On the basis of exclusion and inclusion criteria of tool 14 students were selected as sample (Students scoring below 50% on diagnostic test of learning disability and students scoring above 50% on learning problem checklist). Very few students get score in between 1 to 14 marks and no students can get above score. It further reveals that these students have no more knowledge in Home Science and they have deficiency to receive information, remembering them and also difficulty in organizing the information therefore there are need to teaching strategy and teaching learning material used by the teacher in the classroom.

After administering the teaching learning material based on program learning, score of student in Home Science achievement test was increased in reference to pre and posttest with 27 and 94 respectively. Mean value of pre score test is 1.92 which increased in post score with 6.71. The t-test value of pre score and post score of achievement of LD students in Home Science was found 5.5. T test value was found significant at 0.01 levels i.e. 3.01 and at 0.05 level i.e.2.16 which shows highly significant difference between Pre and Post score of achievement test of LD students.

TIGA and **KAPOOR** (2011) conducted a study on development of a package to enhance competence of learning disabled children. The objectives of the study are (i) to identify children with learning disability in regular schools. (ii) To identify competence among children with learning disability in regular schools. (iii) To design and develop a package for LD children in regular schools. (iv) To find the effectiveness of package in increasing competence among children with learning disability. The sample consisted of 23 learning disabled children from of 5th grade from two school affiliated to U.P. board. Tools were learning disabled identification

Scale (self-constructed) and children's competence scale (self-constructed) were used. Findings of the study are (i) 66 % of the total children have low competence, 30% children have normal competence and 4% children have high competence. (ii) Contents of the package were selected on the basis of needs of learning disabled children and contents of the package were effectively presented in the form of booklets and folders. (iii) After introducing the package, percentage of LD children in high competence categories increased by 4% to 21%, in normal competence categories % of LD children increased by 30% to 39% and in low competence categories % of LD children decreased by 60% to 43%. (iv) Mean value of pre score and post scores of competence of LD children was found to be 3.14 which is significant at 0.01 and shows that there is significant difference between pre and post scores of LD.

The result shows that learning disabled children have low level of competence in comparison to non LD children and they need special assistance to 50 enhance competence. It further reveals that effective package can enhance the competence of the learning disabled children.

TIGA and **VASHISHTHA** (2010) examined the study on social competence as a determinant of self– concept and social anxiety of learning disabled and non-learning disabled adolescents. The objectives of the study are: (i) to study the social competence of learning disabled and non-learning disabled adolescents. (ii) to study the self-concept of learning disabled and non-learning disabled adolescents. (iii) to study the social anxiety of learning disabled and non-learning adolescents. (iv) to study the international effect of self-concept and social anxiety on social competence of learning disabled and non-learning disabled adolescents. Fifty learning disabled adolescents were identified through self-made questionnaire and selected from class IX and X from the selected schools of Agra city.

The findings show that: (i) the CR value of social competence scores of LDA and NLDA groups was found 9.4. CR which is significant at 0.01 level shows that there is significant differences between social competence of leaning disabled adolescents and non-learning disabled students. (ii) CR value of self-concept score obtained in two groups i.e. LDA and NLDA groups was found to be 11.4 which was significant at 0.01 level showing that and non-learning disabled adolescents. (iii) CR value of social anxiety scores of LDA and NLDA groups was found 11.0 which show that there was a significant difference between social anxiety of learning disabled and non-learning disabled adolescents. (iv) the coefficients of multiple determination between the scores of social competence, self-concept and social anxiety of learning disabled adolescents and non-learning disabled adolescents were 0.8 (positive very high correlation) and 0.5 (positive moderate correlation) respectively. These values show significant relationship between self-concept and social anxiety with social competence of learning disabled and non-learning disabled students.

The conclusion of the study is that learning disabled group had low level of social competence in comparison to non-learning disabled adolescents group. Learning disabled group had poor self-concept in comparison to the non-learning disabled adolescent group. Learning disabled adolescents group had higher level of social anxiety than the non-learning disabled group. Social competence depends on self-concept and social anxiety among the groups (learning disabled adolescents and non-learning disabled adolescents). Self-concept and social anxiety are highly correlated in learning disabled adolescents in comparison to non-learning disabled adolescents.

AMRUTH and **DEVIKA** (2009) examined effect of school remediation program on the academic achievement of student with disabilities. The participants of this study were student with disabilities enrolled in one middle school during 2007-2008 school years. This study attempted to determine if a relationship existed between the independent variable, attendance in an after school remediation program and the dependent variable, the achievement test scores earned on the reading and the program. The finding of this research study indicated that program participants demonstrated positive response.

PUSPALATA (2008) conducted a study of relationship between competence and social anxiety of LD children. The study was conducted on a sample of 100 children in the age group of 10-14 years were selected randomly from two schools. Study shows that learning disabled children has low academic competence and higher social anxiety. Result indicates that learning disabled children have low academic competence and is directly related to their social anxiety.

RANI and **VASHISHTHA** (2008) conducted a study on determinants of certain measures of learning disabilities. The objectives of the study are: (i) to develop the tool for identification of learning disabled children in elementary school. (ii) To identify the learning disabled children in elementary school. (iii) To determine Rorschachian measures diagnosing learning disabled children in elementary school. (iv) To evolve Rorschachian measures – based diagnostic model for learning disabilities. The following tools were used: Self constructed tool for measuring learning disabilities and Rorschachian ink blot test. The sample was taken from four school affiliated to C.B.S.E. Board, Delhi. The sample consisted of 50 children (both boys and girls) from 4 - 6 grades. The self-constructed test entitled as 3D-test, related to three areas of learning disabilities dyslexia, dyscalculia and dysgraphia was employed for identification of learning disability. The findings showed that a comparison could be made between learning disabled and non-disabled children in order to discriminatory power of tool. Further it revealed that both groups had distinct features on reading and arithmetic test but it could not be confirmed in relation to language test. Learning disabled children had extroversive tendencies. By psychodramas it was found that learning disabled children had extroversive tendencies.

They are highly responsive to their environment. They are creative in their relationship to objects and people external to them and strive toward goals that have staked out in the external world.

KIRA (2005) conducted a study on race, gender and disability in today's children's literature. Growth in immigration rising birth rates among Hispanic women and yearly increases in the number of disabled students mainstreamed into general classrooms have changed elementary and secondary school classrooms from "homogeneous" to "diverse" settings.

LALL (2001) conducted a study on perceived relations social competence in children with specific disorder of scholastic skills.

This study aimed at examining perceived peer relations and social competence in children with specific development disorders of scholastic skills. A sample of twenty children with specific development disorders of scholastic skills. A sample of twenty children with disorders of scholastic skill aged, seven to twelve years and twenty controls matched on age, class and IQ were taken. The two group were assessed on (i) A semi -structure interview schedule (ii) Malian's intelligence scale for Indian children (MISK) (iii) NIMHANS Index for specific learning disabilities (iv) perceived peer relations questionnaire (v) Interpersonal competence scale – teachers version. Results revealed that children with scholastic skill disorder perceived their relationship with peers as cordial. However teacher found these children as poorer in social competence and in dimensions of academics popularly affiliation and sportsmanship qualities.

PANDIT (2000) conducted a study on factors affecting learning disabilities in mathematics in central region of Nepal. There is a sample of 100 students for conducting the study. 32 students were found to have factors affecting learning disabilities in mathematics in central region of Nepal. The study concluded that the factors related to the children with learning disabilities in mathematics were the poor instruction, parents' adverse behavior to them, and teacher's negligence in the class. It was suggested that the quality of teaching strategies and quality of instruction in the schools must be improved.

BHATTACHARYA (1985). Conducted a study on the alleviation of learning disabilities of the students in life science. There is a tried out technological approach for alleviation of learning disabilities of the students in life science. The sample consisted of 24 students in life sciences. Results of the study indicated that learning through audio-visual materials and techniques caused prolonged retention than by traditional methods.

BHATTACHARYA (1982) conducted a study on Diagnosing and preventing learning disabilities of primary school students in Arithmetic. To diagnose and prevent learning disabilities in arithmetic of primary school. There are 40 samples of students having learning difficulties in reference to mathematics of 10 primary schools. It was found that learning through audio-visual methods caused prolonged retention than traditional methods.

Singh (1981) studied this problem by investigating the effects of peer tutoring in Mathematics skills of learning disabled students. The major question the study attempted to answer was whether the learning disabled who received peer-tutoring made significant gains in Mathematics computation and in the application of Mathematics concepts over the learning disabled pupils who did not receive peer tutoring. Results indicated that peer- tutored group of LD students made significant gains in both Mathematics computation and Mathematics concepts application scores over the non-peer tutored students.

STUDIES CONDUCTED IN AROAD

The various research studies conducted in relation to learning disabilities abroad are as follows:

ANETTE (2010). Conducted a study on learning difficulties and academic competence among children with and without learning disabilities. The aim of this study was to examine learning difficulties as well as academic competence. The sample consisted of 30 learning disabled children. These children were examined for the learning difficulties and academic competence and experimental study was carried out. Result was interpreted as indicating that children with learning disabilities have low academic competence and need special assistance.

SARA(2010) examined promoting social and academic competence in the classroom: An intervention study examining the contribution of the Responsive Classroom approach. Participants included 62 teachers and 157 children at six schools. This exploratory study examined the contribution of the RC Approach over a two-year period. The RC Approach integrates social and academic learning in order to produce classroom environments that are conducive to learning by integrating social and academic learning. Two questions are addressed. First, how does teacher use of RC practices contribute to children's academic and social growth? Second, how is the relation between teachers' use of RC practices and children's academic and social growth moderated by the presence of environmental adversity in the home? Findings showed that teachers' use of RC practices was associated with students' improved reading achievement, greater closeness between teachers and children, better pro-social skills, more assertiveness, and less fearfulness, even after controlling for family risk and children's previous years' performance. Family risk did not moderate the relation between RC practices and children's performance. These findings suggest to the positive contribution of the RC Approach in relation to children's gains over a one year period.

RAY (2008) conducted a study on evaluate the efficiency of the development algebraic literacy Model: Pre passing special educator to implement effective mathematics practices. For student with learning disabilities using a mixed method design the current researcher investigated the usage of the developing Algebraic literacy frame work multiple survey measure were given at pre- mid and post junctures to asses teacher candidates attitudes about mathematics, sealing of efficacy when teaching mathematics and content knowledge surrounding mathematics. Result indicated an increase in perseveres teacher's attitude towards mathematics instruction. Thus study provides preliminary support for utilizing the DAL instruction framework for future special educators.

RUSSELL (2007) presents results of a meta-analysis on writing interventions for students with learning disabilities and draw implications for practice. 13 studies designed to teach students with learning disabilities to write better expository or narrative text were analyzed. Results indicated that the interventions used in the research studies constantly produced strong effects on the quality of student's writing as well as student's sense of efficacy and understanding of the writing process. Findings suggested that 3 components should be part of any comprehensive instructional program. Explicit teaching of (a) the steps of the writing process, (b) the critical dimensions of different writing genres should be provided, as well as (c) structures for giving extensive feedback to students on the quality of their writing from either teachers or peers.

MADISON (2006) presented grounded theory and he aimed at understanding how members of learning disabilities (LD) teams in 9 Saudi study public elementary schools perceived and made sense of students with LD and the context that surrounded the identification process. The data were gathered through semi structured interviews with 13 LD teachers, 10 regular classroom teachers, 9 school counsellors, 6 school principals, and 3 parents. The theory developed in the study revealed that since the information of LD category into Saudi Schools in 1996, there has been conflict over the identity of children experiencing learning difficulties in Saudi School, between on one hand, the official LD discourse created by scientists and policymakers and on the other the local commensurate social discourse created by people in everyday life in Saudi Society. Data indicates that the point at which the two discourses tend to diverge sharply include the notion that: (a) children with LD have disability (b) the cause of children slow achievement lies within children due to neurological damage, and that LD is a life-long phenomenon.

By labelling otherwise normal children's as disabled, the LD discourse raised complex dilemmas at the community level as well as at the individual level, where disability labels have the potential to impact a child's identity and self –worth in negative ways. In response, participants coped with the new LD category by dismissing, de-emphasizing or resisting the unfamiliar, aspects of LD, which in turn affected the identification of students with LD. The identification process –via referrals, evaluation, eligibility and remediation is seen as regular occurrence intended to identify students who need extra help or services rather a process that classifies children into a category of disability. The decision –making atmosphere and the diagnosis of a child as LD generally were regarded as unproblematic. As inclusive placements become an increasingly for students with learning disabilities the need to assist general educators in establishing inclusive classrooms becomes a major priority. Is logical terms, to prioritize the propagation of inclusive practices in general education classroom – practices that would take into account the natural diversity of student populations likely to be present in American Classrooms. Cooperative learning, in the form literature circles, it offered in this study as a highly effective method for laying the groundwork for inclusion. This study rooted in the theory of anchored instruction, attempted to address the need for incorporating inclusive practices by investigating the potential for students with learning disabilities to implement literature circles by viewing video models.

DIMITRIOS (2006). A study on Academic Intrinsic Motivation and Perceived Academic Competence in Greek Elementary Students with and without learning disabilities. The aim of this study was to examine difference in intrinsic motivation and perceived academic competence as well as in their association between 5th and 6th grade students with learning disabilities. The sample consisted of 40 learning disabilities out from 980 Greek elementary students from the metropolitan area of Athens. As predicted, students with LD showed lower intrinsic motivation and perceived academic competence than students without LD almost across all subscales. Exceptions were noticed in intrinsic motivation concerning curiosity/ interest and history subscales as well as perceptions of academic competence in the subjects of history and science. The result was found that among typically achieving students intrinsic motivation was positively and significantly related at a moderate level to perceived academic competence across all subscales, as opposed to students with LD for whom few correlations were found.

FONTENOT (2005) examined the attitudes of rural, suburban and urban public elementary school principals in Texas regarding the inclusion of students with disabilities into the general education classrooms. A three point questionnaire, the “Modified Principles” and inclusion survey, was sent to 733 randomly selected principals, requesting information that could be used to evaluate attitudes toward inclusion of students into the general education classroom setting. There was no significant correlation found between age and attitudes, nor gender and attitudes of principals toward inclusion of students with disabilities. Although a negative correlation was found between full time regular educations teaching experiences in regard to the attitude score of principles toward inclusion of students with disabilities. Neither general education teaching experience nor special education teaching experience was significantly correlated with attitude.

CHRUSTENON (2004) conducted a study to examine the process special education services under the learning disabilities category of particular interest. Qualitative methods were used in the investigation. Three school districts of similar size but very different student demographic compositions were selected as research sites. The results of the investigation indicate that teams generally make an effort to look into exclusivity factors, how this is accomplished often depends on the influential members of the team, particularly the school psychologist.

Differences in student population with regard to demographic characteristics greatly impact the resources at a district's disposal. This in turn, impacts the role special education plays as a resource for addressing academic needs in minority and low income populations. Special education services under the learning disabilities category of particular interest were the exclusionary factors of cultural, environmental and economic deficits, and the role they play with regard to referral, assessment and placement decision making.

BAYER (2003) conducted a study on a descriptive study of teaching strategies used by general education teacher in classroom including student with mild learning disabilities. This study focused on teaching strategies and methodologies successful in general education teacher in grade four through six used in teaching mathematics within an inclusive setting. This study also focused on the rational of how teacher ensure that special education has the opportunity to engage in successful learning experience during mathematics instruction by using ongoing and continuous assessment. The study included how student with learning disabilities benefited from an inclusive setting and how teachers' choice of specific instruction strategies were based on individual student needs. The result can offer assistance to teacher who a restruggling to implement such strategies.

MOCK (2003) conducted a study on identifying students with learning disabilities. The Individuals with Disabilities Education Act is to be reauthorized late in 2003. Thus, adopting the problem solving model assumes the superiority of clinical judgement over statistical judgement in identifying students with learning disabilities. Research comparing statistical and clinical prediction has yielded relatively consistent results. Statistical prediction methods have proven more accurate than clinical method even when (a) the algorithm used for prediction is simplistic; (b) the clinical judge has access to equal or greater amounts of information or (c) the regression variables are weighted equally. He investigated the difference between statistical and clinical judgement relative to the identification of students with learning disabilities in reading. Participants were asked to provide demographic information and to specify the importance that they ascribed to the variables: (a) IQ (b) reading achievement (c) difference between intelligence and achievement (d) response of instruction and (e) the exclusion of mental retardation; when identifying with learning disabilities in reading.

Results indicated that clinical and statistical judgement yielded different results. Statistical judgement, across both conditions, yielded cases in which IQ exceeded achievement. Clinical judgement yielded case studies in which response to instruction was poor, irrespective of IQ and standardized regarding measures. When asked what criteria they used, participants in the current study weighted the variables in the following order of importance, from most to least important (a) difference between IQ and reading achievement (b) reading achievement (c) response to instruction and (d) the exclusion of mental retardation. Although participants gave "Difference between IQ and Reading Achievement" the highest mean importance weighting, this variable never achieved statistical significance as a predictor of clinical judgements. "Reading Achievement" in combination with "Response to Instruction" was found to be satisfactorily significant predictor of clinical judgements at the whole sample level. Limitations, implications and suggestions for future research are provided.

JAMES and **DEBORAH** (2002) conducted a study on classroom behaviour and the academic progress of learning disabled students. A total of 43 learning disabled (LD) students who were identified in grades 1-3 were followed up in their second year of special education services. Teachers completed the Classroom Behaviour Inventory (CBI) for each LD student and for randomly selected classmates, and both groups of students were observed with the SCAN system in regular classroom settings. Group difference in teacher perceived task orientation, independence, and verbal expressiveness replicated previous findings with CBI for this LD sample. SCAN observations partially replicated previous results in that LD children interacted with teachers more often than classmates. Multiple regression analysis indicated that both measures of behaviour were predictive of reading achievement during year 1 when the LD children were identified and that the CBI predicted academic progress from one year to the next. Result indicated that both teacher ratings and observational evidence converged on the importance of task –oriented behaviour, independent functioning, and socially appropriate behaviour in understanding the poor achievement of LD students.

BAYS (2001) presented a grounded theory and describe how the supervision of special education instruction occurs in public elementary schools in rural setting. Nine elementary schools in three rural districts in the State of Virginia participated in this study. Interview data was collected from 34 participants including special and general education teachers, principals and directors of special education. The grounded theory suggests that the supervisor' role is assigned to the principal: (i) Monitoring for legal compliance supervision of instruction for students of disability, and (ii) Evaluation of teachers supervision. The outcome of negotiating competing priorities and contextual factors is a dispersal of responsibility for supervision to three groups of educators. Principal as a primary supervisor: utilizes three strategies to address supervision: the observation evaluation process (ii) supervision by disability and class. Their separate legal development doesn't constitute an institutional conflict.

Result indicated that for the most part the political discord among rights struggle on the basis of race, sex disability and class has entailed a contest for political movement energies and for political attention of particular legal rights conceptions. At the same time educational rights on the basis of socioeconomic class founded upon particular legal form of material resource equalization evidence the potential to develop in the basic institutional coherence with right on the basis of race as well as sex and disability. By contrast the school choice movement in the form of charter and voucher school legislation actually with those on the basis of race, sex and disability. Individual must in effect choose between the concrete, legal attainment of such rights versus those on the basis of race, sex and disability.

FRANTZ (2000) examined the effectiveness of the infusion of remedial reading instruction derived from the Reading Component Model (RCM), on the reading achievement of children with learning disabilities and Title I class rooms. RCM is composed of two major components, word recognition and comprehension and poor functioning of either component can affect reading performance. Remedial instruction is based on the weak component. In contrast, the discrepancy model, a model that is predominant in U.S. schools, classifies students in two categories; those with learning disabilities and the without learning disabilities, but does not, however prescribe any particular instructional remediation. Twelve teachers from grades 2 through 6 provided the names of 151 children in their classrooms who were experiencing difficulty in reading. Complete evaluation data were collected from 130 students using differential diagnostic procedures designed to locate and identify the weak component that may cause the suspected deficits. Results indicated that 43% of the poor readers from both treatment and control groups had weakness in decoding skills only 33% had weakness in both decoding and comprehension skills received 10 hours of phoneme awareness training and 10 hours of comprehension strategy instruction. Results indicated that treatment groups irrespective of category did not make significant statistically positive gains from teachers indicated positive outcomes for the treatment groups. Recommendations are made for multifaceted evaluation measures and longer intervention.

CONCLUSION

It is evident from the above mentioned studies that only a few studies have conducted with the help of instructional and teaching learning material in international perspective on learning disabilities although a number of studies in this area is either related with exploring various dimensional issues of learning disabilities expressing psycho-clinical investigation. In India, it is almost a virgin's field of educational research where a very few studies are available on this topic.

It may appear that as the apex bodies are now a day's focusing attention on Inclusive Education, the researcher are taking initiative in this field which needs gross attention at secondary level. In the next chapter methodology of the present study will be discussed.

Chapter III

Methodology

INTRODUCTION

This study focused on teachers' perceptions towards the inclusion of learners with mental disabilities in schools. There are many challenges that influence teachers' perceptions towards the inclusion of learners with mental disabilities in the regular classrooms which include lack of expertise, inadequate resources, lack of policy direction and lack of supervision. From the findings it was recommended were made basing on the research findings and conclusions the Schools Psychological Services should organize in-service courses or workshops for regular teachers on Special education.

Teacher training programmes should help inculcate positive attitudes among teachers and provide knowledge and skills to handle students with mental disabilities in regular classrooms. In-service training through seminars, workshops or courses should help teachers acquire knowledge and skills to be competent inclusive. There should be an inclusive education policy to fully cater for the educational needs of learners with mental disabilities in inclusive settings.

RESEARCH DESIGN

A research design is the arrangement of conditions for collection and analysis of data in a manner that aims to combine relevance to the research purpose with economy in procedure. The present study has been employed through survey method.

Method and its Procedures

Research design is the conceptual structure within which research would be conducted. The function of research design is to provide for the collection of relevant information with minimal expenditure of effort, time and money. The preparation of research design, appropriate for a particular research problem, involves the consideration of the following:

1. Objectives of the research study.
2. Method of Data Collection to be adopted
3. Source of information—Sample Design
4. Tool for Data collection
5. Data Analysis— qualitative and quantitative

1. Objectives of the Research Study

Objectives identified to answer the research questions have to be listed making sure that they are:

a) Numbered, and

b) Statement begins with an action verb.

2. Methods of Data Collection

There are two types of data.

Primary Data— collected for the first time

Secondary Data—those which have already been collected and analysed by someone else.

Survey Method

The present study is based on survey method. This approach is most suited for gathering descriptive information.

Advantages of Survey Method:

-can be used to collect many different kinds of information

-Quick and low cost as compared to observation and experimental method.

Limitations

The present study is limited to Elementary Schools in Sivagangai District. Only 250 Elementary teachers in these schools are taken as samples for the present study.

STATEMENT OF THE STUDY

Problem of the present study is as follows: *"Problems Faced In Teaching for Disabled Children in Elementary Schools at Sivagangai Educational District"*.

OBJECTIVES OF THIS STUDY

The present study has the following objectives,

8. To find out the difference between the mean score of **Male and Female** teachers in respect of a study on the problems faced in teaching disabled children in Elementary Schools.
9. To find out the difference between the mean score of **Rural and Urban** area in respect of a study on the problems in faced in teaching disabled children in Elementary Schools.
10. To find out the difference between the mean score of **Government and Private** School in respect of a study on the problems in faced in teaching disabled children in Elementary Schools.
11. To find out the difference between the mean score of **B.Ed., and DT.Ed** in respect of a study on the problems in faced in teaching disabled children in Elementary Schools.
12. To find out the difference between the mean score of **Tamil** and **English** medium in respect of a study on the problems in faced in teaching disabled children in Elementary Schools.
13. To find out the difference between the mean score of **Trained and Untrained** teachers area in respect of a study on the

problems in faced in teaching disabled children in Elementary Schools.

HYPOTHESES OF THE STUDY

1. There is significant difference between the mean scores of **male and female** teachers in respect of a study on the problems faced in teaching disabled children in Elementary Schools.
2. There is significant difference between the mean scores of **rural and urban** area teachers in respect of a study on the problems faced in teaching disabled children in Elementary Schools.
3. There is a significant difference between the mean scores of **Government and Private** school teachers in respect of a study on the problems faced in teaching disabled children in Elementary Schools.
4. There is a significant difference between the mean scores of **B.Ed., and D.TEd** qualification teachers in respect of a study on the problems faced in teaching disabled children in Elementary Schools.
5. There is a significant difference between the mean scores of **Tamil and English** medium school teachers in respect of a study on the problems faced in teaching disabled children in Elementary Schools.
6. There is a significant difference between the mean scores of Trained teachers in Special Education and Untrained teachers in Special Education area in respect of a study on the problems faced in teaching disabled children in Elementary Schools.

LIMITATION OF THE STUDY

Even though many attempt has been made to make the study more precise and objective as possible, the investigator in the present study noted a few limitation which comes as follows:

The present study is limited only to the following variables. Only 21 schools in Sivagangai district have been randomly selected for this study and therefore the study is limited to Sivagangai district.

1. Since, the research is a Survey Study the number of students are 250 from Sivagangai Educational District.
2. 21 Schools were selected for the present study .
3. Limited variables have been administered for the Study.
4. Gender
5. Location of School
6. Type of School
7. Medium of Instruction
8. Teachers Education and Teacher Qualification
9. Trained in Special Education

SURVEY METHOD

What is a survey? According to Kerlinger (1973), survey research involves the studying of large and small populations selecting and studying samples chosen from the populations to discover the relative incidence, distribution and interrelations of sociological and psychological variables. It is a method of obtaining information about a population from a sample of individuals. Surveys can provide a quick, inexpensive and accurate means of obtaining information from a large group of people. If you want to know about the opinions, attitudes and perceptions of respondents, the survey is an appropriate method of collecting data. Besides, describing surveys can also be used to explain the relationship and differences between variables. The term sample survey is often used because a sample which is representative of the target population is used. The survey method is widely used in the social sciences, education, business and medicine.

A field of applied statistics, survey methodology studies the sampling of individual units from a population and the associated survey data collection techniques, such as questionnaire construction and methods for improving the number and accuracy of responses to surveys.

Statistical surveys are undertaken with a view towards making statistical inferences about the population being studied, and this depends strongly on the survey questions used. Polls about public opinion, public health surveys, market research surveys, government surveys and censuses are all examples of quantitative research that use contemporary survey methodology to answer questions about a population. Although censuses do not include a "sample", they do include other aspects of survey methodology, like questionnaires, interviewers, and nonresponse follow-up techniques.

The present study adopted the survey design. This assisted to assess influence of various factors which can be manipulated by schools. The study was a research which sought to determine teachers' perceptions towards the inclusion of learners with mental disabilities. As such the survey was the most appropriate for searching and looking into perceptions held by schools. The technique was used in order to come up with the correct number of respondents needed, and was also used to avoid biasness in choosing the respondents.

RESEARCH TOOL

Factual material or data unknown or unearthed so far, is essential is every study. They can be obtained from many sources, direct or indirect. Relevant data, adequate in quantity or quality should be collected, using a systematic procedure. For collecting new, unknown data, required for the study of any problem, one may use various devices. These devices or instruments employed in the collection of data are called tools.

The general type of data gathering instrument used in survey research is called "Questionnaire". It is used to collect factual information from target population. Investigators should consider the four basic standards of survey questionnaires.

They are as follows:

1. Mode of presentation of items in the questionnaire
2. Common items for all individual respondents
3. Ability to respond the items in the questionnaire
4. Willing to respond the items in the questionnaire

Type of the questions and mode of responding the items are important to obtains appropriate response. In the present study, limited response "agree", "disagree" and "Neutral" is used for the scoring procedures in the questionnaire. It was given to ten students among the sample selected. Then the questionnaire was presented to experts for comments. The advice which is gives by the experts has been incorporated in the present questionnaire. The developed questionnaire has been administered among the teachers.

Construction of Research tool

For the present study, Questionnaire is constructed with "Agree", "Disagree" and "Neutral" type response. The tool consists of 25 statements regarding the use of helping tool in teaching. The response is "Agree", "Disagree" and "Neutral".

The research tools are constructed with relevant questionnaire and it was validated. The pilot study was conducted by the researcher. The questionnaire was given to ten teachers in Municipal Primary School, Sivagangai DT", which was considered as a tool for pilot study. From the response given by them validated. All of them answered negatively "disagree" for the item no:25, (Ie) Do you have any problem while teaching the lesson in class room with mental disabilities student and normal students? Then the questionnaire was presented to experts for comments from the advice given by them the tools was further refined. Item no. 25 was restructured.(ie) Are you able to teach the class for mental disabilities students with normal student? The developed questionnaire

Samples of the Study

Sampling may be defined as "the selection of the part of an aggregate or totality, on the basis of which a judgement or inference about the aggregate or totality is made".

There are totally 250 samples were selected for the investigation. These are selected through the Random Sampling technique. These are selected randomly from the 21 Schools in the Sivagangai District.

SAMPLING FRAME FOR THE PRESENT STUDY

S.No	Name of The School	Nature of The School	Female Teacher	Male Teacher	Total
1	Sakkandhi	Government	7	4	11
2	Alish Millar - Sivagangai	Government	5	6	11
3	Panchayat Union – Appakudipatti	Government Primary School	4	5	9
4	Punitha Susaiappar - Sivagangai	Government	9	6	15
5	Ramakrishna, Sivagangai	Government	9	9	18
6	Panchayat Union Primary School – Sivagangai	Government	8	6	14
7	Punitha Fransis, Sivagangai	Government	6	3	9
8	Gandhiji, Mulaikulam	Government	8	7	15
9	Kumaarapatti	Government	5	5	10
10	Arunachalam Chettiyar Sivagangai	Government	9	6	15
11	Muslim Primary School, Sivagangai	Government	6	4	10
12	Kottai Moolai, sivagangai.	Government	7	5	12
13	Panchayat Union Primary School, Komaalipatti	Government	5	6	
14	Bala Bharathi Primary School - Vetriyur	Private	4	5	9
15	Dhandayudapani Primary School – Kundrakudi	Private	3 9	6	
16	Adhi Dravidar Primary School - Adikkaram	Private	4	6	10
17	Vivekananda, Sivagangai	Private	5	4	9
18	Mannar Midle Schol, Sivagangai	Private	9	7	16
19	Roman Catholic Sivagangai	Private	7	7	14
20	PUPS, Keela pongodi	Private	5	6	11
21	Nachiappan Chettiyar Alavaakottai	Private	7	5	12
		Total			250

Description of Research Tool and Scoring Procedure

This section deals with the scoring procedures of the tools employed in the present investigation. “Agree”, “Disagree” and

"Neutral" type is used in the questionnaire. The responses are "Agree", "Disagree" and "Neutral" totally, there 25 statements are present the questionnaire. These statements are deal with the using of helping tool in teachings among the primary and secondary teachers.

These 25 statements are mixed up with positive statements and negative statements.

The Scoring Procedure for positive statements comes as follows:

Agree – 3

Disagree -2

Neutral – 1

The Scoring Procedure for negative statements comes as follows:

Disagree – 3

Neutral -2

Agree - 1

Pilot Study

Pre-testing of the research instruments for specialist teachers was done at School. It involved ten (10) teachers The rationale for conducting the pre-test or pilot study was establish whether teachers were able to understand the items in the questionnaire. The pre-test was also conducted to establish approximately how long it would take to respond to one questionnaire. The knowledge helped in planning for the actual study as it provided a rough estimate of how many teachers could be targeted in a day, thereby helping in establishing the amount of time.

Validity of the Tool

The investigator established content validity in the study. The items are based on the usage of Helping tool in teachings, that are verified by experts in the field educationalist by seeking their opinion in relation to its objectivity and worthiness of items and these measures established the validity for present study.

Reliability of the Tool

After collecting data in the pilot study, the investigator attempted to find out the reliability for the questionnaire on the usage of helping tool in teachings. The reliability of the tool refers to the internal consistency observed in measurement with different set of equivalent items. In this study pearson product moment formula and spearman Brown prophecy formula used to identify the reliability value. The reliability value is

$$R = 2r \,/\, 1+r$$
$$= 2x0.09 \,/\, 1+0.9$$
$$= 0.9$$

The reliability value of the test is 0.9 and thereby the test is said to have reliability.

SAMPLING TECHNIQUE USED

For present study, simple random sampling is selected as sampling technique. It's the most popular sampling technique. It's the basis for other types of probability sampling. Through this technique 250 samples were selected for the investigation from 21 schools located at Sivagangai District.

COLLECTION OF DATA

Researchers point out that direct face to face data collection procedure is more valuable than the mailed questionnaire approach. In the present study, direct questionnaire administration approach was employed in order to ensure objectives collection of data from the respondents. This is preferred because it enhances high response rate and the researcher had an opportunity to clarify the doubts raised by the respondents.

In the process of data collection from the respondents, necessary permission was obtained from the principals of the schools. Having obtained permission from the principals, the validated questionnaire was administered to the teachers. Prior to the tool administration, proper explanation were offered by the investigation and the mode of responding the items in the questionnaires. The respondents were assured that the data collected would be kept in utmost confidential and would be used for statistical interpretation only.

A close rapport was maintained with the respondents to create an open and friendly environment. The friendly approach in the data collection procedures would help to objective and valid data from the respondents. No time limit was fixed while responding the items in the questionnaires. The respondents were asked to respond all the items in the questionnaires. Thus, the above attempts were made successfully to collect objective data from the target group.

ANALYSIS OF DATA

For simple analysis of the results, basic statistics such as central tendency and cross tabulation were used in order to generate the required data for discussion. Data analysis included the using of qualitative and quantitative methods, which involved data reduction, editing and coding in readiness for analysis. For efficient processing, SPSS software for windows was used to accomplish data analysis. The end results were concluded using percentages and tables.

STATISTICS TECHNIQUES USED

In the process of analyzing and interpreting the data, the following statistical techniques were employed to arrive at valid conclusions after the consultations with experts in computing.

6. The usage of helping tool in teaching frequencies was calculated.
7. Mean and standard deviation were calculated.
8. 't' test was used to find out the significant difference between the two mean scores.

Statistical Techniques Used

Arithmetic Mean (M)

The mean of distribution is commonly understood as arithmetic average. The term guide-point averages familiar to teacher is a mean value.

It is computed by the dividing the sum of all the scores by the no. of scores. It is probably most useful of all statistical measures for in addition to the information that it provides. It is the base from many others in important measures is computed.

$M = X_1 / N$

Arithmetic Mean from a frequency distribution

Some time it is more convenient to desire mean from a frequency distribution. An additional column may be opened to record the products of frequency distribution. The total of this frequency distribution will be divided by the total of 'f' (i.e.) N to get mean.

Mean = A +Σfd / N]i

Where, A = assumed mean value

I = school interval

N = sum of frequency

Standard Deviation (σ)

Standard deviation is more accurate than the average deviation to calculate standard deviation, individual deviations must be obtained. Then the individual deviations are squared and added. The sum of the square deviation is divided by the strength of the school N. The quotient should have square root and this is standard deviations. This is mentioned by a symbol (sigma)

$$\sigma = \sqrt{\Sigma x^2 / N}$$

In case of frequency distribution

$$SD = \sqrt{(\Sigma fd^2 / N) - (\Sigma fd/N)^2} SI$$

This is known as the short cut method of finding.

't' Test

't' test is based on 't' distribution and is a sample mean or judging the significance of difference between the means of the sample in case of small when population variance is not known. In case of two samples paired t-test is used for judging the significance of the co-efficient of sample and partial correlation. The relevant test statistic is calculated from the sample data then compared with its probable value based on t-distribution at a specific level of significance for concerning degree of freedom for accepting or rejecting the null hypothesis. The test applied only in case of small samples when population variance is not known.

$$t = [X1 - X_2]\sqrt{\frac{S12}{n1} + \frac{S22}{n2}}$$

X1 = mean of first group
X_2 = mean of second group
S1 = SD of the first group
S2 = SD of the second group
n1 = number of the teachers in the first group
n2 = number of the teachers in the second group

The degrees of the freedom should be computed by use in the formula df = (N-1)+(N-2) and using that obtain the 't' values at 0.05 and 0.01 levels of significance from the 't' table.

Drawing Inference

vIf the obtained 't' value is greater than the table value, then reject the hypothesis and conclude that there is a significant difference. If the obtained't' value is less than the table value, then retain the null hypothesis and conclude that there is no real difference between two groups.

CONCLUSION

In this chapter, the detailed Methodology for studying the problem is presented. Appropriate hypotheses formulated to put the study in right perspective. The research tools and their construction, their description, sampling technique, data collection procedures are all explained in this chapter. The delimitations of the study are also focused. The next chapter deals with the analysis and interpretation of data collected from the samples.

Chapter IV

Analysis and Interpretations of Data

INTRODUCTION

Through the data are valid, reliable and adequate, they do not serve any useful purpose unless they are carefully processed, systematically classified and tabulated, scientifically analyzed, intelligently interpreted and rationally concluded.

According to Best (1977), "Statistical data describe group behaviours or group characteristics abstracted from a number of individual observation which are combined to make generalization possible. The data after collection have to be purpose at the time of awareness of any type of research. It needs high level of judgement skill, thorough knowledge and technical ability of generalization.

Interpretation of data is an extremely important and useful branch of important and useful branch of statistical facts by themselves has no utility, but interpretation makes it possible to utilize the collected data in various fields of activity of generalization.

In the present study, the following pre-requisites are kept in mind for the scientific interpretation of data collected through relevant tools.

Accurancy of Data

In order to ensure accuracy in data correction, the investigator herself has visited the schools and collected data from the respondents in a perfect way in order to get right conclusion.

Sufficiency of the Data

In this study the data are collected from the teachers with the help of validated questionnaire in order to achieve objectivity and proper interpretation and analysis. It's felt that data collected are sufficient and reliable.

Classification and Tabulation

This is one of the important steps used by the investigator in data analysis in order to get accurate interpretation. In the present study, the collected data are systematically classified and tabulated.

Application of possible Statistical Treatment

Before analysis the data, satisfied experts are consulted for the application of possible statistical treatment. The data are analysed with the appropriate statistical techniques. Hence, these techniques are used for analysis and interpretation of data.

STEPS USED IN ANALYSIS AND INTERPRETATION

In this study, the following steps are employed to analyze and interpret the data.

Step – I Critical Examination of Data

In this step, a critical examination of collection data collected data is done in a holistic approach.

Step – II Categorization

In the process of categorization, attempted are made to classify the data in an independent category and overlapping is avoided. In order to ensure proper categorization of data, the following activities are undertaken.

A Sample classificatory principle is used.

Exhaustive and sufficient categories are made for classifying all responses, district, separate and mutually exclusive categories are identified.

Step-III Coding

Coding is one of the steps of data analysis which involves assigning of numerical to each response of a category. In this study, coding is used to translate the raw data into numerical (symbols) which are counted and tabulated.

Step-IV Tabulation

The investigator has arranged the data orderly in columns and rows to facilitate effective analysis and interpretation of data. Then the data are presented in tabular columns for easy understanding and interpretation of results.

Step-V Statistical analysis and inference

Statistical Analysis is a systematic analysis and it helps to interpret the data in an accurate and precise way. In the present study, the entire data are analysed with the help of statistical techniques.

HYPOTHESES TESTING

DESCRIPTIVE ANALYSIS

This section deals with the descriptive analysis of the data. For descriptive analysis, percentage, mean and standard deviation scores are calculated and the data are interpreted by using the statistics.

HYPOTHESIS - 1

There is no significant difference between Male and Female teachers in respect of a study on the problems faced in teaching disabled students in Elementary Schools.

TABLE 1

The following figure shows the Mean and Standard deviation value in respect of Problems Faced in Teaching Disabled Children in Elementary Schools in terms of their Gender.

Gender	N	M	SD	t' value	Level of significant at .05 level
Male	118	32.53	8.16		
Female	132	32.39	8.45	0.13	Not significant

INTERPRETATION

From the above table,'t' value is **(0.13)**, which is less than the table value **(1.96)**. Hence there is no significant difference between the mean scores of on the basis of the **Gender** in respect of Problems Faced in Teaching Disabled Children.

RESULT:

Hence the hypothesis is **accepted.**

HYPOTHESES -2

There is no significant difference between Rural and Urban teachers in respect of a study on the problems faced in teaching disabled students in Elementary Schools.

TABLE 2

The following figure shows the Mean and Standard deviation value in respect of Problems Faced in Teaching Disabled Children in Elementary Schools in terms of their Locality.

Locality	N	M	SD	t' value	Level of significant at .05 level
Rular	129	30.77	8.2		
Urban	121	34.26	7.98	3.42	significant

INTERPRETATION

From the above table't' value is **(3.42)**, which is greater than the table value **(1.96)**. Hence there is significant difference between the mean scores of using helping tool in developing teaching skill among mentally disabled students on the basis of their **locality** in respect of Problems Faced in Teaching Disabled Children.

RESULT:

Hence the hypothesis is **rejected.**

HYPOTHESES -3

There is no significant difference between Government and Private Teachers in respect of a study on the problems faced in teaching disabled students in Elementary Schools.

TABLE 3

The following figure shows the Mean and Standard deviation value in respect of Problems Faced in Teaching Disabled Children in Elementary Schools in terms of their Type of School.

Type of school	N	M	SD	t' value	Level of significant at .05 level
Government	129	30.77	8.2		
Private	121	34.26	7.98	3.42	significant

INTERPRETATION

From the above table 't' value is **(2.04)**, which is greater than the table value **(1.96)**. Hence there is no significant difference between the mean scores of on the basis of the type of their **school** in respect of Problems Faced in Teaching Disabled Children.

RESULT:

Hence the hypothesis is **rejected.**

HYPOTHESE -4

There is no significant difference between B.Ed., and D.TEd., teachers in respect of a study on the problem in faced in teaching disabled students in Elementary Schools.

TABLE 4

The following figure shows the Mean and Standard deviation value in respect of Problems Faced in Teaching Disabled Children in Elementary Schools in terms of their Teachers Qualification.

Teacher's Qualification	N	M	SD	t' value	Level of significant at .05 level
B.Ed.,	180	32.94	8.37		
D. TED.,	70	31.21	8.03	1.51	significant

INTERPRETATION

From the above table't' value is **(1.51)**, which is less than the table value **(1.96)**. Hence there is no significant difference between the mean scores of based on the teacher's in respect of Problems Faced in Teaching Disabled Children on the basis of their Teachers **qualification**.

RESULT:

Hence the hypothesis is **accepted.**

HYPOTHESES -5

There is no significant difference between Tamil and English teachers in respect of a study on the problems faced in teaching disabled students in Elementary Schools.

TABLE 5

The following figure shows the Mean and Standard deviation value in respect of Problems Faced in Teaching Disabled Children in Elementary Schools in terms of their Medium of Instruction.

Medium of Instruction	N	M	SD	t' value	Level of significant at .05 level
Tamil	154	32.81	8.74		
English	156	31.72	9.17	0.93	Not significant

INTERPRETATION

From the above table't' value is **(0.93)**, which is less than the table value **(1.96)**. Hence there is no significant difference between the mean scores of based on the in respect of Problems Faced in Teaching Disabled Children on the basis of the **Medium of Instruction**.

RESULT:

Hence the hypothesis is **accepted.**

HYPOTHESES -6

There is no significant difference between Trained and Untrained teachers in respect of a study on the problems faced in teaching disabled students in Elementary Schools.

TABLE 6

The following figure shows the mean and standard deviation value in respect of Problems Faced in Teaching Disabled Children in Elementary Schools in terms of their Trained Teachers.

Medium of Instruction	N	M	SD	t' value	Level of significant at .05 level
Trained	96	30.82	8.54		
Utrained	154	33.47	7.92	2.45	significant

INTERPRETATION

From the above table't' value is **(2.45)**, which is greater than the table value **(1.96)**. Hence there is no significant difference between the mean scores of based in respect of Problems Faced in Teaching Disabled Children on the basis of the **trained or untrained teachers**.

RESULT:

Hence the hypothesis is **rejected**

CONCLUSIONS

In light of the analysis and discussion of the research findings presented above the following conclusion can be deduced. While teachers can define the concept of inclusion, they have scanty knowledge of the issues obtaining in special needs education more so in inclusion of learners with mental disabilities.

In spite of the scanty knowledge, most teachers agree with the idea that inclusive education is the ideal placement for learners with mental disabilities. Respondents feet that students with mental disabilities do not have learner support they need for learning in inclusive settings due to unavailability of resources.

Learners with mental disabilities benefit in a number of ways from inclusion. Teachers feel that learners with mental disabilities benefit educationally and socially from inclusion.

Respondents perceive that learners with mental disabilities are not readily accepted by their peers in inclusive settings while teachers are very forthcoming. In spite of the fact that teachers readily accept learners with mental disabilities, they feel they have nothing much to offer these students in light of the conflicting constraints and expectations they face. There is no inclusive education policy to fully cater for the educational needs of learners with mental disabilities in inclusive settings. There are many challenges that influence teachers' perceptions towards the inclusion of learners with mental disabilities in the regular classrooms which include lack of expertise, inadequate resources, lack of policy direction and lack of supervision. Teachers perceive pre-service training at college, in-service training as well as staff development at school level as important for them to successfully implement inclusive education.

Chapter - V

Findings and Conclusion

INTRODUCTION

Teacher should make hundreds of decisions every day - decisions about what should be taught, why it should be taught, when it should be taught, how it should be taught, why it should be taught, and to whom it should be taught. Teacher makes decision that affect the learning of individual students and groups of students. Teacher should make decisions that affect students' future learning and academic progress. All of these important decisions will be based on your knowledge, understanding, experience, purposes, values, attitudes, and beliefs.

As the most significant resource in schools, teachers are critical to raise education standards. Improving the efficiency and equity of schooling depends, in large measure, on ensuring that teachers are highly skilled, well resourced, and motivated to perform at their best.

Teaching children with learning disabilities is a big challenge to most parents and teachers. Most people know, or are taught at an early age, how to process information and develop an organized plan or strategy when confronted with a problem. It should not matter whether that problem is social, academic, or job related. Others find such cognitive processes quite difficult. Learning disabilities have only recently been recognized as disabilities.

This neurological disorder causes difficulty in organizing information received, remembering it, and expressing information, and therefore, affects a person's basic functions such as reading, writing, comprehension, and reasoning. However, children with learning disabilities can be taught effective learning strategies that will help them approach tasks more effectively.

NEED FOR THE STUDY

This study focused on teachers' perceptions towards the inclusion of learners with mental disabilities in schools. There are many challenges that influence teachers' perceptions towards the inclusion of learners with mental disabilities in the regular classrooms which include lack of expertise, inadequate resources, lack of policy direction and lack of supervision. From the findings it was recommended were made basing on the research findings and conclusions the Schools Psychological Services should organize in-service courses or workshops for regular teachers on Special education. Teacher training programmes should help inculcate positive attitudes among teachers and provide knowledge and skills to handle students with mental disabilities in regular classrooms. In-service training through seminars, workshops or courses should help teachers acquire knowledge and skills to be competent inclusive. There should be an inclusive education policy to fully cater for the educational needs of learners with mental disabilities in inclusive settings.

STATEMENT OF THE PROBLEM

Problem of the present study is as follows: "*Problems Faced In Teaching for Disabled Children In Elementary Schools At Sivagangai Educational District*".

OBJECTIVES OF THE STUDY

The present study has the following objectives,

1. To find out the difference between the mean score of **Male and Female** teachers in respect of a study on basis of problems faced in teaching disabled children in Elementary Schools.

2. To find out the difference between the mean score of **Rural and Urban** area in respect of a study on basis of problems faced in teaching disabled children in Elementary Schools.
3. To find out the difference between the mean score of **Government and Private** School in respect of a study on basis of problems faced in teaching disabled children in Elementary Schools.
4. To find out the difference between the mean score of **B.Ed., and D.TEd** in respect of a study on basis of problems faced in teaching disabled children in Elementary Schools.
5. To find out the difference between the mean score of **Tamil and English** medium in respect of a study on basis of problems faced in teaching disabled children in Elementary Schools.
6. To find out the difference between the mean score of **Trained** and **Untrained** teachers area in respect of a study on basis of problems faced in teaching disabled children in Elementary Schools.

FINDINGS OF THE STUDY

In light of the analysis and discussion of the research findings presented above the following conclusion can be deduced.

1. The male and female of disabled students are not different in the using helping tool significantly.
2. The localities of the disabled students are different in the using helping tool.
3. The types of the schools of disabled students are not different in the using helping tool significantly.
4. The teacher's qualifications of disabled students are not different in the using helping tool significantly.
5. The medium of instruction of disabled students are not different in the using helping tool significantly.
6. The trained and untrained teachers of disabled students are different in the using helping tool significantly.

SUGGESTIONS FOR FURTHER RESEARCH

1. Experimental studies may be conducted after providing self learning packages to improve the skill in the use of helping tool among the disabled student teachers.
2. It may be appropriate to conduct research studies on remedial teaching for disabled students in order to minimize the difficulties in using the helping tool.
3. Research may be undertaken to evolve suitable methods of teaching disabled students with the trained teachers in order to produce possible results.
4. Research may be undertaken to frame syllabus in order to teach disabled students in an effective way.
5. Research shows that we uncover some important differences for the sub population of students with disabilities and their teachers.
6. Consistent with research on regular education students, we find that in – service professional development for teachers has little effect on their ability to increase the achievement gains of students with disabilities.
7. This suggests current expenditures on professional development might be more efficiently used in other ways to enhance teacher quality and promote student achievement. Further, as with teachers serving the general student population, value added increases with the first few years of experience. Thus there are potential gains from reducing attrition among early – career special education teachers.

RECOMMENDATIONS OF THE STUDY

The following recommendations were made basing on the research findings and conclusions.

1. The Schools Psychological Services should organize in-service courses or workshops for regular teachers on Special education.
2. Teacher training programmes should help inculcate positive attitudes among teachers and provide knowledge and skills to handle students with mental disabilities in regular classrooms.

3. In-service training through seminars, workshops or courses should help teachers acquire knowledge and skills to be competent inclusive.
4. Teachers with specialization in disability studies in regular schools through their administrators should hold staff development workshops to educate the staff on inclusive education and learners with mental disabilities for them to be successfully included.
5. There should be an inclusive education policy to fully cater for the educational needs of learners with mental disabilities in inclusive settings.
6. There is need for thorough supervision; monitoring and evaluation by School Psychological Services and the Special Education in schools where learners with mental retardation are included.
7. Schools, at cluster level, should take an active role in promoting the inclusion of learners with mental disabilities in regular schools.
8. Schools and the Ministry of Education should mobilize resources from donor agencies to cater for the successful implementation of inclusive education.

CONCLUSIONS

After reviewing the above related literature it is found that:

3. There were studies related to different method of teaching at middle school, writing and self-monitoring strategies for eight graders, instructional intervention for writing and spelling performance, novel teaching method on mathematics, differential efficacy of verbal self-instructional training on reflective and impulsive reading disabled, instructional methods for teaching spelling to elementary students with learning disabilities, service delivery ability of general education of middle school students, self-monitoring instructions delivered to students by peers on the participation of students with severe learning disabilities, accomplishment of students with specific learning disabilities and language impairment, story mapping, infusion of remedial

reading instruction, RCM model, social competence, classroom behaviour, teaching strategies, social skills interventions, individualized instruction education program, emotional competence, video models, psychological factors, algebraic literacy model in reference to learning disabilities conducted in abroad.

4. There were studies related to educational provision, inclusive education practices, competence and social anxiety, social remediation program peer tutoring mathematics skills, factor affecting learning disabilities in mathematics and science.
5. It is evident from the above mentioned studies that only a few studies have conducted with the help of instructional and teaching learning material in international perspective on learning disabilities although a number of studies in this area is either related with exploring various dimensional issues of learning disabilities expressing psycho-clinical investigation.
6. It is almost a virgin's field of educational research where a very few studies are available on this topic.
7. It may appear that as the apex bodies are now a day's focusing attention on Inclusive Education, the researcher are taking initiative in this field which needs gross attention at secondary level.

BIBLIOGRAPHY

1. Ainscow, M. (1993).Understanding the development of inclusive schools London. Falmer Press.
2. Badza A.M. & Tafangombe, J. (2010). Inclusion and the Zimbabwean Situation.Harare: Zimbabwe Open University.
3. Browder, D. M. and Snell, M. E. Instruction of students with severe disabilities.4th edition, New York: Macmillan/Merrill.
4. Chimedza, R. and Peters, S. (2001).Disability and special education in African context different voices. Harare: College Press.
5. Creswel, J.W. (2002). Educational Research: Planning conducting and evaluating Qualitative and Quantitative Research. New Jersey:

6. Merill Prentice Hall. Dutoit, P. and Forlin, C. (2009).Cultural transformation for inclusion? A South African perspective. SAGE publications.

7. Forlin, C. (2004). Promoting Inclusivity in western Australian schools.

8. Taylor and Francis LTD. Forlin, C. (2008). Impact of training on pre service teachers attitudes and concerns about inclusive education and sentiments about person with disabilities.

9. Routledge. Hallahan, D.P. & Kauffman, J.M. (1997). Exceptional Learners: Introduction to special Education,7th Edition.

10. Boston: Ally & Bacon. Hardman, M.l, Drew C.L. and Engan, M.W. (1996). Human exceptionality Society school and family 6th Edition. Boston: Allyn and Bacon. The Inclusion of Children with Mental Disabilities: A Teacher's Perspective International Journal of Humanities Social Sciences and Education (IJHSSE)

11. Kisanji, (1997). "Inclusive Education" International Journal inclusive Education, Volume 2, Number 1, pg 55-7.

12. Lander, M.F. & Weaver, H. B. (1997). Inclusive Education 2nd Edition. Needham Heights: Watersun Publishing Company.

13. Mpofu, E. (2000). Education Consideration for Students who are Mentally Challenged/Retarded. Harare: Zimbabwe Open University.

14. Nziramasanga et al (1999). Presidential Commission of Inquiry into Education and Training. Harare: Government Printers.

15. Patton, J.R. and Payne, J.S. (1990).Mental Retardation. Birmingham: Merrill Publishers.

16. Ryndak, D. L., Jackson, L., & Billingsley, F. (2000). Defining school inclusion for students with moderate to severe disabilities: What do experts say. Exceptionality, 8(2), 101–116.

17. Santoli, S. P., Sachs, J., Romey, E. A., & McClurg, S. (2008). A successful formula for middle school inclusion: Collaboration, time, and administrative support. Research in Middle Level Education Online, 32(2), 1–13.

18. Santrock, J.W. (2003). Children, 7th Edition. Boston: McGraw Hill Company.

19. Saunders, M. Lewis, P. and Thornhill, A. (2003). Research Methods for Business Students 3rd Edition England: Pearson Education Limited.

20. Slavin, R.E. (1996). Education for All. Swets and Zeitlinger Publishers.

21. United Nations (1994). "The standard rules on the equalization of opportunities for persons with disabilities" United Nations General Assembly (48th Session)(Resolution 48/96),New York.

22. Zindi, F. (1997). Special Education in Africa. Botswana: Tasalls Publications. AUTHORS' BIOGRAPHY Mrs. Barbra MAPURANGA is a lecturer teaching at the Zimbabwe Open University in the Faculty of Applied Social Sciences. She is the Regional Programme Coordinator responsible for Special Needs and Disability Studies programme. She holds a Master's degree in Special Education. She has co-authored a number of research articles, and course modules published by Zimbabwe Open University.

6. Implementation of Active Based Learning Methodology

Chapter - I

Conceptual Framework

INTRODUCTION

Education research is a field of inquiry aimed at advancing knowledge of education and learning processes and development of the tools and methods necessary to support this endeavor. Education researchers aim to describe, understand and explain how learning takes place throughout the life cycle and how formal and informal processes of education affect learning, attainment and the capacity to lead productive lives. The unifying purpose for education research is to build cumulative and sound knowledge about human and social process of fundamental significance to individuals, to groups and to the larger society.

According to the research, it seems that every new idea in education is research-based, but what does that really mean? This overview is a summary of important concepts and considerations related to research in education.

Education is a purposeful activity. By education we intend to bring certain desirable changes in the students. Education is a conscious effort and as such, it has definite aims and objectives. In the light of these aims the curriculum is determined and the academic achievements of the student are measured.

Education without aim is like a boat without its rudder. Aims give direction to activity. Absence of an aim in education makes it a blind alley. Every stage of human development had some aim of life. The aims of life determine aims of education. The aims of education have changed from age to age and thus it is dynamic because the aims of life are dynamic.

It is science alone that can solve the problems of hunger and poverty, of insanitation and malnutrition, of illiteracy and obscurantism of superstition and deadening customs, of rigid traditions and blind beliefs, of vast resources going to waste of a rich country inhabited by starving millions.

By education I mean an all-round drawing out of the best in child and man's body, mind and spirit **Mahatma Gandhi.**

The highest education is that which does not merely give us information but makes our life in harmony with all existence- **Rabindranath Tagore.**

Education is something, which makes a man self-reliant and self-less- **Rigveda.**

Education according to Indian tradition is not merely a means of earning a living; nor is it only a nursery of thought or a school for citizenship. It is initiation into the life of spirit and training of human souls in the pursuit of truth and the practice of virtue- **Radhakrishnan.**

In a 'traditional' class there is a perception that the most industrious students are those who passively soak up everything the teacher might serve up to them in a suitably 'didactic sauce' only to 'spout it' back word-for-word. It was important, therefore, at the beginning of the course, in the introductory lecture, to stress that participants do not need to repeat things learned word-for-word. Rather we expressed our vision that students evolve into "investigators", starting an independent inquiry into a topic of interest in a self-directed manner. Consequently, facilitating, motivating, enabling and coaching are the key skill-set of the instructor (facilitator) rather than just didactic lectures. At the beginning of the class, illustrated ABL with a famous saying of Confucius that stresses participation as the key to students' learning success.

IMPORTANCE OF EDUCATION

Education has been considered as an instrument of economic, social and political change. The ultimate goal of education is to develop necessary skills among the people. Education for adults is the key element in the rural development Endeavour to involve rural masses a point which they can run their own affair and to enable them to become self reliance by increasing productivity through their dedication and hard work.

An individual's education starts from birth and extends up to death. The process of education can be hastened through study and instruction. An individual is educated not only in the classroom, college and universities, but also in the play fields, place of work and worship-social gathering etc. Education paves way for the development and perpetuation of nation culture.

Education can be regarded as a process. That is the continuous experiences that are engaged in by the learners develop his innate potentialities. Education as a product represents the developed skills, knowledge and attitudes that result from the learner's participation in learning process.

THE MODERN AIMS OF EDUCATION

1. To prepare the young to enter the world of work and earn for living.
2. To develop the wholesome personality.
3. To actualize the potentialities, talents and capacities of the child.
4. To contribute to the social harmony.

5. To help the individual to enjoy life.
6. To develop a desirable or good philosophy of life.
7. To promote individual excellence.
8. To create scientific spirit in the minds of the young.

In modern age, education is regarded as an essential expenditure and productive investment. Whatever expenditure is incurred on educational plans, equipment, buildings and other expenses is an investment, the return of which is received in the form of useful, dynamic and efficient citizens who contribute more and more to greater and greater economic welfare of the country which provides them such useful education.

ACTIVITY BASED LEARNING

Activity Based Learning (ABL) is a methodology where children of different ages are grouped together in one class, and each learns at his or her own pace through a series of activities and cards arranged in the form of a learning ladder, with the teacher acting as a facilitator of children's learning.

IMPORTANCE OF ACTIVE LEARNING

Active learning is a term used to identify teaching methods that require students to be actively involved in the learning process. The term is sometimes used to contrast against so-called passive methods of teaching, though this may be too simplistic, because no pedagogy can succeed without actively engaging students at some stage. Nevertheless, some teaching approaches are thought to be too passive.

ACTIVITY - BASED LEARNING (ABL) MODULES (JOYFUL LEARNING)

The ABL approach is unique and effective to attract out-of -school children to schools/AIE centers. The teachers who are involved in implementing this method have developed activities for each learning unit which facilitated readiness for learning, instruction, reinforcement and evaluation. ABL has transformed the classrooms into hubs of activities and meaningful learning.

ABL – AN INNOVATIVE APPROACH

The ABL concept has been taken from the Rishi Valley practices. This has been introduced in the Corporation Schools of Chennai with slight modifications. Seeing the success of the scheme this has been introduced in the Panchayat Union Schools.

Initially, a core team was asked to investigate the current practices of classroom process and find out the reasons for the low achievement of children. As the team members had rich exposure in the field of primary education they had strong faith on children, parents, teachers and the government that they would not be responsible for low achievement of children. Then, after close study in some of the schools in the corporation area, the team identified the following as the malady of conventional process.

STUDENT-CENTERED TEACHING AND LEARNING

In the traditional approach to college teaching, most class time is spent with the professor lecturing and the students watching and listening. The students work individually on assignments, and cooperation is discouraged.

Student-centered teaching methods shift the focus of activity from the teacher to the learners. These methods include **active learning**, in which students solve problems, answer questions, formulate questions of their own, discuss, explain, debate, or brainstorm during class; **cooperative learning**, in which students work in teams on problems and projects under conditions that assure both positive interdependence and individual accountability; and **inductive teaching and learning**, in which students are first presented with challenges (questions or problems) and learn the course material in the context of addressing the challenges. Inductive methods include inquiry-based learning, case-based instruction, problem-based learning, project-based learning, discovery learning, and just-in-time teaching. Student-centered methods have repeatedly been shown to be superior to the traditional teacher-centered approach to instruction, a conclusion that applies whether the assessed outcome is short-term mastery, long-term retention, or depth of understanding of course material, acquisition of critical thinking or creative problem-solving skills, formation of positive attitudes toward the subject being taught, or level of confidence in knowledge or skills.

TEACHER DOMINATES THE CLASSROOM ALWAYS

1. Rare use of teaching learning materials.
2. Most of the time the lecture method was followed.
3. Importance was given to rote learning.
4. Teachers are under the assumption that they know everything and children do not know anything.
5. Teacher assumes uniform learning pace and uniform level of achievement among children.
6. The gap between teacher and children are more.
7. Focus is given on teaching rather than learning.
8. No scope to cover the loss of learning during the period of absence of children.
9. Multi grade and multi level is not addressed.
10. Traditional way of evaluation.
11. Absence of joyous based extra activities.
12. Absence of play way and learning by doing activities.
13. Less chance for mutual and self learning.
14. Coverage of syllabus by the teacher and not by the children.
15. Classroom with fewer facilities for learning activities.
16. Instructional materials neither intensive nor attractive.
17. Lack of learning freedom - more of time restricted environment.

To overcome the above malady in teaching learning process a suitable strategy called Activity Based Learning (ABL) was evolved to be implemented in the Schools.

IMPLEMENTATION OF ABL APPROACH

Implementation of this approach was divided into four phases viz.

1. Preparation Capacity Building Phase
2. Experimental Phase

3. Extension Phase and
4. Evaluation Phase

During capacity building phase a core team consisting 4 programme coordinators and selected 26 practicing teachers were trained by Rishi Valley Project people three (or) four times repeatedly during 2003 and 2004. The four co-coordinators with I to V and experience in the background along with the teachers developed the module.

1. The ABL approach was experimented for one year in selected 13 schools in 10 zones during (2003) the experimental phase.
2. Since printed cards were not available at that time photocopies of the same were used in the classrooms.
3. During this stage, only classes I & II were integrated. The ultimate idea is to integrate up to class IV.
4. As the results were encouraging, this approach was extended to all 264 schools in Chennai Corporation during 2004.
5. During this phase, learning cards for classes I & II (4 subjects) and teachers manual were prepared, printed and distributed.
6. In the year 2005, class III was integrated with class I & II.
7. Workbooks for classes I & II for four subjects were prepared, printed and distributed during 2004-2005.
8. Training of classroom teachers and other Staff
9. Experimental school teachers handling class I & II were trained initially and recurrently with reasonable time in ABL methodology during 2003 and 2004 under capacity building phase.
10. Appraisal and review meetings were conducted periodically for smooth conduct of the programme.
11. To enhance resource support a team of 100 members ten in each zone / block were trained sufficiently in the ABL methodology (Teacher instruction) who in turn trained all the classroom teachers handling classes I to III and other teachers also who are handling IV to VIII.

12. For effective monitoring and supervising of the ABL, all BRTEs, HM's, DEOs, CEOs and ADPCs, Supervisors, AEEOs were trained by core team members in various cycles during 2004-2005.
13. Teachers and Headmasters are also trained and oriented by visiting model schools and other schools of appreciable performance and interaction with successful teachers.
14. Apart from these, teachers were provided on the spot support by expert team periodically and regularly.
15. A resource centre was functioning to offer all time support to teachers at Corporation Middle School, Ranganathan Street, Nungambakkam.
16. The Process of ABL approach
17. Competencies are split into different parts/units and converted into different activities.
18. Each part/unit is called a milestone.
19. In each subject, the relevant milestones are clustered and linked as chain and this chain of milestones is called LADDER.
20. Each milestone has different steps of learning process and each step of learning process is represented by logo.
21. Milestones are arranged in a logical sequence from simple to complex and also activities in each milestone.
22. To enable the children to organize in groups group cards are used.
23. Evaluation is inbuilt in the system. Separate cards / activities are used for this purpose.
24. Each child is provided with workbook/worksheet for further reinforcement activities.
25. Children's progress is recorded through annual assessment chart.
26. Each milestone has different type of activities such as introduction, reinforcement, practice, evaluation, remedial and enrichment activities represented by different logos.

BENEFITS OF ABL APPROACH

1. Children learn on their pace.
2. Provision of more time for self-directed learning and teacher directed learning is reduced considerably.
3. Group learning, mutual learning and self learning are promoted.
4. Teachers teaching time is judiciously distributed among children. Only needy children are addressed by teachers.
5. Children's participation in every step is ensured in the process of learning.
6. Evaluation is inbuilt in the system it is done without the child knowing it.
7. Rote learning is discouraged and almost no scope for rote learning.
8. Periodical absence of child from school is properly addressed.
9. Classroom transaction is based on child's needs and interests.
10. Freedom to child in learning as he chooses his activity.
11. Multi grade and multilevel in learning is effectively addressed.
12. No child can move to the next higher step of learning unless attains the previous one.
13. Sense of achievement boosts child's confidence and morale.
14. Attractive cards and activity create interest among children.
15. Scope for child's development in creative and communicative skills.
16. Children will have a feel of security as they sit in rounds in the groups.
17. Children are allowed to move in the classroom as they choose their activity.

Moreover the distance between the teacher and the child is largely reduced and the teacher acts as a facilitator rather than teacher.

The ABL concept is used in selected regular schools in the State apart from 6,000 AIE centers. The ABL cards which can match the pace of learning have been placed permanently in Block Resource

Centers. This ground–breaking approach has been tried out experimentally in a few schools (10 schools per block). After field-testing of the ABL modules and Self Learning Material kits are to be used in other schools. The Directorate of Teacher Education, Research and Training and Directorate of Elementary Education have been involved in implementing this programme including imparting training for the same. Yet, another silent revolution in Innovative Education.

ACTIVITY-BASED LEARNING PEDAGOGY

Activity-based learning or ABL describes a range of pedagogical approaches to teaching. Its core premises include the requirement that learning should be based on doing some hands-on experiments and activities. The idea of activity-based learning is rooted in the common notion that children are active learners rather than passive recipients of information.

If child is provided the opportunity to explore by their own and provided an optimum learning environment then the learning becomes joyful and long-lasting.

Activity-based learning started sometime in 1944 around World War II when a British man David Horsburgh came to India and finally decided to settle down there. He was an innovative thinker and charismatic leader. He started teaching in Rishi Valley School. He joined the British Council and worked in Chennai and Bangalore for many years.

After his voluntary retirement, he located a 7-acre (28,000 m^2) site in Kolar District and opened his school, Neel Bagh. Neel Bagh was based on an innovative idea of Horsburgh and known for its creative methods in teaching well-planned learning materials. With his wife Doreen and his son Nicholas, Horsburgh developed a diverse curriculum, which included music, carpentry, sewing, masonry, gardening, as well as the usual school subjects, English, mathematics, Sanskrit, and Telugu.

These pedagogic materials were systematically planned, with sketches and drawings and an occasional touch of humor. Later Horsburgh created a magnificent library in Neel Baugh that was accessible to teachers and students.

This initiative of Horsburgh was later proved to be one of the pioneer and milestones in ABL. In modern time ABL is the method of education followed in the Corporation schools of Chennai, from 2003, as an effort to provide special schools for children who had been freed from bonded labor.

PHILOSOPHY OF ABL

The philosophy of ABL finds its antecedents in the common notion that learning can be best when it is initiated by the surrounding environment and motivated by providing optimum opportunities to learn. A fearless and freedom to express environment always adds to best learning outcomes characteristics

The key feature of the ABL method is that it uses child-friendly educational aids to foster self-learning and allows a child to study according to his/her aptitude and skill. Under the system, the curriculum is divided into small units, each a group of Self Learning Materials (SLM) comprising attractively designed study cards for English, Tamil, Maths, Science and Social Science. When a child finishes a group of cards, he completes one "milestone". Activities in each milestone include games, rhymes, drawing, and songs to teach a letter or a word, form a sentence, do maths and science, or understand a concept. The child takes up an Exam Card only after completing all the milestones in a subject. If a child is absent one day, he/she continues from where he/she left unlike in the old system where the children had to learn on their own what they missed out on.

PROBLEMS FACED BY TEACHERS IN ABL METHOD

There are numerous individual learning theories attempting to find answers to the problems of helping students learn and adapt to new situations; two stand out: behaviorist theory (B.F. Skinner) and cognitive theory (Jean Piaget). Behaviorist theory states that knowledge exists independently and outside of people, i.e. only small bits of information are transferred to learners, with learning success achieved only when a connection is established between a stimulus and a response (credited to the work of B.F. Skinner). The second theory, cognitive theory, stresses the importance that learning is a result of the interaction of a particular structure and a person's own psychological environment. In this theory, learning modifies the student's "world of knowledge" by interaction processes, so that he or she acquires new insights or changes old ones. Activity-based learning (ABL) theory is a cognitive-learning theory which is considered a "constructivist" learning theory (Hein, 1991). Essentially, a learner "constructs" his own microcosms of knowledge from past knowledge and/or current experiences and interacting with data. He or she actively seeks new information, and is actively engaged in the process in the way s(he) gains, assimilates, and utilizes knowledge. The facilitator engages learners in outlining real-world problems in the first place instead of starting with a classification of problem-solving methods. (Therefore, the theory is also referred to as problem-based learning theory). Integrating ABL elements is thus a promising way to enhance students' learning experiences.

Increased recognition of the importance of non cognitive skills – self regulation, motivation, perseverance

1. Non cognitive skills affect schooling, returns to schooling, dropout rates (Heckman, Stixrud and Urzua 2006)
2. Effect of non cognitive skills (for many outcomes) is similar to that of cognitive skills
3. Non cognitive skills importantly influence development of cognitive skills and learning capability
4. Gaps in non cognitive skills also appear early, and are partly reduced by controlling for mother's ability and education, family income and family structure.

NEED OF THE STUDY

The study will more light into the Activity Based Learning method implementation problems towards teachers among the various schools in Pudukkottai District.

The basic argument for Activity Based Learning arises out of the rather fragmentary nature of much of our present day evaluation. Problems are one barrier in an analytic process. In order to evaluate each individual student as objectively as possible, it is necessary to break down the student's total performance or total behavior pattern in relation to a particular course of study. This task is performed through a precise statement of objectives, which sets down the abilities, skills and behavior expected from students at the end of courses as a result of having followed them. The flow in this approach is that it implies that the whole person is made of isolated reactions.

We know however that no single aspect of student's behavior can be understood without reference to the total behavior pattern, i.e., without reference. A way of redressing the balance is through Activity Based Learning carried out by the own teacher who is in a unique position to see the student as whole person as well as to help with the evaluation of his progress should be continuous.

In this sense, written tests, oral questioning and discussion projects, reports, class work, homework etc. are all considered to be evaluation measures that causes burden among the teachers.

A teacher use of Activity Based Learning is looking for signs which show the growth of thinking processes and the development of those varying abilities towards which the teaching is aimed; he is more concerned with signposts than the whole itinerary.

The research therefore continuous and educational researchers all over the world all still seeking a breakthrough is elucidating this phenomenon for a better understanding. The outcome of the study is therefore expected to stimulate and to avoid problems upon Innovative Teaching methods like Activity Based Learning introduced among Teachers. With a view to enhancing the educational development activity instead of method is in the need to investigate.

SCOPE OF THE STUDY

This study focused on the problems of teachers in primary schools with regarding the implementation of ABL method. Also this study is intended to offer deeper insights into theory and practice of Problems Faced by Teachers in the Implementation of Active Based Learning Methodology in Pudukkottai Educational District. Concerning practice, this research project might serve as help to school teachers as well as a guide to future ones to overcome their problems. This research may contribute in filling a gap of references about the present study.

STATEMENT OF THE PROBLEM

Problems founded in the implementation of Active Based Learning Methodology study provides information and various reports on the educational progress of students learning outcomes through

Evaluation in teaching and learning process. Thus it helps in predicting the future success of the learner through active based outcomes by suggesting value judgments.

Thus, to investigation made to find the opinion of school teachers entitled as *"Problems Faced by Teachers in the Implementation of Active Based Learning Methodology in Pudukkottai Educational District"*.

OBJECTIVES OF THE STUDY

The objectives for the study are

1. To find out the significant difference between the mean scores of Problems Faced by Teachers in the Implementation of Active Based Learning Methodology with respect to their gender as Male and Female.
2. To find out the significant difference between the mean scores of Problems Faced by Teachers in the Implementation of Active Based Learning Methodology with respect to their type of school as Government and Aided School.
3. To find out the significant difference between the mean scores of Problems Faced by Teachers in the Implementation of Active Based Learning Methodology with respect to their type of school as Aided and Private school.
4. To find out the significant difference between the mean scores of Problems Faced by Teachers in the Implementation of Active Based Learning Methodology with respect to their type of school as Private and Government school.
5. To find out the significant difference between the mean scores of Problems Faced by Teachers in the Implementation of Active Based Learning Methodology with respect to their family nature as Nuclear and Joint family.

6. To find out the significant difference between the mean scores of Problems Faced by Teachers in the Implementation of Active Based Learning Methodology with respect to their locality as Rural and Urban area.
7. To find out the significant difference between the mean scores of Problems Faced by Teachers in the Implementation of Active Based Learning Methodology with respect to their Working Experience as <5 and > 5 years.

HYPOTHESES OF THE STUDY

1. There is no significant difference between the mean scores of Problems Faced by Teachers in the Implementation of Active Based Learning Methodology with respect to their gender as Male and Female.
2. There is no significant difference between the mean scores of Problems Faced by Teachers in the Implementation of Active Based Learning Methodology with respect to their type of school as Government and Aided School.
3. There is no significant difference between the mean scores of Problems Faced by Teachers in the Implementation of Active Based Learning Methodology with respect to their type of school as Aided and Private school.
4. There is no significant difference between the mean scores of Problems Faced by Teachers in the Implementation of Active Based Learning Methodology with respect to their type of school as Private and Government school.
5. There is no significant difference between the mean scores of Problems Faced by Teachers in the Implementation of Active Based Learning Methodology with respect to their family nature as Nuclear and Joint family.
6. There is no significant difference between the mean scores of Problems Faced by Teachers in the Implementation of Active Based Learning Methodology with respect to their locality as Rural and Urban area.

7. There is no significant difference between the mean scores of Problems Faced by Teachers in the Implementation of Active Based Learning Methodology with respect to their Working Experience as <5 and > 5 years.

LIMITATIONS OF THE STUDY

The limitations for the study are as follows;

1. The investigation is restricted to 160 primary School teachers opinion about Problems Faced by Teachers in the Implementation of Active Based Learning Methodology was considered.
2. The data were collected from Pudukkottai Educational District only.
3. The variables were limited to the study framed and highly reliable tool was given as questionnaire.
4. The survey was conducted in the year 2014-2015.

CONCLUSION

This chapter deals with need, significance of the study, scope, key term definition and limitations. The next chapter deals with the collection of literature review for the present study.

Chapter - II

Review of Related Literature

INTRODUCTION

Research takes advantages of the knowledge which has accumulated in the past as a result of constant human Endeavour. It can never be undertaken in isolation of the work that has already been done on the problems which are directly or indirectly related to the study proposed by a researcher. A careful review of the research journals, books, dissertations, thesis and other sources of information on the problems to be investigated is one of the important steps in planning of any research study. Practically all human knowledge can be found in books and libraries. Unlike other animals that must start a new with each generation, man builds up on the accumulated and recorded knowledge makes possible progress in all areas of human endeavor.

THE PURPOSE OF THE REVIEW OF LITERATURE

A review of related studies is explicit, systematic and reproducible method for identifying, evaluating and interpreting the existing body of recorded work produced by scholars. A study review is a critical summary and assessment of the range of existing materials dealing with knowledge and understanding in a given field. The main objectives of review of related studies are mentioned below.

Cataloging variables significant for research

When researcher makes a careful review of the literature, becomes aware of the significant variables in the concerned area of research.

A careful review also helps researcher in selecting the variables falling within the scope of researcher's interest, in defining and operational variables, which are conceptually and virtually significant.

2. Avoidance of repetition

A review of studies helps researcher in evading any duplication of work done earlier. A careful review always aims at understanding previous studies and signifying their efficacy for the intended study.

3. Amalgamation of previous studies

A careful review facilitates researcher to bring together and emulate previous studies related to the intended study.

4. Determining importance and relationship in relevant variables

An evaluation of the literature permits researcher in finding out significant variables. A perfect literature review contributes beyond the stage of simply listing variables to offer an analytical study on the chosen area.

In the present study, studies are classified in to two, studies in abroad and studies in India.

CLASSIFICATION OF REVIEW OF RELATED STUDIES

In the present study, the investigator has classified in to two main classes. They are;

A. Related Indian studies

B. Related foreign studies

STUDIES CONDUCTED IN INDIA

Fatima Nasser, (2014) Problems Faced by Primary School

Teachers .The study identified the problems faced by primary school teachers from the viewpoints of school administrators based on such domains as: curriculum issues, students, local community, school building, facilities, scientific devices and to identify whether there is variation in the availability degree of such problems faced by teachers attributed to school administrative experience, or the academic qualification. A two-part questionnaire was developed based on to measure problems faced by primary school teachers within Irbid Governorate, and adjusted in light of the comments of the judges who validated the study instrument. The first scale measures the demographic characteristics of participants, whereas the second part measures problems faced by primary school teachers as perceived by the school administrators within Irbid Governorate. Sample (N=100) was representative of the public primary school administrators within Ibid Governorate. Results indicated problems faced by teachers; and found statistically significant differences (á=-0.05) attributed to the academic qualification effect on the problems faced that are related to the local community. Further, no statistically significant differences ((á=-0.05) were found attributed to experience effect on all domains. In light of the results, the authors called for increasing the funds allotted for school buildings, student numbers to accommodate classroom size, greater involvement of teachers in curriculum design and development. It is also recommended to set up remedial plans for poor achievers, help students pay greater attention to homework assignments, and invite parents to periodically hold meetings about the teaching process.

Graves, Michael F.; Juel, Connie; Graves, Bonnie B. (2014), Melding what has been learned from research, theory, and experience, this book presents a comprehensive plan for assisting students in becoming lifelong readers and attaining the level of critical literacy crucial for success in the 21st century. Chapters begin with a brief personal statement or scenario to spark interest in the topic and to suggest major themes. Next comes a chapter overview, then the body of the chapter, followed by a section on "Special Needs and Special Talents," and concluding remarks. Chapters conclude with ideas for observing classrooms, talking with parents and teachers, or further investigation; annotated references; and children's literature citations. Chapters in the book are (1) Reading and Learning to Read;

(2) Reading Instruction; (3) Emergent Literacy; (4) Word Recognition; (5) Vocabulary Development; (6) Scaffolding Students' Comprehension of Text: Teacher-Directed Approaches; (7) Guiding Students toward Independence in Reading; (8) Teaching for Understanding in Content Areas; (9) Writing and Reading; (10) Literacy Instruction for Non-Native Speakers of English; (11) Classroom Assessment; and (12) Classroom Portraits. Each chapter contains references.

Solomon Melesse (2013), Implementation of Active Learning Strategies: Perceptions of Primary School Teachers. The study tries to investigate the contribution of primary school teachers' peer- and self- assessment for effective implementation of active learning in their actual classrooms. In this study, areas in which self-reflection and peer assessment include three broad categories, such as methods of teaching and learning, instructional resource utilization, and assessment techniques employed by teachers in actual classes. The study was carried out on randomly selected primary school teachers of Bahir Dar town (the Capital City of Amhara Region, Ethiopia). Using multistage sampling, five schools were randomly selected out of 25 government primary schools found in Bahir Dar town, Amhara Region, Ethiopia. And then, 50 of the teachers were randomly selected from a total of 157 teachers found in the five selected primary schools residing in Bahir Dar town. Of these sample teachers, 32 were females and 18 were males. Data collection checklists were employed to gather information from teachers about their state of using peer-and self-assessment as a means for promoting the implementation of active learning in their respective classes. The results indicated that teachers' peer- and self- assessment are insufficient in promoting active learning in primary schools of Bahir Dar town. This study, therefore, proposes means and ways of improving the roles and status of teachers in using active learning in primary schools of Bahir Dar town as suggested in the current ETP of Ethiopia.

Beijaard, Douwe (2012), Problems Faced by Primary School Teachers, which teachers can use to enhance student learning. It appears difficult for teachers to give qualitatively good feedback, especially during active learning. In this context, teachers should provide facilitative feedback that is focused on the development of meta-cognition and social learning. Aims: The purpose of the present study is to contribute to the existing knowledge about feedback and to give directions to improve teacher feedback in the context of active learning. Sample: The participants comprised 32 teachers who practiced active learning in the domain of environmental studies in the sixth, seventh, or eighth grade of 13 Dutch primary schools. A total of 1,465 teacher-student interactions were examined. Methods: Video observations were made of active learning lessons in the domain of environmental studies. A category system was developed based on the literature and empirical data. Teacher-student interactions were assessed using this system. Results: About half of the teacher-student interactions contained feedback. This feedback was usually focused on the tasks that were being performed by the students and on the ways in which these tasks were processed. Only 5% of the feedback was explicitly related to a learning goal. In their feedback, the teachers were directing (rather than facilitating) the learning processes. Conclusions: During active learning, feedback on meta-cognition and social learning is important. Feedback should be explicitly related to learning goals. In practice, these kinds of feedback appear to be scarce. Therefore, giving feedback during active learning seems to be an important topic for teachers' professional development.

Bent, Gert Jan; Bakx, Anouke; den Brok, Perry (2011), Concerns about the decreasing quality of geography education within primary schools can be linked to a decrease of time spent on geography education and, for example, to low achievement on national or school-specific tests. Learning outcomes for geography stay behind in relation to what experts believe that pupils should perform. Results indicate that pupils would like to gain more theoretical knowledge and get more help from teachers to apply actual and conceptual knowledge within new subject content. Pupils also wish to have more active, inquiry-based teacher activities during the lessons, and to be actively coached and motivated by the teacher.

Westwood, Peter (2011), The Problem with Problems: Potential Difficulties in Implementing Problem-Based Learning as the Core Method in Primary School Mathematics. This viewpoint paper presents the writer's opinion that while the use of problem solving as the core method for learning mathematics is valid and reasonable in secondary schools (where students generally possess the necessary prior skills and strategies) there are many obstacles to applying the same method in primary schools, particularly in the early years. In addition to acquiring a conceptual understanding of number, young learners—and older students with learning difficulties—need to develop automaticity in recalling basic number facts and in applying computational procedures. To do this they require both active experience with number relationships and direct teaching with guided and independent practice. There is no hard evidence that most students achieve adequate mastery of basic numeracy skills simply by engaging in exploratory problem solving. Drawing on the relevant literature the writer identifies and analyses the potential difficulties associated with using such an approach as a main method for teaching primary mathematics.

Martlew, Joan; Stephen, Christine; Ellis, Jennifer (2011), Problems Faced by Primary School Teachers interest in a more play-based pedagogy commonly described as Active Learning. The research reported in this article is an exploration of moves towards creating an active play-based learning environment in six Primary classrooms in Scotland and is concerned with

(i) The children's experiences in such a play-based active learning environment in school and

(ii) Their teachers' perspectives on this pedagogical innovation and their roles in supporting the learners.

This study examined experiences and perspectives within and across each of the six child-centered and play-focused classes. The main findings suggest that the role of the teacher varies between what could be considered as teacher-intensive and teacher-initiated activities. "Active" or "play-based" learning was interpreted differently by teachers; play in some classrooms was peripheral rather than integral to the learning process and curriculum-embedded.

Kocyigit, Sezai, (2010), Starting primary education is one of the most important changes that children encounter in early childhood. Moreover, especially within the last twenty years, as an outcome of the idea that children are active learners, listening to children's ideas about their learning, lives, and experiences has gained importance. In this sense, this study is thought to be significant in terms of its aim to analyze the transition to primary school according to the thoughts of children and to offer suggestions for preschool education. For this purpose, the study was conducted with 55 children who were attending 7 independent kindergarten schools in Ayden city center. The participants were selected by a systematic sampling method. The study was conducted using a phenomenological design. For the data collection, a mosaic approach including different verbal and visual techniques that allowed the children to express themselves comfortably was used. The data were analyzed by descriptive analysis using the Qualitative Analysis program. According to the findings of the study, preschool age children described primary school as big, crowded, complex, and distant. They referred to their family, teachers, and television as information sources. Further, they thought that there were many rules in primary school and they could never play. When the dialogues were considered in general, nearly all of the interviews included negative thoughts. It is thought that this case stems from the lack of right information about primary school.

Engidaw, Berhanu (2010), Problems Faced by Primary School Teachers perceptions and practices of active learning and the constraints to implementing them in the English Department of Bahir Dar University. A mixed study approach that involves a quantitative self administered questionnaire, a semi-structured lesson observation guide, and qualitative in depth interviews was used to obtain relevant data. Information on what perceptions and attitudes teacher trainers and teacher trainees' hold towards active learning, how often they use such methods, and what factors constrain teacher trainers from implementing active learning methods are obtained through the questionnaire. In-depth interview of teacher trainers and classroom lessons observation were used to extrapolate the subjects' responses from the questionnaire. The findings indicated that both teacher trainers and teacher trainees employed Active learning. Teacher trainers used pair and group work more than they use other active learning methods. Teacher trainees on the other hand used more group work, reflection and whole class discussion. No statistically significant difference was noted in the perceptions of teacher trainers and trainees towards active learning. Overall, the study results indicated that there was a shift from the traditional teacher fronted lecture to student centered active learning, which is desirable. While the study findings indicate that both teacher educators and trainee teachers have positive perceptions towards Active Learning, the particular methods they use in their classroom tended to be dictated by the peculiarities of the classroom contexts they work in. The findings point towards a need among teacher practitioners to make informed decisions in choosing active learning methods that suit the specific realities of the classroom they work in. The findings have implications to teacher trainers at the university and trainee teachers working in high schools.

Zayapragassarazan, Z.; Kumar, Santosh (2010),Problems Faced by Primary School Teachers learning experiences and lecture courses may not suit all their learning needs. Effective learning involves providing students with a sense of progress and control over their own learning. This requires creating a situation where learners have a chance to try out or test their ideas. This testing is ideally accomplished by connecting students' ideas to concrete experience and that's where the "active" part of the learning comes in. Active learning involves providing opportunities for students to meaningfully talk and listen, write, read, and reflect on the content, ideas, issues, and concerns of an academic subject. This article briefly describes about some of the popular active learning strategies that have resulted in enhanced learning and are widely followed across the medical schools globally.

STUDIES CONDUCTED IN ABROAD

Cheng, Yuan-Wen; Ren, Lillian (2014), Job satisfaction and job stress have been shown to be consistently related in a range of school education studies. The purpose of this research was to investigate how well the job satisfaction of resource room teachers in Taiwan may be predicted through an understanding of their job stress and demographic characteristics. Method: A total of 153 elementary resource room teachers in Taoyuan were questioned using a self-report questionnaire. Following the questionnaire, 10 veteran resource room teachers were asked to provide further insight into their work. Results: For the 135 participants, both the working condition dimension of job stress and education level were significant predictors of job satisfaction. The results are discussed in terms of the Taiwan context. Conclusions: Along with initiatives to improve the professional qualifications of teachers, some changes may assist in improving the job satisfaction of resource room teachers and extending their careers in Taiwan.

Jocoy, Christine L.; Liu, Yan; Bradford, Michael (2013), Problems Faced by Primary School Teachers in a course, many others stick to conventional teaching methods. They are often deterred by suggestions that it can be difficult to implement active learning where students have no prior knowledge of a subject, that active learning requires too much work of lecturers and students, and that there are significant institutional constraints to implementing active learning. In this article the authors draw on their experiences of utilizing active learning in five different countries before dispelling myths which continue to constrain the uptake of active learning methods. Finally, they provide simple guidelines for successful integration of active learning in geography courses.

Westwood, Peter (2013), This viewpoint paper presents the writer's opinion that while the use of problem solving as the core method for learning mathematics is valid and reasonable in secondary schools (where students generally possess the necessary prior skills and strategies) there are many obstacles to applying the same method in primary schools, particularly in the early years. In addition to acquiring a conceptual understanding of number, young learners—and older students with learning difficulties—need to develop automaticity in recalling basic number facts and in applying computational procedures. To do this they require both active experience with number relationships and direct teaching with guided and independent practice. There is no hard evidence that most students achieve adequate mastery of basic numeracy skills simply by engaging in exploratory problem solving. Drawing on the relevant literature the writer identifies and analyses the potential difficulties associated with using such an approach as a main method for teaching primary mathematics.

Mansell, Jim; Beadle-Brown, Julie; Bigby, Christine (2013), Active support is an effective intervention to support engagement of residents with intellectual disability in group homes. This survey explored resident characteristics of the people supported by organizations implementing active support, the provision of active support, its procedures and systems, and resident engagement in meaningful activity and relationships. Method: Information was collected through questionnaires and direct observation of 33 group homes from 6 organizations in Victoria, Australia, with a 5-10-year history of implementing active support. Results: Residents with lower support needs were engaged with little staff contact or assistance. Use of active support systems and structures was mixed. Only one organization consistently provided good active support. Conclusions: Administrative systems and structures are not sufficient to change staff interaction and thus resident experience. Shared supported accommodation services may represent an inefficient use of resources for more able residents, as staff resources are not maximized to support for resident engagement.

Leung, Shuk-kwan S. (2013), This paper reports a study about how a teacher educator shared knowledge with teachers when they worked together to implement mathematical problem posing (MPP) in the classroom. It includes feasible methods for getting practitioners to use research-based tasks aligned to the curriculum in order to encourage children to pose mathematical problems. Techniques, challenges, and strategies of implementing an MPP focus were also reported.

Tan, Susan M. K.; Bell, Cathy K.; Hunt, Jeffrey (2013), Problem-based Teaching represents a major development and change in educational practice that continues to have a large impact across subjects and disciplines worldwide. It would seem that child and adolescent psychiatry, because of its inherently integrative, bio-psycho-social nature and emphasis on teamwork and collaboration, would be a specialty learned optimally through PBL. Thus, there was a need to establish an international group where experiences in implementing PBL in child and adolescent psychiatry could be shared. This article reports on the first meeting and plans of the Problem-Based Learning in Child and Adolescent Psychiatry (CAP) Special Interest Study Group (SISG), held at the annual meeting of the American Academy of Child and Adolescent Psychiatry. Methods: Through international collaboration and information-sharing, the SISG aims to promote knowledge among Child and Adolescent

Psychiatrists on PBL, to explore evaluation methods of PBL in CAP, and to discuss development of PBL-based curricula. Results: Problem-based learning represents a major change in education that has had a large impact across disciplines worldwide. Conclusion: The core steps in PBL are the following: presentation of the initial problem; discussion of the problem, and development of learning objectives; independent learning focused on the objectives; and discussion, exploration of new ideas, and discovery of solutions in the reconvened group. Different from the traditional teacher's role, the PBL tutor is an active facilitator who guides learners to identify issues and ways to learn, rather than a "content expert" who provides facts.

Orr, Taylor; Flowers, Jim (2012), The goal of formal education is student learning. By emphasizing experimentation in the classroom or lab, students learn about the results of a particular inquiry. But more importantly, they learn to refine their approach to learning by creating new knowledge rather than merely remembering what they have been told. An inquiry approach where students gain experimentation skills can impact how they learn and their approach to problem solving long after school has ended. A subject area that is fertile with opportunities for implementing experimentation into its curriculum is technology and engineering education, because of its focus on problem- and project-based learning. This article discusses several ways of incorporating experimentation into technology education: teacher-directed experiments, student-selected experimental methods, student-selected and student-found topics, and utilizing an inquiry approach.

Cole, Rebecca (2011), Given the current focus on student outcomes, use of the problem-solving model to plan interventions is one method by which school psychologists can hold themselves accountable for implementing counseling interventions that have a positive impact on student behavioral outcomes and mental health. This study surveyed school psychologists about their general counseling practices, as well as their application of the problem-solving model when designing and implementing counseling interventions. A total of 283 Nationally Certified School Psychologists completed an online survey based on current research and best practices for behavioral interventions. Results indicated that counseling is typically provided to general and special education students in group and individual formats. Infrequently, students are recommended for discontinuation and in most cases because counseling goals have reportedly been met. Most often respondents indicated using many general components of the problem-solving model including defining and establishing the behavior of concern (e.g., behavioral definition, problem validation), as well as those involved in determining what should be done about it (e.g., goal setting, intervention plan development). Less frequently did they report monitoring and determining the effectiveness of counseling interventions (e.g., formative and summative evaluation, decision-making plan), as well as problem-analysis. These results suggest that school psychologists apply many of the steps of the problem-solving model in accordance with federal special education laws, especially when defining target behaviors and planning interventions. These results, however, also call into question the degree to which these school psychologists engage in progress monitoring and data-based decision making. The quality and frequency of baseline and progress monitoring data collection may not enable accurate comparison of student behavior and demonstration that behavioral improvement has been made. Further research is needed to determine barriers and facilitators to objective data gathering in practice settings. Implications for school psychology training programs include knowledge of practices to focus on in order to help new and current practitioners make a paradigm shift from assessors to researchers and active problem-solvers who consistently and effectively implement all aspects of the problem-solving model and consult with other school professionals to gather and evaluate behavioral data and demonstrate accountability.

Stenhouse, Vera L.; Jarrett, Olga S. (2011), Problems Faced by Primary School Teachers, the authors initiated a "Problem Solution Project" (PSP) in the second year a two-year urban certification and Master's program. The PSP, designed to promote empowerment of first-year urban teachers and their students, involves both service learning. In 2004, the authors began implementing a PSP in the program's first year, to enable pre service teachers to experience civically engaged learning using a student centered, participatory approach. The purposes were to: (a) encourage pre service teachers' own active practice and participation in identifying problems and forging solutions and (b) model how they might conduct a PSP in their own classrooms the following year. This article describes five years of implementing first-year problem solution projects.

McCoy, Leah P., Ed. (2010), This document presents the proceedings of the 18th Annual Research Forum held June 26, 2013, at Wake Forest University in Winston-Salem, North Carolina. Included are the following 13 action research papers: (1) Developing Oral Language Ability in the Secondary Spanish Classroom Using the Interpersonal and Presentational Modes of Communication (Sophia Bauers); (2) Problem-Based Learning and Student Attitudes in Mathematics (Caitlin Boone); (3) "Grammar-Drama": An Exploration of Teaching Grammar through Performing Arts (Kaylin Bugica); (4) Mining for Gold on the Silver Screen: Using Film to Develop Active Literacy Skills (Beau Burns); (5) Influences of Reflective Writing in High School Biology (Laurel Clapp); (6) Multicultural Perspective Taking in Social Studies Education (Angelina Cobb); (7) Using Primary Sources to Evoke Historical Empathy (Christina Cobb); (8) Computers and Problem-Based Learning in Mathematics (Hannah Everhart); (9) Developing Empathy through Identity Enactment Techniques (Caroline Fisher); (10) Literature 2.0: An Exploration of Character using Edmodo (Christina McClain); (11) Flipping the High School Mathematics Classroom (Allison Mousel); (12) Environmental Literacy Meets English: How Students Think about Sense of Place in the Classroom (Michael Short); and (13) How Implementing Interactive Geometric Software Affects Students' Achievement, Engagement, and Attitude Towards Mathematics (Matthew Tysinger). (Individual papers contain references, tables, and figures.)

Santos, Afonso (2010), The objectives were to: i) describe the experience of implementing Problem-Based Learning in an online course over three consecutive academic years, ii) analyze the learning environment generated, iii) discuss impacts on students' active participation, based on the analysis of their interactions. The participants were 30 students, working in five groups, and four tutors. All the interactions of each member of the five groups and their tutors in the discussion forums were identified and counted. The interactions identified were subjected to content analysis. The results showed a great variability in the degree of participation of each member of the group as well as the development of a group dynamic that did not appear to depend on the activity of each tutor. Moreover, in most groups, tutors reduced their participation during the semester. Regarding the ways students participated, and despite the individual variability observed, most students kept actively involved in the work contrarily to what research has shown about the uneven students' participation in online courses. Two categories of interactions were identified in the groups according to the underlying objectives: learning-problem solving and group functioning. Whereas all groups were able to solve the problems under investigation, only a few demonstrated self-regulation capabilities leading to a great cohesion among the group members. The discussion of the results generated some guidelines for future investigations regarding the use of PBL in online environments.

Yi, Zeng; LuXi, Zhang (2010), In the past few years, many students have begun to lose interest in science and information and engineering technology courses because they find them too boring and hard to learn. To strengthen this field of education and stimulate students' motivation and interest in learning, this study introduces a theoretical pedagogical framework based on cooperative learning theory and tailored to the realities of the university education system in China. In the framework, a group in a class is treated as a system that goes through different stages and is subject to different input instructions and output outcomes. Based on this structure, teachers' interventions serve as feedback for controlling inputs to promote the correct operation of the system. This study aims to promote the development of a cooperative learning model for university students. A case study of the application of the framework shows that it has positive and active effects on student learning.

Kapanadze, Marika; Eilks, Ingo (2010), After the collapse of the former Soviet Union, many Central and Eastern European countries underwent significant change in their political and educational systems, among them Georgia and Moldova. Reforms in education sought to overcome the highly centralized educational system of the former Soviet Union as well as to conquer the teacher-centered paradigm in schools that was both dominant in these countries during pre- and post-Soviet times. National reforms demanded more student-active and problem-based science education under the heading of hands-on and inquiry-based learning. Unfortunately, in many cases, the curricula, teaching materials, and teacher training facilities were inadequate in implementing these reforms successfully. In the case of science education, this paper reflects upon how European Union (EU) initiatives can help the countries in Central and Eastern Europe in their reform efforts. Reflection is performed in relation to the cross-regional TEMPUS IV project Sails (Student Active Learning in Science). SAM envisages countries strengthening their capacities to promote contemporary science education through investments in science teacher education curricula and infrastructure. The current paper discusses the potential of such EU projects for aiding reform in science education in EU-neighboring countries.

Cho, Moon-Heum; Rathbun, Gail (2009), Teacher Professional Development and Problems Faced by Primary School Teachers is critical for educational improvement in higher education. However, one of the main concerns in TPD is that the traditional workshop format constrains active participation and the consequent creation of usable knowledge for teaching. In response to this challenge, we developed a series of teacher-centered online Teacher Professional Development programmes using a problem-based learning approach. We created opportunities for participants to engage in the programmes and to construct usable knowledge that could be immediately applied in their own class contexts. The study presents examples of findings, and lessons learned for successful implementation of teacher-centered programmes in higher education. This study will be particularly beneficial to the practitioners who plan to implement programme for teachers.

Lee, Seung Hwan; Hoffman, K. Douglas, (2009), Based on the popular television show the “Iron Chef,” an innovative marketing activity called the “Iron Inventor” is introduced. Using the creative problem-solving approach and active learning techniques, the Iron Inventor facilitates student learning pertaining to the step-by-step processes of creating a new product and exposes students to the challenges associated with the new product development processes. End-of-semester assessments reveal the Iron Inventor as a superior method in enhancing student satisfaction. More specifically, the Iron

Inventor activity increases students' creative input, enhances topic knowledge, engages participation, fosters relationships, and builds class enthusiasm.

Demirel, Turgay; Baydas, Ozlem (2008), The numbers of project competitions and interest in this kind of competition have been steadily increasing in Turkey. Accordingly, it is important to determine what challenges teachers and students may face while preparing themselves for project competitions, so that recommendations may be made to overcome these challenges. This study investigated challenges faced by secondary school students and their project advisors. The teachers' own solutions for the difficulties that were encountered are presented at the end. Both quantitative and qualitative research approaches were used in the data collection and analysis processes. One hundred twenty-one teachers participated in this study. The identified challenges include the students' lack of requisite information and skills, insufficient financial and technical support, the students' lack of interest, and problems with cooperation from universities. The recommended solutions include improving financial and technical support, revising education programs to be more project-based, and strengthening cooperation with universities.

Edwards, Richard (2007), In highlighting the importance of problem-based learning in the development of 21st century skills, (Yun Jo) An (2013) identified the challenges faced by novice teachers in its implementation and suggested strategies to support them. This commentary explores two aspects mentioned in the article, assessment and the role of collaboration, and argues that they need greater critical consideration if the implementation of problem-based learning is to be effective. The role digital technologies can play is discussed and some implications for teacher education are considered.

Mielants, Eric; Weiner, Melissa F. (2007), This article addresses the difficulty of local-level qualitative educational research in Amsterdam in light of changes related to contemporary political discourse on decades of immigration, especially from the 1970s onward, and increasingly critical assessments of Dutch education in the literature. It considers recent developments in the Netherlands while taking into account similar processes elsewhere in the European Union, with the aim of understanding taboos and problems associated with research on immigration, racism, and discrimination. Specifically, we utilize one researcher's efforts to gain access to educationally based field sites to focus attention on the links between contextual political discourses and policies excluding immigrants with efforts to sociologically examine the experiences of immigrants. We conclude with a discussion of broader challenges faced by social scientists, including the benefits and disadvantages of having outsider status, attempting to utilize ethnographic methodology abroad when scrutinizing politically sensitive topics.

Terriquez, Veronica (2007), Problems Faced by Primary School Teachers developing members civic capacity. Yet few empirical studies examine how and the extent to which civic skills transfer across distinct and separate civic contexts. Focusing on Latino immigrant members of a Los Angeles janitors' labor union, this article fills a void by investigating union members' involvement in an independent civic arena—their children's schools. Analyses of random sample survey and semi-structured interview data demonstrate that labor union experience does not simply lead to more civic engagement, as previous research might suggest. Rather, conceptual distinctions must be made between active and inactive union members and between different types of civic engagement. Results show that active union members are not particularly involved in plug-in types of involvement, which are typically defined and dictated by school personnel. Instead, active union members tend to become involved in critical forms of engagement that allow them to voice their interests and exercise leadership. Furthermore, findings suggest that the problem solving, advocacy, and organizing skills acquired through union participation do not uniformly influence members' civic engagement. Experience in a social movement union serves as a catalyst for civic engagement for some, while it enhances the leadership capacity of others.

Lamonica, Aukje K.; Boeri, Miriam (2005), This study examines patterns of use of prescription drugs and methamphetamine. We drew our sample from a study about 130 active and inactive methamphetamine users and focused on 16 participants with a recent history of methamphetamine and prescription drug use. We collected in-depth interviews to explore relationships in use trajectory patterns. The qualitative methods we used in this study followed the constant comparison process developed by grounded theory methods and analytical ethnography, which is based on familiarity with the social setting and developing propositions while conducting a research study. We used a triangulation of methods and analysis and included qualitative data, such as participant observation notes and in-depth interviews, as well as quantitative data that we collected in drug history matrices. Five themes emerged from the coding of the interview transcripts: (1) sequential polydrug use; (2) concurrent polydrug use (3) temporary substitution of preferred drug; (4) consequential-based use; and (5) switching from using methamphetamine to using prescription drugs. The trajectory patterns of methamphetamine and prescription drug use complicates treatment significantly.

Ampuero, David; Miranda, Christian E (2005), The present study explores the outcomes of teaching empathy and critical thinking to solve environmental problems. This investigation was done throughout the duration of an environmental education course within a primary school located in central Chile. A community-based research methodology was used to understand the formation of empathy and critical thinking. The findings reveal a significant benefit in using empathy strategies to engage students regarding the thinking processes involved with solving environmental problems. Using these elements as teaching techniques for environmental education courses can be very helpful in reaching the aims of creating a sustainable citizenry.

Grenier-Boley, Nicolas (2004), Certain mathematical concepts were not introduced to solve a specific open problem but rather to solve different problems with the same tools in an economic formal way or to unify several approaches: such concepts, as some of those of linear algebra, are presumably difficult to introduce to students as they are potentially interwoven with many types of difficulties as formal ones and far away from the actual knowledge of the students. The purpose of this paper is to propose a methodology for studying the introduction of such concepts in linear algebra during tutorial sessions at the beginning of university, the wording of the concepts being yet presented during lectures. For this purpose, we amend a general methodology of Parries, Robert and Rogalski inside the general framework of Activity Theory. This methodology lets us take into account several specificities of these concepts and studies the mathematical activity the teacher organizes for students and the way he manages the relationship between students' actual activities and mathematical tasks. We also present an implementation of this methodology based on a French university course to illustrate our approach and discuss its possibilities.

Hollenbeck, James (2004), Science educators define a learning environment in which the problem drives the learning as problem based learning. Problem based learning can be a learning methodology/process or a curriculum based on its application by the teacher. This paper discusses the basic premise of Problem base learning and successful applications of such learning. PBL enables students to develop skills, and inquiry methodology to solve problems for the future. This important teaching application will better prepare our students to meet a global future. A 15-item cited bibliography is included.

Juergensmeyer, Erik (2004), The methodology of community-based action research provides concrete strategies for fostering effective community problem solving. To argue for a community research pedagogy, the author draws upon past and present scholarship in action research and participatory action research, experiences teaching an undergraduate writing course revolving around action research, and conversations with community members who have benefitted from student research.

Leung, Nelson (2004), Due to the successful implementation of knowledge management (KM) in many commercial organizations, KM has been recently extended to higher education institutions to manage scholar knowledge, and institution policies and procedures. To address the lack of insight in regards to the engagement of tertiary students to manage knowledge at a course level, a KM methodology is proposed to allow students to interact with lecturers in and outside large lecture halls to create, disseminate, use and evaluate knowledge. The proposed methodology provides electronic, telecommunication and manual channels to allow students to ask questions in lectures when they fail to understand any incoming knowledge delivered by academics regardless of time and space constraints. Knowledge developed based on students' questions can further be evaluated and extended using mechanisms to comment and recommend features. In additional, students are able to create new knowledge and to solve problems using incoming knowledge as the methodology which can enhance knowledge understanding throughout the learning process. The proposed methodology was applied to a business computing course at an undergraduate level, conducted in an offshore campus of an Australian university in the third trimester of 2012. The methodology was evaluated using quantitative analysis. The findings show that the majority of the students agreed the computerized tool incorporated in the methodology could enhance their learning experience by allowing students to ask for, share, discuss and extend knowledge. In particular, the knowledge management system provided additional channels and a platform for those who are passive and preferred not to seek help from lecturers directly, due to cultural or other reason.

Gardner, Andrew W. (2003), Brief functional analysis is an abbreviated assessment methodology derived from traditional extended functional analysis methods. BFAs are often conducted when time constraints in clinics, schools or homes are of concern. While BFAs have been used extensively to identify the function of problem behavior for children with disabilities, their utility with typically developing children has been questioned. This systematic review evaluates empirical studies, in which BFAs were employed with typically developing children to identify function of problem behavior. Twelve articles were reviewed and coded for quality indicators based on specific single-subject design criteria. Nine studies were considered to have acceptable quality and were summarized according to practice dimensions such as settings, therapists, problem behavior, and behavioral functions. Results suggest that BFA meets the standards for an empirically supported assessment methodology for typically developing children. Evidence is strongest for parents and teachers to serve as therapists when disruptive behavior is of concern.

Davis, Nancy T.; Callihan, Laurie P. (2003), This article examines the multiple methodologies used in educational research and proposes a model that includes all of them as contributing to understanding educational contexts and research from multiple perspectives. The model, based on integral theory (Wilber in a theory of everything. Shambhala, Boston, 2000) values all forms of research as true, but partial. Consideration of objective (exterior) forms of research and data and subjective (interior) forms of research and data are further divided into individual and collective domains. Taking this categorization system one step further reveals eight indigenous perspectives that form a framework for considering research methodologies. Each perspective has unique questions, data sources, methods and quality criteria designed to reveal what is "true" from that view. As science educators who guide our students' research, this framework offers a useful guide to explain differences in types of research, the purpose and validity of each. It allows professional science educators to appreciate multiple forms of research while maintaining rigorous quality criteria. Use of this framework can also help avoid problems of imposing quality criteria of one methodology on research data and questions gathered using another methodology. This model is explored using the second author's dissertation research. Finally a decision chart is provided to use with those who are starting inquiries to guide their thinking and choice of appropriate methodologies to use when conducting research.

Schechter, Chen (2001), This article aims to reinterpret principal preparatory programs to also include the collective learning-from-success process (success-based learning), thus providing a complementary instructional framework on how to prepare principals for today's public school reality. Design/methodology/approach: The discussion reviews the core leadership capacities for today's and tomorrow's principal ship and the need to rethink principal preparatory programs accordingly. The interrelationship between problems and learning is described, coupled with the possibilities and limitations of problem-based learning. Success-based learning is then described, enumerating its potentials and pitfalls. Findings: The paper finds that focusing on both learning from problems and learning from successes in leadership education may better develop prospective principals' leadership capacities necessary to lead schools in a dynamic environment. Originality/value: The paper highlights the need to conceptualize and empirically investigate problem-based learning and success-based learning as interrelated instructional frameworks that are both necessary to develop effective future leaders.

John Dewey, ABL is not a completely new teaching style because it can be traced back at least as far as Socrates and Humboldt. However, it has been discovered by progressive educators. For a long time, it seemed that universities neglected to think about the process of learning, since it is a highly active process in which it is imperative to convince students to speak, read, write, and think deeply. "The thinking required while attending class [traditionally has been] low level comprehension that goes from the ear to the writing hand and leaves the mind untouched". In contrast, the success of ABL is to make students feel responsible for their learning and to support their own individual development.

For several years ABL has been implemented in teaching-learning curricula in a variety of settings from private schools (e.g., Montessori schools) to universities. Applications can be found in medicine, science and engineering and more recently, also in operations management classes (e.g., Kanet and Barut, 2003). Recently, the Harvard Business School even created a committee on activity-based learning aimed at integrating students' extracurricular activities with their academic experiences in the classroom.

Activity -Based Learning is an umbrella term that refers to several models at instruction that focuses the responsibility of learning on the learners. Activity-Based Learning is a procedure where students actively engage in the lesson rather than just sitting, listening and absorbing the lesson. It is a method of teaching that enables students to be involved in reading, writing, discussion, practical activities, analysis and evaluation of the topic under discussion.

The models of Activity- Based Learning suggest that all learning activities involve some kind of learners' experiences which emphasizes observing and doing (Kathleen, 1996). These also promote students involvement and actively engaging with material to enhance the recall of information according to Bruner in Azuka. Learning becomes more perfect when theoretical knowledge is supplemented by learning all possible life supporting skills which can only be enhanced through Activity- Based Learning method in teaching. Learning can be termed meaningful in the life of the learners when they learned or acquired knowledge, facts, ideas, concepts, skill, behaviors and attitudes are transferred to thinking and action of the learners. To effectively carryout activity- based learning in classrooms, the teachers are advised to adhere strictly to the following: learning experiences should be arranged to create motivation and interest in the students to learn concept by doing; teacher should move away from telling or lecturing method and embrace the use of activity- based learning; teacher should make sure that the learning experiences are arranged according to the need of the learners and make them search and gather more information in the teaching and learning of; and learning experiences should become challenging to the students and stimulate them for more self activities. Others are that learning experiences should energize the improvement of their thinking abilities, decision-making abilities, intellectual resourcefulness and discipline in life; learning experiences should be inspiring, able to relate them to life situations and bring about desirable change in behavior thus leading to the development of personality (Mathew, 2000). The reasons while teachers are advised to embrace activity-based learning is that students understand concepts better when they are engaged in learning experiences which help to enhance higher retention in the learners and provide opportunities for them to think for themselves.

CONCLUSION

The review has revealed the extent of contribution of educationalists and research periodicals in the area of the present study. The next chapter deals with methodology.

Chapter - III

Methodology

INTRODUCTION

Research methodology involves systematic procedures starting from the initial identification of the problem to its final conclusions. Its role is to carry on the research work in a scientific and valid manner. This chapter deals with methodological procedures used in the present study. These procedures were selected based on the previous pertinent studies. In this chapter, the investigator explained objectives, Assumptions, Hypotheses, Research Methods, Data Collection, Data Analysis and Delimitations of the study.

Methodology occupies on important place is and kind of research methods or methodology refers to the way the study is conducted. It refers to the design through which validity of result is to be established. It is pointed at that the success of any research largely depends on the suitability of the method and the tools techniques used to collect reliable and valid data.

RESEARCH DESIGN

1. Selection of dependent variables and categorical variables.

2. Construction of tools to measure the Problems Faced by Teachers in the Implementation of Active Based Learning Methodology.
3. Methods of establishing the reliability, validity and item analysis of the tool constructed.
4. Sampling procedure adopted in this study and Scheduling the survey method

RESEARCH PROCEDURE

1. Problem Selection
2. Plotting The Variables
3. Development Of Tools
4. Selection Of Sample
5. Administration Of Tools
6. Collection Of Data
7. Data Analysis And Interpretation
8. Test Of Hypotheses
9. Findings And Evaluation

METHOD AND ITS PROCEDURES

J. Mouly, has said, "No category of educational research is more widely used than the type know variously as the survey and description research the board classification comprise a variety of specific techniques on procedures all similar from the stand point of purpose that is, to establish the status of the phenomenon under investigation".

For the present study, the investigator followed the Normative Survey method; the word 'survey' indicated the gathering of the data.

The normative survey method uses statistics and values considered normal for the group being surveyed to understand and collect data on a specific subject. The normative survey method is sometimes referred to as descriptive research as well. All of the information gathered in this type of survey should always be compared to the social norms for the group being surveyed and tested.

Normative data, data that characterize what is usual in a defined population at a specific point or period of time, are of enormous importance to primary care. Such data, which seek to describe rather than explain phenomena, are essential for:

a) describing the natural history of conditions in the community;

b) developing standards of care for primary level and

c) establishing appropriate for primary care research.

In all studies designed to obtain normative data, methodological issues need careful attention. Especially important in studies which seek normative data are precise characterization of the study population, clear definition and measurement of phenomena and appropriate interpretation and generalization of results.

In order to realize the above said objectives **Normative Survey Method** is employed. Normative Survey Methods studies, describes and interprets what exists at present. They are concerned with existing conditions or relations, prevailing practices, beliefs and attitudes etc. Such investigations are termed in research literature as Descriptive Survey or Normative Survey. The term "Normative" implies the determination of typical conditions or practices.

The term "Survey" suggest the gathering of evidences related to prevailing conditions or practices.

STATEMENT OF THE PROBLEM

Problems founded in the implementation of Active Based Learning Methodology study provides information and various reports on the educational progress of students learning outcomes through Evaluation in teaching and learning process. Thus it helps in predicting the future success of the learner through active based outcomes by suggesting value judgments. Thus, to investigation made to find the opinion of school teachers entitled as *"Problems Faced by Teachers in the Implementation of Active Based Learning Methodology in Pudukkottai Educational District".*

OBJECTIVES OF THE STUDY

The objectives for the study are

1. To find out the significant difference between the mean scores of Problems Faced by Teachers in the Implementation of Active

Based Learning Methodology with respect to their gender as Male and Female.

2. To find out the significant difference between the mean scores of Problems Faced by Teachers in the Implementation of Active Based Learning Methodology with respect to their type of school as Government and Aided School.
3. To find out the significant difference between the mean scores of Problems Faced by Teachers in the Implementation of Active Based Learning Methodology with respect to their type of school as Aided and Private school.
4. To find out the significant difference between the mean scores of Problems Faced by Teachers in the Implementation of Active Based Learning Methodology with respect to their type of school as Private and Government school.
5. To find out the significant difference between the mean scores of Problems Faced by Teachers in the Implementation of Active Based Learning Methodology with respect to their family nature as Nuclear and Joint family.
6. To find out the significant difference between the mean scores of Problems Faced by Teachers in the Implementation of Active Based Learning Methodology with respect to their locality as Rural and Urban area.
7. To find out the significant difference between the mean scores of Problems Faced by Teachers in the Implementation of Active Based Learning Methodology with respect to their Working Experience as <5 and > 5 years.

HYPOTHESES OF THE STUDY

The Hypotheses for the study are;

1. There is no significant difference between the mean scores of Problems Faced by Teachers in the Implementation of Active Based Learning Methodology with respect to their gender as Male and Female.
2. There is no significant difference between the mean scores of Problems Faced by Teachers in the Implementation of Active

Based Learning Methodology with respect to their type of school as Government and Aided School.

3. There is no significant difference between the mean scores of Problems Faced by Teachers in the Implementation of Active Based Learning Methodology with respect to their type of school as Aided and Private school.
4. There is no significant difference between the mean scores of Problems Faced by Teachers in the Implementation of Active Based Learning Methodology with respect to their type of school as Private and Government school.
5. There is no significant difference between the mean scores of Problems Faced by Teachers in the Implementation of Active Based Learning Methodology with respect to their family nature as Nuclear and Joint family.
6. There is no significant difference between the mean scores of Problems Faced by Teachers in the Implementation of Active Based Learning Methodology with respect to their locality as Rural and Urban area.
7. There is no significant difference between the mean scores of Problems Faced by Teachers in the Implementation of Active Based Learning Methodology with respect to their Working Experience as <5 and > 5 years.

DELIMITATIONS OF THE STUDY

The limitations for the study are as follows;

1. The investigation is restricted to 160 primary School teachers opinion about Problems Faced by Teachers in the Implementation of Active Based Learning Methodology was considered.
2. The data were collected from Pudukkottai Educational District only.
3. The variables were limited to the study framed and highly reliable tool was given as questionnaire.
4. The survey was conducted in the year 2014-2015.

RESEARCH TOOLS

The investigator herself constructed a research tool on identification of different Problems Faced by Teachers in the Implementation of Active Based Learning Methodology.

CONSTRUCTION OF RESEARCH TOOL

Before constructing the research tools, the investigator visited a few schools located in and around Pudukkottai District. To identify Problems Faced by Teachers in the Implementation of Active Based Learning Methodology on the basis of the construction of the research tool. The problems are collected one and referred very carefully by the investigator and then the question items were selected. These items were pooled to frame the research tool for the present study.

SAMPLES OF THE STUDY

After finalizing the research tool the investigator collected 160 samples from the primary and upper primary level school teachers in and around Pudukkottai District. Both male and female teachers response were recorded with few variables and with some sub variables.

DESCRIPTION OF THE RESEARCH TOOL AND SCORING PROCEDURE

A questionnaire on Problems in the Implementation of Active Based Learning Methodology observation categorized with 30 statements in different evaluation based aspects. All the items of the questionnaire are focusing on varieties of Active Based Learning Methodology. All the items are open ended type.

The personal data sheet was prepared to collect the information on personal and institution related details of teachers working at primary school level such as gender, school management, family nature, locality, , teaching experience and annual income of the teachers were considered.

It is a three point of likert's types of tool consist "Agree", "Disagree", "Strongly Disagree". The inventory consists of 30 statements which related Problems in the Implementation of Active Based Learning Methodology.

PILOT STUDY

The investigator conducted pilot study in few School located at Pudukkottai district. Before administering the research tool, the investigator gave some instructions regarding how to answer for all questions. Then the investigator allowed them to give their response for the each and every item of the questionnaire statements.

After getting response from the respondents, the investigator gave frequencies for the correct response and these frequencies were converted into scores.

The collected samples were considered for finding the reliability, validity and consistency level of the tool.

VALIDITY OF THE TOOL

In validation process, the investigator used two measures in order to establish validation of tools. The investigator established content validity.

To find out the validity of research tool as *"Problems Faced by Teachers in the Implementation of Active Based Learning Methodology in Pudukkottai Educational District"*.

RELIABILITY OF THE TOOL

The split-half method of reliability has been used to establish the reliability of the scale. The coefficient of correlation between the odd and even numbers scores are found separately for the tool based on implementation of Active Based Learning Methodology responded by the teachers.

The reliability test has been calculated by using the Spearman-Brown formula.

$$r_{11} \frac{2r^{oe}}{1+r^{oe}}$$

$$= \frac{2x0.79}{1+0.79}$$

$$= 0.88$$

Hence the present tool, Problems Faced by Teachers in the Implementation of Active Based Learning Methodology has the reliability value 0.88 and it is said to be highly reliable.

SAMPLING TECHNIQUE USED

The sampling procedure is used to collect the data is random sampling. The investigator collected samples from various school teachers located in an around Pudukkottai District.

The term population means the aggregate number of totality of objects or individuals regarding which references are to be made in a sampling study. A population is any group of individuals that have one or more characteristics common that are in the research.

A population refers to any collection of specified group of human beings or non-human entities such as objects, educational institutions and time and Geo-graphics areas.

A sample is a small portion of a population selected for analysis. By observing the sample certain inferences may be made about population.

For studying any problem it is difficult to study to whole population or universe studying the entire universe is not viable in many ways, it is therefore convenient to pick up a sample out of the universe proposed to be conversed by the study.

Sampling means selecting a given number of people from a defined population. By target population, we mean all the members of a real or hypothetical set of people events or objects to which we wish to generalize the results of our research, if sampling is done by the researcher he can search conclusion about an entire population that are likely to be correct with in a small margin of error by studying a relatively small sample.

To cover the entire population is an impossible task for any survey or research. What is feasible and generally practiced is to study a sample representative of the population. Therefore a sample of 160 primary school teachers had been drawn by **Random Sampling** method for the present study. The sample consists of both men and women teachers from Government, Aided and Private schools in Pudukkottai District.

COLLECTION OF DATA

The investigator herself visited the schools teachers located in and around Pudukkottai, by getting permission from the headmasters of various schools. Before administering the research tool the investigator explain the aim and purpose of the study and then administered the research tool for school teachers. Then the investigator asked all the teachers to respond for each and every item that are given in the questionnaire.

The responses were recorded and the demographic particulars were collected from the teachers. The collected data were used for data analysis. After collecting data, the investigator gave frequencies for all the question items and then entered in master table as frequencies and those were converted into scores for analysis.

ANALYSIS OF DATA

The researchers tried to make this study as objective as possible. The data were collected through the survey by visits.

The analysis of data was done using the earn differences't' test to find out significant differences in Problems Faced by Teachers in the Implementation of Active Based Learning Methodology using variables given.

The data collected were tested in total. In differential level of the scores with independent variables were compared. The hypotheses were tested using "t" test at 0.05 level of significance.

STATISTICAL TECHNIQUES USED

Descriptive statistics were used to describe the sample with reference to the variables taken for the study. In the differential analysis the significant of difference between the groups was studied using't' test .

DESCRIPTIVE STATISTICAL ANALYSIS

It is concerned with numerical description of a particular group observed. Any similarity to those outside the group cannot be taken for granted. The data describe one group only.

Simple educational research involves descriptive statistics and provides valuable information about the nature of a particular group or class.

Data collected from tests have little meaning or significance until they have been classified or rearranged in a systematic way.

ARITHMETIC MEAN

The mean of a distribution is commonly understood as the arithmetic average. It is computed by dividing the sum of all scores by the number of scores.

$$x = \frac{\Sigma x_1}{n}$$

$$x = \frac{\Sigma x_1}{n}$$

$$s = \sqrt{\frac{\Sigma(x_1 - x)^2}{n-1}}$$

MEDIAN

Median is defined as the midpoint of a given distribution. It is the point which divides the given distribution exactly into two halves.

MODE

Mode is that measure which occurs most frequently. It is the popular measure or the most often repeated score in a distribution.

STANDARD ERROR

The population standard deviation of many measurements of a mean of n samples. It is estimated by the standard deviation of one measurement of the mean divided by the square root.

STANDARD DEVIATION (S.D)

Standard Deviation is the square-root of the mean of the squares of the deviations of all the items from the arithmetic mean. It is represented by the letter 'ó'.

RANGE:

Maximum value minus minimum value. (Usually increases as n

increases, making it a poor measure of the dispersion or spread of the population values)

THE LEVEL OF SIGNIFICANCE

The rejection or acceptance of a null hypothesis is based upon some level of significance as a criterion.

TWO – TAILED TEST

If a null hypothesis is established that there is no significant difference between the mean I.Q. scores one would be concerned only with a difference.

t – TEST

Thee test of significance of the difference between two means is known as t-test. It involves the computation of the ratio between experimental variance (Observe difference between two sample means) and error variance (the sampling error factor).

When small samples are involved, the t-table is used to determine statistical-significance, rather than the normal probability table.

This concept of small sample size was developed around 1915 by William Sealy Gusset, consulting tacticians for Guinness Breweries of Bublin, Ireland. Gusset's t-critical values, carefully calculated for small samples are reproduced in the t-distribution table.

The t-critical values necessary for rejection of a null hypothesis are higher for small samples of a given level of significance.

Each t-critical value for rejection is based upon the appropriate number of degree of freedom. The t- test would be based upon this formula.

$$t = \frac{M_1 \quad M_2}{SED}$$

$$SED \quad \sqrt{\frac{SD^2}{N_2} \quad \frac{SD^2}{N_2}}$$

$$DF \quad (N_1 - 1) + (N_2 - 1)$$

CONCLUSION

The research procedure adopted in this study was discussed in the chapter. The data collected as 160 data were interpreted in the upcoming chapter. The data were analyzed with suitable statistical techniques and interpreted.

Chapter - IV

Analysis and Interpretation of Data

INTRODUCTION

One of the important parts of any investigation is analysis and interpretation of data. The data collected in any field of activity becomes meaningful and useful only when there are subjected to statistical analysis and inference.

Analysis of data means studying the organized material in order to discover inherent facts. The data are studied from as many angles as possible explore the few facts. Once the research data have been collected data analysis has been made. Then the research interpreting is essentially needed to state whether the result shows the research data become meaningful after they are being analyzed and interpreted.

The analysis and interpretation of data involves the objective material in the possession of the research and his subjective reactions and desires to device from the data.

ANALYSIS OF DATA

Analysis of data mean studying the tabulated materials in orders to determine inherent fact of meaning. It involves the breaking down of the existing complex factors into simple parts and putting them together in an arrangement for the purpose of interpretation.

According to Pearson, "Analysis is a research technique for objective, systematic and quantitative description of the manifest content of communication".

According to Cristofer, "Analysis is an important phase of the classification and summation of data into a summary"

According to Prestly, "The discovery of order in the phenomena of nature, not withstanding their complexity and apparent confusion is rendered possible by process of analysis and synthesis which are foundation stone of all scientific methods".

After, collection the data from the respondents, the investigator gave frequencies for the correct responses and these frequencies were converted into scores and then investigator calculated the scores.

These scores were used to identify the level of *"Problems Faced by Teachers in the Implementation of Active Based Learning Methodology in Pudukkottai Educational District".*

TESTING OF HYPOTHESES

Analysis is a technique of social research which presents qualitative data in an objective, systematic and quantitative.

The investigator also tests the significance to find out the significant difference between the various groups of demographic variables in *"Problems Faced by Teachers in the Implementation of Active Based Learning Methodology in Pudukkottai Educational District".*

The following are the Hypotheses to be tested;

HYPOTHESIS: 1

There is no significant difference between the mean scores of Problems Faced by Teachers in the Implementation of Active Based Learning Methodology with respect to their gender as Male and Female.

TABLE: 1

The table given below shows the mean, standard deviation and "t" values of Problems Faced by Teachers in the Implementation of Active Based Learning Methodology with respect to their gender as Male and Female.

Gender	N	M	SD	df	't' value	Level of Significance at 0.05
Male	34	75.85	5.28			
Female	126	74.86	4.88	158	0.986	Not Significant

INTERPRETATION

The computed table value of **t = 0.986** is smaller than the critical table value at 0.05 level of significance (i.e.) 1.96 for df = 158, which implies that there is no significant difference in the mean scores of Problems Faced by Teachers in the Implementation of Active Based Learning Methodology with respect to their gender as Male and Female.

RESULT

Hence the null hypothesis is accepted.

HYPOTHESIS: 2

There is no significant difference between the mean scores of Problems Faced by Teachers in the Implementation of Active Based Learning Methodology with respect to their type of school as Government and Aided School.

TABLE: 2

The table given below shows the mean, standard deviation and "t" values of Problems Faced by Teachers in the Implementation of Active Based Learning Methodology with respect to their type of school as Government and Aided School.

School Management	N	M	SD	df	't' value	Level of Significance at 0.05
Government	66	75.39	5.35			
Govt. Aided	30	75.27	5.06	94	0.106	Not Significant

INTERPRETATION

The computed table value of **t = 0.106** is smaller than the critical table value at 0.05 level of significance (i.e.) 1.96 for df = 94, which implies that there is no significant difference in the mean scores of Problems Faced by Teachers in the Implementation of Active Based Learning Methodology with respect to their type of school as Government and Aided School.

RESULT

Hence the null hypothesis is Accepted.

HYPOTHESIS: 3

There is no significant difference between the mean scores of Problems Faced by Teachers in the Implementation of Active Based Learning Methodology with respect to their type of school as Aided and Private school.

TABLE: 3

The table given below shows the mean, standard deviation and "t" values of Problems Faced by Teachers in the Implementation of Active Based Learning Methodology with respect to their type of school as Aided and Private school.

School Management	N	M	SD	df	't' value	Level of Significance at 0.05
Govt. Aided	30	75.27	5.06	92	0.581	Not Significant
Private	64	74.64	4.55			

INTERPRETATION

The computed table value of **t = 0.581** is smaller than the critical table value at 0.05 level of significance (i.e.) 1.96 for df = 92, which implies that there is no significant difference in the mean scores of Problems Faced by Teachers in the Implementation of Active Based Learning Methodology with respect to their type of school as Aided and Private school.

RESULT

Hence the null hypothesis is accepted.

HYPOTHESIS: 4

There is no significant difference between the mean scores of Problems Faced by Teachers in the Implementation of Active Based Learning Methodology with respect to their type of school as Private and Government school.

TABLE: 4

The table given below shows the mean, standard deviation and "t" values of Problems Faced by Teachers in the Implementation of Active Based Learning Methodology with respect to their type of school as Private and Government school.

School Management	N	M	SD	df	't'	Level of Significance at 0.05
Private	64	74.64	4.55			
Government	66	75.39	5.35	128	0.862	Not Significant

INTERPRETATION:

The computed table value of **t = 0.862** is smaller than the critical table value at 0.05 level of significance (i.e.) 1.96 for df = 128, which implies that there is significant difference in the mean scores of Problems Faced by Teachers in the Implementation of Active Based Learning Methodology with respect to their type of school as Private and Government school.

RESULT:

Hence the null hypothesis is accepted.

HYPOTHESIS: 5

There is no significant difference between the mean scores of Problems Faced by Teachers in the Implementation of Active Based Learning Methodology with respect to their family nature as Nuclear and Joint family.

TABLE: 5

The table given below shows the mean, standard deviation and "t" values of Problems Faced by Teachers in the Implementation of Active Based Learning Methodology with respect to their family nature as Nuclear and Joint family.

School Management	N	M	SD	df	't' value	Level of Significance at 0.05
Nuclear	133	75.20	4.80			
Joint	27	74.41	5.77	158	0.666	Not Significant

INTERPRETATION

The computed table value of **t = 0.666** is smaller than the critical table value at 0.05 level of significance (i.e.) 1.96 for df = 158, which implies that there is no significant difference in the mean scores of Problems Faced by Teachers in the Implementation of Active Based Learning Methodology with respect to their family nature as Nuclear and Joint family.

RESULT

Hence the null hypothesis is accepted.

HYPOTHESIS: 6

There is no significant difference between the mean scores of Problems Faced by Teachers in the Implementation of Active Based Learning Methodology with respect to their locality as Rural and Urban area.

TABLE: 6

The table gave below shows the mean, standard deviation and "t" values of Problems Faced by Teachers in the Implementation of Active Based Learning Methodology with respect to their locality as Rural and Urban area.

Locality	N	M	SD	df	't' value	Level of Significance at 0.05
Rural	72	75.32	5.29			
Urban	88	74.86	4.71	158	0.575	Not Significant

INTERPRETATION

The computed table value of **t = 0.575** is smaller than the critical table value at 0.05 level of significance (i.e.) 1.96 for df = 158, which implies that there is no significant difference in the mean scores of Problems Faced by Teachers in the Implementation of Active Based Learning Methodology with respect to their locality as Rural and Urban area.

RESULT

Hence the null hypothesis is accepted.

HYPOTHESIS: 7

There is no significant difference between the mean scores of Problems Faced by Teachers in the Implementation of Active Based Learning Methodology with respect to their Working Experience as <5 and >5 years.

TABLE: 7

The table given below shows the mean, standard deviation and "t" values of Problems Faced by Teachers in the Implementation of Active Based Learning Methodology with respect to their Working Experience as <5 and >5 years.

Working Experience	N	M	SD	df	't' value	Level of Significance at 0.05
<5 Years	86	74.80	5.10			
>5 Years	74	75.38	4.82	158	0.739	Not Significant

INTERPRETATION

The computed table value of **t = 0.739** is smaller than the critical table value at 0.05 level of significance (i.e.) 1.96 for df = 158, which implies that there is no significant difference in the mean scores of Problems Faced by Teachers in the Implementation of Active Based Learning Methodology with respect to their Working Experience as <5 and >5 years.

RESULT

Hence the null hypothesis is accepted.

CONCLUSION

In this chapter the collections of data were tabulated, analyzed and interpreted. The next chapter deals with the summary findings and conclusion of the present investigation on "Problems Faced by Teachers in the Implementation of Active Based Learning Methodology in Pudukkottai Educational District".

Chapter - V

Findings and Conclusion

INTRODUCTION

Education is the systematic development and cultivation of the natural powers. Education includes all the processes that develop human ability and behaviors. It is an organized and sustained instruction designed to communicate a combination of knowledge, Skills and understanding valuable for all the activities of life.

Active Based Learning is not an end in itself but means for creating and maintaining a learning environment that is optimal, given the intended curriculum. Since classroom management skills affect the quality and quantity of the learning and teaching core, learning for the 21st century demands acquisition of a range of teachers classroom skills and broad areas of knowledge, and the development of set attitudes among teachers.

A teacher's problems in implementing the ABL have special qualities that are a potential source of stress. Classrooms are closed. Crowded spaces in which many people with differing abilities and priorities are forced to use limited resources to achieve a broad range of personal, institutional and social goals. Teachers have to face a classroom full of students every day, negotiate potentially stressful interactions with parents, administrators, counsellors and other teachers; contend with relatively low school budget and ensure students meet increasingly strict standards. Thus to find the study the topic was chosen. This chapter deals with the summary, findings and conclusions of the investigation followed by the suggestion.

STATEMENT OF THE PROBLEM

Problems founded in the implementation of Active Based Learning Methodology study provide information and various reports on the educational progress of students learning outcomes through Evaluation in teaching and learning process. Thus it helps in predicting the future success of the learner through active based outcomes by suggesting value judgments. Thus, to investigation made to find the opinion of school teachers entitled as "*Problems Faced by Teachers in the Implementation of Active Based Learning Methodology in Pudukkottai Educational District*".

OBJECTIVES OF THE STUDY

The objectives for the study are

1. To find out the significant difference between the mean scores of Problems Faced by Teachers in the Implementation of Active Based Learning Methodology with respect to their gender as Male and Female.
2. To find out the significant difference between the mean scores of Problems Faced by Teachers in the Implementation of Active Based Learning Methodology with respect to their type of school as Government and Aided School.
3. To find out the significant difference between the mean scores of Problems Faced by Teachers in the Implementation of Active Based Learning Methodology with respect to their type of school as Aided and Private school.
4. To find out the significant difference between the mean scores of Problems Faced by Teachers in the Implementation of Active Based Learning Methodology with respect to their type of school as Private and Government school.

5. To find out the significant difference between the mean scores of Problems Faced by Teachers in the Implementation of Active Based Learning Methodology with respect to their family nature as Nuclear and Joint family.
6. To find out the significant difference between the mean scores of Problems Faced by Teachers in the Implementation of Active Based Learning Methodology with respect to their locality as Rural and Urban area.
7. To find out the significant difference between the mean scores of Problems Faced by Teachers in the Implementation of Active Based Learning Methodology with respect to their Working Experience as <5 and >5 years.

HYPOTHESES OF THE STUDY

The Hypotheses for the study are

1. There is no significant difference between the mean scores of Problems Faced by Teachers in the Implementation of Active Based Learning Methodology with respect to their gender as Male and Female.
2. There is no significant difference between the mean scores of Problems Faced by Teachers in the Implementation of Active Based Learning Methodology with respect to their type of school as Government and Aided School.
3. There is no significant difference between the mean scores of Problems Faced by Teachers in the Implementation of Active Based Learning Methodology with respect to their type of school as Aided and Private school.
4. There is no significant difference between the mean scores of Problems Faced by Teachers in the Implementation of Active Based Learning Methodology with respect to their type of school as Private and Government school.
5. There is no significant difference between the mean scores of Problems Faced by Teachers in the Implementation of Active Based Learning Methodology with respect to their family nature as Nuclear and Joint family.

6. There is no significant difference between the mean scores of Problems Faced by Teachers in the Implementation of Active Based Learning Methodology with respect to their locality as Rural and Urban area.
7. There is no significant difference between the mean scores of Problems Faced by Teachers in the Implementation of Active Based Learning Methodology with respect to their Working Experience as <5 and >5 years.

FINDINGS OF THE RESEARCH

The following are the findings for the hypotheses framed

FINDING - 1

There is no significant difference in the mean scores of Problems Faced by Teachers in the Implementation of Active Based Learning Methodology with respect to their gender as Male and Female.

RESULT: ***Hence the null hypothesis is accepted.***

FINDING - 2

There is no significant difference in the mean scores of Problems Faced by Teachers in the Implementation of Active Based Learning Methodology with respect to their type of school as Government and Aided School.

RESULT: ***Hence the null hypothesis is accepted.***

FINDING - 3

There is no significant difference in the mean scores of Problems Faced by Teachers in the Implementation of Active Based Learning Methodology with respect to their type of school as Aided and Private school.

RESULT: ***Hence the null hypothesis is accepted.***

FINDING - 4

There is significant difference in the mean scores of Problems Faced by Teachers in the Implementation of Active Based Learning

Methodology with respect to their type of school as Private and Government school.

RESULT: ***Hence the null hypothesis is accepted.***

FINDING - 5

There is no significant difference in the mean scores of Problems Faced by Teachers in the Implementation of Active Based Learning Methodology with respect to their family nature as Nuclear and Joint family.

RESULT: ***Hence the null hypothesis is accepted.***

FINDING - 6

There is no significant difference in the mean scores of Problems Faced by Teachers in the Implementation of Active Based Learning Methodology with respect to their locality as Rural and Urban area.

RESULT: ***Hence the null hypothesis is accepted.***

FINDING - 7

There is no significant difference in the mean scores of Problems Faced by Teachers in the Implementation of Active Based Learning Methodology with respect to their Working Experience as <5 and >5 years.

RESULT: ***Hence the null hypothesis is accepted.***

SUGGESTIONS FOR THE FURTHER RESEARCH

The following are some of the suggestions given for further study:

1. A similar study test may be under taken at district level.
2. A correlative study will be conducted among teacher in different schools.
3. A similar study may be under taken at teacher's level at various districts.
4. A similar study may be under taken in different subject teacher's evaluation.

5. Comparative study may conduct to different Educational District.

RECOMMENDATIONS OF THE STUDY

1. Every school should be provided with all necessary materials and equipment for the use of ABL in schools
2. Teachers should have enough periods to accommodate the use of ABL in the classroom
3. Workshops and seminars should be organized for the training and re-training of teachers on how to use ABL in classes.
4. All Tertiary Institutions in charge of preparation of teachers should ensure that teachers are properly prepared on the use of ABL in schools.

CONCLUSION

This study considered the attitude of school teachers towards Problems Faced by in the Implementation of Active Based Learning Methodology. Activity based learning is a new teaching strategy that is in vogue in every subject and everywhere in the world. The study revealed that school many teachers in understand the ABL methods and the need for their use in schools. In fact many of the teachers prefer ABL to the conventional method of teaching. But many others are still facing the problems of effective use of ABL in schools. Hence, there is need for a continuous retraining of teachers and provision of instructional materials to schools to facilitate the utilization of ABL in schools. The study revealed that the major problems of the use o ABL methods in schools are lack of instructional materials and time. Hence, teachers must embrace the use of ABL in the teaching and learning of in schools.

BIBLIOGRAPHY

1. Anandalakshmy, S. (2007). Activity Based Learning: A Report on an Innovative Method in Tamil Nadu. Chennai: SSA State Project Directorate.
2. Activity Based Learning (ABL). New Initiatives and Projects: *Special Efforts towards Quality Improvement.* Sarva Shiksha Abhiyan, Tamil Nadu.

3. Anandalakshmi. S. (2007) Activity Based Learning – A report on an innovative method in Tamil Nadu. Annual Status of Education Report (Rural). (2007).

4. Bloom, B. S. (1984). The 2-sigma problem: The search for methods of group instruction as effective as one-to-one tutoring. *Educational Researcher, 13(6),* 4-16.

5. Bredderman, T. (1983). Effects of activity based elementary science on student outcomes. *Review of Educational Research, 53(4),* 499-518

6. DPE (2010). Program Document Third primary Education Development (PROG 3), Draft for Appraisal. Dhaka: Directorate of Primary Education.

7. De, A., Dreze, J., Shiva Kumar, A. K., Noronha, C., Pushpendra, Rampal, A. et al. (1999). *Public report of basic education in India (PROBE),* Oxford University Press, USA.

8. Dyck, N., & Pemberton, J.B. (2002). A model for making decisions about text adaptations. *Intervention in School and Clinic, 38*(1), 28-35.

9. Edyburn, D.L. (2003). Reading difficulties in the general education classroom: A taxonomy of text modification strategies. *Closing the Gap, 21*(6), 1, 10-13, 31.

10. Gauthama, G. (2008). Active Learning Methodology, Sarva Shiksha Abhiyan. Chennai: SSA State Project Directorate.

11. Gardner, Howard. Frames of Mind: The Theory of Multiple Intelligences. New York: Basic, 1983Garner, R. (1987). *Metacognition and reading comprehension.* Norwood, N.J: Ablex Publishing.

12. Goswami, U. (2004). Neuroscience and education. *British Journal of Educational Psychology, 74,* 1-14.

13. Kingdon, G. G. (2007). The progress of school education in India. *Oxford Review of Economic Policy, 23(2),* 168-195.

14. Mani, M. N. G. (2005). Inclusive education. Prabuddha Bharatha.

15. Maxwell, S. E. & Delaney, H. D. (2004) Designing Experiments and analyzing Data: A model comparison perspective, Second Edition, Lawrence Erlbaum Associate.

16. Morse, J. M. & Richards, L. (2002). *Readme first: A user's guide to qualitative methods.* Sage Publications, Thousand Oaks:CA.

17. Munakata, Y., Casey, B. J., and Diamond A. (2004). Developmental cognitive neuroscience: Progress and potential. *Trends in Cognitive Science, 8(3),* 122-128.

18. National Council for Educational Research and Training (n.d.). India: Educational policies and curriculum at the upper primary and secondary education levels.

19. National Curriculum Framework, 2005. National Council for Educational Research and Training. ABL Methodology.

20. Nehru, A., and Raghupathi, H. (2011). ASER 2010: Shocking primary learning report card. *Special Report, Education World: The Human Development Magazine, March 2011.*

21. Panda, B. N. (2006). Critical pedagogy: Teaching for equality and Justice. *Journal of Indian Education, 32(2),* 22-32.

22. Prema, P., Subbiah, S., Ramnath, R., & Subramanian, S. (2009). Instructional and nurturant effects of activity-based-learning-an impact study in selected districts in Tamil Nadu. Alagappa University, A report submitted to the SPD, SSA-TN.

23. Ramesh Babu, B. (2007). Schooling for social transformation. *Journal of Indian Education, 33(1),* 5-15.

24. Ramchandar, K (2010). ABL Reform in Tamil Nadu-An evolution not a revolution.

25. Rose, D H., A. Meyer, G. Rappolt and N. M. Strangman (2002). T*eaching Every Student in the Digital Age: Universal Design for Learning.* Alexandria, VA, ASCD Press.

26. Sarva Shiksha Abhiyan (n.d.). Achievements under SSA.

27. Sarva Shiksha Abhiyan (2009). Activity Based Learning: Effectiveness of ABL under SSA, Centre for Educators and Sarva Shiksha Abhiyan. Chennai: SSA State Project Directorate.

28. Sainath, P. (1996). *Everybody loves a good drought: Stories from India's poorest districts.* Penguin, India.

29. School Scape and SSA-Tamil Nadu. (2008) Activity Based Learning: Effectiveness of ABL under SSA June 2007-April 2008. Report by SchoolScape and SSA-Tamil Nadu.

30. Singal, N. (2006). An ecosystemic approach for understanding inclusive education: An Indian case study. *European Journal of Psychology in Education, 21(3)* 239-252.

31. Sirohi, V. (2006). Quality improvements in elementary education through pedagogical innovations. *Journal of Indian Education, 32(1),* 5-17.

32. Suydam, M. N., & Higgins, J. L. (1977). Activity – based learning in elementary school mathematics: recommendations from research. Mathematics Education Reports, ERIC Center for science, math and environmental education, Ohio State University. ED144840.

33. Swarup, S. (2006). Education of children with special needs. *Journal of Indian Education, 32(2),* 68-74The Multi-Grade Methodology. Rishi Valley Institute of Educational Research.

34. The Right of Children to Free and Compulsory Education Act, 2009, Government of India.

35. Vasantha Devi, V., Rajagopalan, S. S., and Jayakumar, R. (2008) *Activity Based Learning in Tamil Nadu Primary Schools.* A report prepared on the suggestion of the Hon ble Minister for school Education, Thiru.Thangam Thennarasu and the Special Project Director of SSA, Thiru.M.P.Vijayakumar.

36. Vijaykumar, M. P., Venkatesan, R., Kannappan, S., & Sekhar, R. (2009). Time on task of teachers and students in Tamil Nadu. *Research report by Tamil Nadu State Mission of Education for All, State Project Directorate, Tamil Nadu.*

37. Yadav. S.K. (2007). Implementation of school curriculum at primary stage in different states. *Indian Education Review, 43(1),*107-119.

